Going to Court to Change Japan

Going to Court to Change Japan

Social Movements and the Law
in Contemporary Japan

EDITED BY
PATRICIA G. STEINHOFF

CENTER FOR JAPANESE STUDIES
THE UNIVERSITY OF MICHIGAN
ANN ARBOR   2014

Published by the Center for Japanese Studies,
The University of Michigan
1007 E. Huron St.
Ann Arbor, MI 48104-1690

Library of Congress Cataloging-in-Publication Data

Going to court to change Japan : social movements and the law in contemporary Japan /
Edited by Patricia G. Steinhoff.
    p. cm. -- (Michigan monograph series in japanese studies ; no. 77)
    Includes bibliographical references and index.
    ISBN 978-1-929280-83-4 (pbk. : alk. paper) -- ISBN 978-1-929280-84-1 (ebook : alk.
paper)
    1. Law reform--Japan. 2. Law--Social aspects--Japan. 3. Courts--Japan. 4. Procedure
(Law)--Japan. 5. Justice, Administration of--Japan. 6. Japan--Social policy. 7. Sociological
jurisprudence. I. Steinhoff, Patricia G., 1941- editor.

    KNX470.G65 2014
    340'.30952--dc23

                2014032100

This book was set in Times New Roman, with titles in Cambria.

This publication meets the ANSI/NISO Standards for Permanence of Paper
for Publications and Documents in Libraries and Archives (Z39.48—1992).

Printed in the United States of America

Contents

PREFACE

The impetus for this book began a decade ago, with panel presentations at the Association for Asian Studies by graduate students who were studying social movements in Japan that had used lawyers and support groups to make legal challenges. As the publication project took shape, we added scholars who had done research on other interesting cases, and Daniel Foote graciously agreed to reprise his role as panel discussant to provide a legal perspective on the case studies.

Alas, it has taken even longer to get this book into print than the usual lengthy gestation period for an edited volume, and the graduate students who listed this forthcoming publication on job applications are now tenured professors. Most of our authors have written elsewhere about their social movement research, but without the central focus on lawyers, support groups, and litigation that characterizes their chapters for this volume. The chapter by Karen Nakamura is a substantial revision and rearticulation of chapter 6 of her monograph *Deaf in Japan: Signing and the Politics of Identity* (Ithaca, NY: Cornell University Press, 2006). Some of the background segments of chapter 1 are adapted from my "Doing the Defendant's Laundry: Support Groups as Social Movement Organizations in Contemporary Japan," *Japanstudien, Jahrbuch des Deutschen Instituts für Japanstudien* 11 (1999). We thank the publishers for permission to use these materials.

My introduction provides a basic overview of the Japanese legal system at the time these studies were conducted. Since then the Japanese government has introduced an array of legal changes concerning issues raised in the case studies, which did not affect any of the cases directly. Conversely, some of the creative legal strategies used in these cases may have indirectly affected subsequent legal changes, although of course the Japanese authorities would resist that interpretation. Foote's concluding chapter describes these recent legal reforms and discusses what impact they have had to date. Despite the reforms, social movements today still have to contend with most of the same problems as they use the courts to try to change Japan.

My thanks to the anonymous reviewers who provided constructive comments, and to Bruce Willoughby for getting it into print at last. I hope this volume will raise awareness of the many ways that social movements in Japan work with support groups and lawyers to bring about change, and will inspire others to do similar research into other social movements.

Patricia Steinhoff
August 2014

INTRODUCTION

Patricia G. Steinhoff

This book examines the relationship between social movements and the law in bringing about social change in Japan. Six fascinating case studies take us inside social movements that have taken up causes as disparate as death by overwork, the rights of the deaf, access to prisoners on death row, consumer product safety, workers whose companies go bankrupt, and persons convicted of crimes they did not commit. Each chapter chronicles many attempts to bring about change through use of the courts and assesses their frequent failure and occasional success. Along the way we learn much about how the law operates in Japan as well as how social movements mobilize and innovate to pursue their goals using legal channels.

To those unfamiliar with Japan's judicial system and more familiar with the Anglo-American system, many regular practices of the Japanese judicial system are quite shocking. Japan's modern system was initially crafted during the Meiji era based on German and French models; hence, it followed the Continental legal tradition to produce comprehensive criminal and civil law codes and codes of procedure that were designed to be administered by elite bureaucrats to protect the interests of the emperor-centered state over its subjects. In contrast, a reading of Japan's current Constitution, enacted during the Allied Occupation, would suggest that contemporary Japanese have the same legal rights and protections as people in countries following the Anglo-American legal system, which is based on the common law tradition of protecting the rights of citizens in relation to the state.

In fact, however, when the war ended, most of Japan's prewar law codes were carried over along with virtually all of the personnel who administered them. Consequently, major aspects of the old system have remained in practice up to the present. For example, the 1922 Code of Criminal Procedure was revised in 1948 in an effort to shift from an inquisitorial system to a more Anglo-American adversary system, but it remains strongly inquisitorial, with judges and prosecutors far more powerful than defense lawyers (Abe 1957). Foote (2010) argues that the Japanese judiciary has shaped criminal justice policy by interpreting the Constitution and code changes very narrowly in deference to prosecutors, "granting broad authority to the prosecution and limiting rights and protections for suspects and defendants, often in the face of rather explicit language in the Constitution, at times buttressed by even more detailed language in the Code."

Similarly, some changes were made to the Code of Civil Procedure in 1948, also with the purpose of making the adjudication of civil claims more adversarial, but practice quickly reverted back toward the earlier practice of an inquisitorial judge dominating the proceedings. Even today, many civil actions are brought by parties without legal counsel (Taniguchi 2007). Reflecting this elite bureaucratic orientation, Japan did not even have an administrative procedures law until the mid-1990s, despite some earlier attempts to produce one (Uga 2007)

The Penal Code of 1907 remained in force with only minor changes until the 1990s, despite several unsuccessful efforts to draft a new one (Matsuo 2007). The Civil Code of 1896 has also remained in force along with the Commercial Code that was partially amended in 1950, and there was little change in the way contracts were written and treated in Japan until well into the 1980s (Uchida and Taylor 2007). Certainly there were specific laws passed over the years, but the basic framework of both civil and criminal law, and the way disputes were resolved and crimes were prosecuted, remained relatively unchanged until reform efforts began to take shape in the 1990s.

Although very recent reforms to the judicial system have been enacted that promise to alter some of these practices, they are just coming into effect, and their impact will not be known for some time. The research for the studies in this volume was conducted under the rules and practices that prevailed throughout the postwar period and into the first decade of the twenty-first century. The following are the distinctive features of the Japanese system as of the period of study, emphasizing those that differ from Anglo-American expectations and practices as they relate to the studies presented here.

PROFESSIONAL PERSONNEL: JUDGES, PROSECUTORS, AND LAWYERS

The two main types of bureaucratic officials in the prewar Japanese judicial system, judges and procurators (renamed prosecutors), carried over to the postwar system quite directly. Lawyers had somewhat marginal status and roles in the prewar system but were elevated to formal parity with judges and prosecutors in the deliberate effort to create an adversarial system for postwar Japan. All three receive the same types and levels of training in postwar Japan, and then they move into different types of positions.

Law is an undergraduate major in Japan, intended to prepare students as generalists to enter the government bureaucracy or private corporations and not to fill positions in the judicial system. Until the introduction of Western-style graduate law schools in 2004, all judges, prosecutors, and lawyers in postwar Japan followed the same route to enter their careers. They first had to pass the Legal Examination, for which, similar to university entrance exams, "passing" was limited to the number of places available in the Legal Training and Research Institute, an agency of the Supreme Court that provided a two-year apprenticeship program (reduced in the late 1990s to one and a half years). The program provides practical training for future judges, prosecutors, and lawyers, with courses taught by active professionals and rotating paid apprenticeships in courts, prosecutors' offices, and law offices.

The number of applicants passing the Legal Examination grew from 265 in 1949 to about 500 by the early 1960s, and it remained at that level until the beginning of the 1990s, at which time various pressures led to a doubling of the number passing over the course of the decade. These numbers were sufficient to fill available slots for judges and prosecutors, but they severely constrained the number of lawyers in Japan. In the late 1980s and 1990s, business interests in Japan began pressing for an increase in the number of lawyers. Some suggest that the initial increases in numbers came about because it was becoming harder to fill the available slots for prosecutors, which also implies that more candidates wanted to become lawyers. Until the institution of the new system of legal education, the pass rate had hovered at around two to three percent of applicants since the mid-1960s; most of those passing had taken the exam several times and were in their late twenties or older when they succeeded (Rokumoto 2007). Upon completion of the legal training program, candidates must sit for a final examination, but typically the vast majority of trainees pass that examination. At that point, all successful candidates are officially considered to be trained lawyers and officers of the court, certified to become judges at the district court level, prosecutors in the national bureaucracy, or to practice law. (There are also positions at the lowest level of the judiciary: summary court judges, filled by persons who have not attended the legal training institute who cannot move up to become judges at district, family, or other higher courts.)

The first two positions, judge and prosecutor, are elite positions in the national bureaucracy, under separate bodies. Instructors assigned from these bodies to teach in the legal training institute use their posts to recruit promising new candidates. Prosecutors are career bureaucrats within the Ministry of Justice, where they enjoy status and salary levels equal to judges and a high level of independence. They are assigned to various positions in prosecutors' offices in major cities that change as part of the regular rotation of bureaucratic officials, and they also may rise to fill top-level positions in the ministry (Johnson 2002;

Tachi 2003). Judges are part of an independent bureaucracy under the authority of the Supreme Court. They are appointed for renewable ten-year terms, but most remain in the judiciary until they retire at the age of sixty-five, moving from post to post within the judiciary just like career bureaucrats in other parts of the Japanese government (Haley 2007). The fact that all judges and prosecutors belong to two elite bureaucracies in a unified national judicial system facilitates a high level of uniformity and predictability in the way prosecutorial and judicial decisions are made. Those who do not take positions in these two bureaucracies may practice law independently, and persons who resign or retire from positions as judges or prosecutors may also work as lawyers.

The environment in which Japanese lawyers work is very different from that in the United States. The Japanese Civil Code does not allow for punitive damages, and there are no juries to make unpredictable awards, so lawyers do not undertake civil lawsuits on a contingency fee basis in hopes of winning big settlements. Until the 1980s there were virtually no large business law firms in Japan providing legal advice to business clients (Nagashima and Zaloom 2007). In addition, large corporations did not employ in-house lawyers because the nature of contracting in Japan and the way companies operated did not require such legal expertise until Japanese businesses began to work in a multinational environment. Except for the few large business law firms that have emerged in the past two decades, most independent law firms in Japan are very small general practices.

However, since very early in the postwar era many lawyers have worked for labor union federations and other organizations affiliated or loosely allied with the major opposition political parties in Japan, the Socialist Party and the Communist Party, which were highly attuned both to Constitutional issues and to the adversarial use of the courts to bring about social change. As a result of this combination of factors, the very small pool of practicing lawyers in Japan also contains a relatively high proportion of what in the United States would be called "cause lawyers" (Sarat and Scheingold 1998), who are willing to take on some cases from a commitment to social justice, in addition to the regular legal practice that pays their bills.

How Trials Are Conducted

Trials in Japan are not continuous. Both criminal trials and civil lawsuits are conducted through half-day or whole-day sessions about once a month until they conclude, often with a gap of some months between the end of the trial and the formal decision. There are no juries, and all except summary proceedings are heard by a panel of three judges at varying levels of seniority. Because both judges and prosecutors are professional bureaucrats subject to routine transfers, it is not uncommon for the judges in civil and criminal trials, and even the prosecutors in criminal trials, to change midway through the trial because they have been reassigned.

Despite what the Constitution says and the early postwar efforts to make oral pleadings and witness testimony the centerpiece of trials, they remain heavily centered on the paper documents that are entered into the trial record. At least until recent amendments aimed at streamlining trials by implementing rather strict pretrial adjustment procedures, plaintiffs and defendants in civil trials, and prosecutors and defense lawyers in criminal trials, have prepared for just the next few sessions of the trial, beginning with the submission of documents and their acceptance or rejection by the judges. Typically, judges also have focused their attention mainly on the upcoming sessions of a trial based on the new sets of documents that have been submitted for those sessions. The discontinuous nature of trials and the possibility that judges may be transferred in the middle of trial proceedings greatly increase the judges' dependence on written documents. The final decisions may be rendered by judges who were not in court or assigned to the case when witnesses testified, and therefore can only rely on the documentary record.

Moreover, until the very recent reforms that are just beginning to be implemented, rules of discovery have been extremely limited in both civil and criminal cases. Essentially, lawyers and defendants only learn what evidence the other side has to offer when it is submitted to the court piecemeal, document by document, throughout the intermittent trial. They have had no right to learn what other conflicting or exculpatory evidence the other side might hold that it does not choose to present to the court. They can only see what evidence is going to be presented when it is added to the documentary record, often just one trial session in advance of when it will be utilized, and they must then scramble to rebut or defend against it.

Even under the newly revised procedures for discovery, one must request specific items in the possession of the other side. If the defense does not know what those items might be, it cannot ask the court to compel the other side to disclose them (Soldwedel 2008). The lack of discovery hobbles the defense in both civil and criminal cases, but it is particularly damaging to criminal defense. However, there are many other peculiarities of the Japanese criminal justice system that shock observers accustomed to the Anglo-American system with its strong presumption of innocence and protections for criminal defendants.

THE JAPANESE CRIMINAL JUSTICE SYSTEM

Criminal law and criminal procedure textbooks and judicial precedents proclaim that the presumption of innocence is a basic tenet of Japanese law, yet nowhere in such basic documents as the Constitution, the Penal Code, and the Code of Criminal Procedure is there a clear stipulation that a person is innocent until proven guilty beyond a reasonable doubt. The Constitution spells out a number of protections for defendants, but not this most basic of protections. The Penal Code spells out crimes and punishments, while the Code of Criminal Procedure describes the procedures for treating "the accused" and accords to prosecutors the determination of whether there is sufficient evidence of guilt to charge the person with a crime. The judges are then required to set forth the evidence on which the person was found guilty. According to the Code of Criminal Procedure, a person can be found "not guilty" if the court finds that there was no crime committed, and the possibility that the evidence was insufficient to establish guilt is offered as an afterthought. In short, if a person is formally charged with a crime and goes to trial, there is a strong presumption that the defendant must be guilty. The court assumes that it is the prosecutor's duty to bring a case to trial only if the evidence clearly establishes the defendant's guilt. The presumption of guilt is so strong that a person who is found not guilty is entitled to restitution from the state, and there are informal punishments for prosecutors who have made the error of taking a case to trial that they might lose (Johnson 2002).

In a clear continuation from its Continental inquisitorial roots, Japan's criminal justice system remains very heavily oriented to confession, which is regarded as the pinnacle of evidence and also as the key to subsequent remorse and rehabilitation. Although confession alone is not sufficient for conviction, confession is overwhelmingly the primary focus of criminal investigation. Both police and prosecutors have very wide latitude in highly "enabling" circumstances to obtain confessions. They may hold suspects for up to twenty-three days of interrogation in a police jail before formally charging them with a specific offense or releasing them. Most suspects confess within the first three days, before it is even necessary to take the suspect before a judge to obtain permission for additional time for interrogation. And although the official limit is two ten-day periods of additional interrogation, that time can be extended seemingly indefinitely by the simple expedient of charging someone with one offense at the end of the twenty-three days, and then immediately rearresting the person on suspicion of another crime.

Although suspects are constitutionally entitled to a lawyer, the state does not provide lawyers for indigent persons until after charges have been filed (although the recent reforms attempt to rectify this with a new state system that many defense lawyers mistrust). Even when a suspect does have a lawyer, access to the client is severely restricted, and lawyers are never permitted to observe interrogations, which may be conducted for up to twelve or fourteen hours a day.

A major feature of the Japanese criminal justice system that seems very strange to those accustomed to the Anglo-American system is that the suspect or defendant does not actually write his or her own confession statement. Instead, these are documents constructed and written up by police and prosecutors from the interrogation and other evidence, which the person is then urged to sign. Such constructed "confessions" are admitted into the court record in evidence as the person's own signed confession document. After days of interrogation, the exhausted arrestee may be cajoled, coerced, or tricked into signing a false confession statement, often with the argument that the document's contents may be denied later when the person goes to court. And although the Constitution states clearly that "confession made under compulsion, torture or threat, or after prolonged arrest or detention shall not be admitted in evidence," (Article 38) in fact courts routinely accept such confession statements even when the defendant testifies vigorously in court that the statement was coerced after prolonged arrest and detention. In the same manner, written statements constructed by prosecutors from questioning of witnesses are often entered into the documentary court record instead of calling the witness to testify in court and be subject to cross-examination.

One further feature of Japanese criminal justice that is common to Continental legal systems but differs substantially from the Anglo-American system is the interpretation of double jeopardy. Following the initial decision in District Court, both the prosecution and the defense are allowed to appeal the decision, and the appeals court can retry the facts of the case anew. The prosecution frequently appeals if the sentence is regarded as too light, or in the rare instance when a defendant has been found not guilty. Article 39 of the Constitution states, "No person shall be held criminally liable for an act which was lawful at the time it was committed, or of which he had been acquitted, nor shall he be placed in double jeopardy." However, Japanese courts do not follow the Anglo-American understanding of double jeopardy, but have interpreted an appeal of the first decision to be a continuation of the original trial process; thus, it is not regarded as double jeopardy for the prosecution to appeal an acquittal. Double jeopardy does not apply until a case has been fully appealed all the way to the Supreme Court, and the Supreme Court has confirmed a final decision.

RESEARCH ON LAW AND SOCIETY IN JAPAN

There is now a substantial body of literature in English on the subject of law and society in Japan. We have come a very long way from the work by Kawashima Takeyoshi (Kawashima 1963) that suggested the Japanese people were culturally predisposed not to take their claims to court. That position has been refuted effectively by scholars of Japanese law who have pointed out several structural barriers to pressing claims through the Japanese legal system (Haley 1978; Ramseyer 1988; Miyazawa 2001) and have shown why such claims are often pursued through alternative means. More recently, Eric Feldman (2007) has provided a more nuanced reading of Kawashima's work as not exclusively culturalist but as based on modernization theory expectations about how Japan would change in the future. He traces the wide range of subsequent studies of dispute resolution in

Japan as part of Kawashima's broad legacy, whether they take a cultural, institutional, law and economics (rational choice), or case studies approach. He sees the recent efforts to change the Japanese legal system as consistent with Kawashima's basic predictions about the future of Japanese dispute resolution.

Similar debates have colored the English language literature on the use of the courts for criminal cases. The Japanese criminal justice system attracted attention in the 1970s and 1980s because the rates of crime and prosecution appeared very low in comparison to U.S. statistics, although they were not out of line with other European countries. Several studies argued that because the Japanese criminal justice system emphasizes confession, and police and prosecutors have great freedom to obtain confessions through lengthy interrogations without the presence of a defense lawyer, very few criminal cases ever go to court for a full trial (Castberg 1990; Westermann and Burfeind 1991; Thornton and Endo 1992). While it is true that the vast majority of criminal cases are resolved with a confession and a single court session, there are still many contested cases that require a full trial, plus appeals and requests for retrial, that keep the criminal courts busy. The best studies of the criminal justice system (Miyazawa 1992; Johnson 2002) have taken a close look at the daily practices of the police and prosecutors that underlie the statistics and have shown us why it produces these results.

USING THE COURTS TO PRODUCE SOCIAL CHANGE

The studies in this volume point out that in addition to ordinary civil and criminal matters, cases are also contested through Japanese courts for the explicit purpose of producing social change. Although such cases are indistinguishable in official statistics, they are sustained through the legal system by social movement groups working in concert with cause lawyers. The phenomena of cause lawyering and of social movements supporting lawsuits in order to bring about social change are well-known in other countries (Sarat and Scheingold 1998; Sarat and Scheingold 2001; Scheingold and Sarat 2004; Sarat and Scheingold 2005). The present volume contributes to our understanding of how cause lawyers and social movements undertake such activities in the particular circumstances of the Japanese legal system.

In a seminal study, Frank Upham (1987) demonstrated that after a series of legal disputes had pushed for social change in several disparate fields, Japanese courts crafted solutions that regularized the claims process into administrative arrangements. The hallmark of these arrangements was the flexibility they left to bureaucratic discretion, rather than creating firm rights and remedies, a situation Upham termed "bureaucratic informality." Upham focused primarily on the legal processes and their outcomes, but a close reading of his case studies makes it clear that in addition to the individuals whose claims made up the actual legal cases,

8

cause lawyers and social movement organizations provided the driving force that brought about social change.

The studies contained in this volume aim to broaden our understanding of the use of the courts to bring about social change in Japan by focusing on the social movement component in the equation. In my own research on Japanese New Left groups that ran afoul of the law because of their confrontational political actions, I discovered that they brought their struggles into the courts with the aid of trial support groups. In reading the accounts of other scholars who had done field work in Japanese social movements, it seemed that such support groups constituted a much broader form of social movement activity.

This volume is intended to test that idea, by inviting other scholars who have done extensive fieldwork on a particular social movement to look at how their movement has used legal cases to pursue its goals. For some, this was already a main thrust of their work; for others, it required going back into their field notes to think about their movement in a new way. Some of the cases we document stretch back to the 1960s, while others are more recent in origin, and many continue today. All of the case studies are based on extensive participant observation and interviews with the social movement organizations, but they rely equally on the newsletters and other print materials that social movements produce, in order to document the complexities of long-running legal actions and extend the time frame of the research. Each study also provides some background on the Japanese legal context that underlies the case, which supplements the basic outline provided above.

The resulting studies have expanded the original focus on individual trial support groups to encompass the role of larger social movement organizations and labor unions as institutionalized support groups that back extensive, long-running legal campaigns, and to highlight the critical role of cause lawyers in helping social movements utilize the courts. The authors of the six case studies are social scientists, not lawyers: three are sociologists, two anthropologists, and one a political scientist. To balance the presentation of the case studies with appropriate legal expertise, noted Japanese legal scholar Daniel Foote has provided a commentary that also highlights recent and pending changes in the basic structure of the Japanese legal system itself.

Each of the case studies stands on its own as a detailed account of how a social movement has persisted against heavy odds to pursue a cause through the use of the courts. The studies are linked through common themes, and the ordering of the chapters reflects some of these. The first of these themes is the great difficulty that individuals or small groups in Japan have in mounting legal challenges in the face of strong social expectations and the overwhelming power of their adversaries, be they corporations or the state itself. While cause lawyers provide the necessary expertise to navigate the legal system, social movement organizations and trial support as a form of social movement activity provide the energy and constant dedication that keeps the principals in the legal case from giving up the fight or accepting a partial solution. Every chapter details legal cases that stretch for years or even decades, requiring patience and dogged determination to keep the momentum going against heavy odds.

A second, related theme is that despite very generous protections in the Japanese Constitution and in various bodies of law, Japanese citizens tend not to know about their rights and thus do not believe they have a chance to succeed against more powerful adversaries. Hence, the first task of cause lawyers and social movements is to teach clients their rights and thereby persuade them to pursue redress. This is no easy task, as the case studies document eloquently. For many of these participants, rights-consciousness is an entirely new and radically different way of thinking about themselves, their social relations, and their place in the wider society. Social movement organizations can mediate between the formal and technical realm of the law and the everyday social experience of individuals who are faced with a specific problem. They help to transform the individual's private problem into an example of a broader social issue that can be addressed through a combination of collective action and legal strategy. This transformation does not happen quickly, and it must be constantly reinforced through the personal relationships and steady support that the social movement members provide to the criminal defendant or civil plaintiff.

The studies pay particular attention to the relationship between the social movement and the lawyers who handle their cases. These relationships range from major labor union federations that donate their staff lawyers to assist a small union with its legal challenges, to a social movement that uses a hotline to recruit cases for its cause lawyers to pursue, and one that produced its own homegrown lawyer out of the movement itself. Unlike the American situation in which many large, national social movement organizations have staff lawyers who pursue the group's agenda, most of the studies in this volume involve cause lawyers who work for very modest fees or *pro bono* and can only handle these cases by using the social movement participants as unpaid paralegal assistants. Students of social movements have long pointed out that volunteer labor is a prime resource that makes social advocacy possible, but the range of tasks that social movement activists perform for these Japanese legal cases goes well beyond the standard array of social movement activities that require willing hands.

The chapters also point to the rewards that trial support for legal cases brings to the social movement as a whole and to its participants. Some of the authors point to changes in laws or legal practices that have resulted from the social movement's challenges, while others claim only small victories in individual legal cases. In some cases the social movement was actually created by the need for trial support, while other groups got involved in it as a secondary activity that related in some way to their main purpose. Yet underlying all of the studies is the sense that the social movement itself has been invigorated and enhanced by its foray into the legal system, and that social movement members who participate in support for a legal case have found their involvement to be personally rewarding and even life changing.

Despite these common themes running through the volume, each of the case studies puts us inside the world of one particular movement, with its own unique problems and specific legal context. Only when all the studies are brought together does it become apparent that they reflect some broader characteristics of Japanese society and the Japanese legal system. The volume as a whole thus contributes to our understanding of both law and society, but the reader's greatest pleasure will come from the fascinating glimpse that each author gives us of a hidden pocket of contemporary Japan.

Chapter 1, "No Helmets in Court, No T-Shirts on Death Row: New Left Trial Support Groups" by Patricia Steinhoff, examines how New Left student movements and their supporters in the late 1960s refashioned existing elements into a trial support system that permitted them to move their fight from the streets into the courts, after a major crackdown on violent protests produced mass arrests and indefinite detentions. The chapter identifies the major organizational features of the resulting institution of trial support groups and thus provides a foundation for several of the other chapters. It then shows how one trial support group, whose defendants received death penalties in 1979 and 1980 that have not yet been carried out, has found innovative ways to use the courts to maintain contact with their prisoners and to bring about broader changes in the treatment of prisoners awaiting the death penalty in Japan.

Chapter 2, "*Karōshi* Activism and Recent Trends in Japanese Civil Society: Creating Credible Knowledge and Culture" by Scott North, follows with a quite different social movement that supports the surviving family members of persons who have died suddenly from overwork. He shows how a substantial social movement has grown out of the efforts of cause lawyers, medical professionals, and small support groups to find and pursue individual cases of *karōshi*, or death by overwork. Along the way, they have produced changes in the official definitions and criteria for *karōshi* and have established a number of legal precedents. In this instance, the trial support group for one case led to a national movement using some methods that are similar to the New Left cases. However, instead of having a continuous hotline that responds to arrests, this movement opens a well-advertised hotline for a short time each year in order to find new cases to pursue, a practice that has been now replicated in other social movements. North also shows how *karōshi* lawyers and support groups must battle company and labor union resistance in order to obtain critical evidence and must pursue their cases not only through the regular courts but also through a thicket of administrative agencies.

In Chapter 3, "Courting Justice, Contesting 'Bureaucratic Informality': The Sayama Case and the Evolution of Buraku Liberation Politics," John Davis examines one of the famous *enzai* or false prosecution cases, in which a member of the Buraku minority was apparently falsely convicted of murder. A major national social movement, the Buraku Liberation League (BLL), took up the case when they suspected that the defendant had been singled out and charged with the crime solely because of his minority status. Davis shows us how strong BLL support challenged what would otherwise have been a simple murder case that the police had quickly solved. He traces not only how the case itself has progressed but also how it has been used within the BLL and has attracted widespread support outside the organization. His account captures the symbolic aspects that energize social movements, and provides a lively sense of what it is like to participate in social movement rallies and demonstrations in Japan. Legal efforts to improve the status of the Buraku minority also constituted one of Upham's case studies. While Davis supports and utilizes Upham's work, his analysis provides a strikingly different view that foregrounds the role of the BLL in pursuing one iconic legal case that has ramifications well beyond the Buraku movement.

Chapter 4, "Becoming Unforgettable: Leveraging Law for Labor in Struggles for Employment Security" by Christena Turner, examines how strong labor laws enabled the workers in a small shoe factory to fight back when the parent company drove their small subsidiary into bankruptcy. With support and guidance from large labor unions, the workers took legal actions that enabled them to take control of the factory and its materials and continue production while the bankruptcy proceeded slowly through the courts. Turner shows how the resources of a major union federation helped the workers learn how to organize and become a social movement in their own right, while their control of the factory kept them employed so they could continue to fight their legal battles in court. Although Turner has written a monograph about the same case and another similar one (Turner 1999), this chapter focuses more directly on the lengthy sequence of legal actions that the workers took with the aid of the larger labor unions and labor lawyers. The case is intriguing because of the highly unusual situation of workers gaining control of production while their company was in bankruptcy, but it also raises important legal issues concerning the status of workers in subsidiary firms.

Then in Chapter 5, "Suing for Redress: Japanese Consumer Organizations and the Courts," Patricia Maclachlan chronicles the efforts of a consumer organization of housewives to improve product safety through a series of legal challenges using cause lawyers. As in the *karōshi* case, the group had to battle administrative agencies to change their focus and policies, as well as suing manufacturers. Their efforts raised questions of who has legal standing to bring cases to court and resulted in changes in the ability of organizations to bring something similar to class action lawsuits. She also shows how this activity involved legal efforts to gain access to information about faulty consumer products that was held by government bureaucracies, and thus led into the freedom of information movement of the 1980s and 1990s.

Chapter 6 rounds out the case studies with Karen Nakamura's study, "No Voice in the Courtroom: Deaf Legal Cases in the 1960s." Nakamura traces the roots of activism within the deaf community to the same late 1960s protest generation examined by Steinhoff, but with a rather different trajectory. She shows how the early period of activism produced the first deaf lawyer in Japan, who then led a series of legal challenges to overturn highly restrictive and paternalistic regulations that prevented deaf and hard-of-hearing adults from participating in the normal activities of Japanese society. Like Maclachlan, she emphasizes the important role of cause lawyers in making it possible for social movement organizations to pursue social change through the courts. Nakamura also shows how the organization she studied won several court battles and then turned away from the legal strategy as it became a nonprofit organization (NPO) providing services through government contracts.

The volume concludes with a chapter by Daniel Foote, "Cause Lawyering in Japan: Reflections on the Case Studies and Justice Reform." A legal scholar of Japan who now teaches at the University of Tokyo, Foote brings his legal perspective to bear on the social movement case studies, highlighting the connections among the different cases and pointing to ways these movements make creative use of legal resources. He emphasizes how many times these efforts fail, but that they also sometimes win. And as each of the case studies suggests, sometimes these efforts do result in social changes that go well beyond the specific individual case that was taken to court. It is more difficult to achieve such general changes in Japan, both because the legal system itself relies less on precedent, and because the bureaucratic orientation Upham pointed out also makes it more difficult to trace the connection between individual cases that challenge the system and the eventual social changes that may come about indirectly. Foote's chapter goes beyond analysis of the case studies, to contribute additional information about many recent and some still-pending changes in the Japanese legal system that may affect the ability of social movements to bring such challenges in the future.

REFERENCES

Abe, H. (1957). Criminal Procedure in Japan. *The Journal of Criminal Law, Criminology, and Police Science* 48 (4): 359–68.

Castberg, A. D. (1990). *Japanese Criminal Justice*. New York, Praeger Publishing.

Feldman, E. A. (2007). Law, Culture, and Conflict: Dispute Resolution in Postwar Japan. In *Law in Japan: A Turning Point*, ed. D. H. Foote, 50–79. Seattle and London, University of Washington Press.

Foote, D. H. (2010). Policymaking by the Japanese Judiciary in the Criminal Justice Field. *Hōshakaigaku* [Sociology of Law] 72: 6–45.

Haley, J. O. (1978). The Myth of the Reluctant Litigant. *Journal of Japanese Studies* 4.

Haley, J. O. (2007). The Japanese Judiciary: Maintaining Integrity, Autonomy, and the Public Trust. In *Law in Japan: A Turning Point*, ed. D. H. Foote, 99–135. Seattle and London, University of Washington Press.

Johnson, D. T. (2002). *The Japanese Way of Justice: Prosecuting Crime in Japan*. Oxford and New York, Oxford University Press.

Kawashima, T. (1963). Dispute Resolution in Contemporary Japan. In *Law in Japan: The Legal Order in a Changing Society*, ed. T. Kawashima and Arthur von Mehren, 41–72. Cambridge, MA, Harvard University Press.

Matsuo, K. (2007). The Development of Criminal Law in Japan Since 1961. In *Law in Japan: A Turning Point*, ed. D. H. Foote, 312–33. Seattle and London, University of Washington Press.

Miyazawa, S. (1992). *Policing in Japan: A Study on Making Crime*. Albany, NY, State Universty of New York Press.

Miyazawa, S. (2001). Administrative Control of Japanese Judges. In *Japanese Law in Context: Readings in Society, the Economy, and Politics*, ed. C. J. Milhaupt, J. M. Ramseyer, and M. K. Young, 79–83. Cambridge, MA and London, Harvard University Asia Center, Harvard University Press.

Nagashima, Y., and E. A. Zaloom (2007). The Rise of the Large Japanese Business Law Firm and its Prospects for the Future. In *Law in Japan: A Turning Point*, ed. D. H. Foote, 136–52. Seattle and London, University of Washington Press.

Ramseyer, J. M. (1988). Reluctant Litigant Revisited: Rationality and Disputes in Japan. *Journal of Japanese Studies* 14 (1): 111–23.

Rokumoto, K. (2007). Legal Education. In *Law in Japan: A Turning Point*, ed. D. H. Foote, 190–232. Seattle and London, University of Washington Press.

Sarat, A., and S. Scheingold, eds. (1998). *Cause Lawyering: Political Commitments and Professional Responsibilities*. New York, Oxford University Press.

Sarat, A., and S. Scheingold (2001). *Cause Lawyering and the State in a Global Era*. New York, Oxford University Press.

Sarat, A., and S. Scheingold (2005). *The World's Cause Laywers Make Structure and Agency in Legal Practice*. Stanford, CA, Stanford University Press.

Scheingold, S., and A. Sarat (2004). *Something to Believe In: Politics, Professionalism, and Cause Lawyering*. Stanford, CA, Stanford University Press.

Soldwedel, A. F. (2008). Testing Japan's Convictions: The Lay Judge System and the Rights of Criminal Defendants. *Vanderbilt Journal of Transnational Law*.

Tachi, Y. (2003). *Investigation Against Corruption by Public Prosecutors in Japan. ICAC-Interpol Conference*. Hong Kong, United Nations Asia and Far East Institute for the Prevention of Crime and the Treatment of Offenders.

Taniguchi, Y. (2007). The Development of an Adversary System in Japanese Civil Procedure. In *Law in Japan: A Turning Point*, ed. D. H. Foote, 80–98. Seattle and London, University of Washington Press.

Thornton, R. Y., and K. Endo (1992). *Preventing Crime in America and Japan: A Comparative Study*. Armonk/London, M. E. Sharpe, Inc.

Turner, C. L. (1999). *Japanese Workers in Protest: An Ethnography of Consciousness and Experience*. Berkeley/Los Angeles/London, University of California Press.

Uchida, T., and V. L. Taylor (2007). Japan's "Era of Contract." In *Law in Japan: A Turning Point*, ed. D. H. Foote, 454–82. Seattle and London, University of Washington Press.

Uga, K. (2007). Development of the Concepts of Transparency and Accountability in Japanese Administrative Law. In *Law in Japan: A Turning Point*, ed. D. H. Foote, 276–303. Seattle and London, University of Washington Press.

Upham, F. K. (1987). *Law and Social Change in Postwar Japan*. Cambridge, MA, Harvard University Press.

Westermann, T. D., and J. W. Burfeind (1991). *Crime and Justice in Two Societies: Japan and the Unites States*. Pacific Grove, CA, Brooks/Cole Publishing Company.

CHAPTER 1

No Helmets in Court, No T-Shirts on Death Row: New Left Trial Support Groups[1]

Patricia G. Steinhoff

At the entrance to every district court building in Japan, and outside every court-room inside these buildings, a sign lists the rules of behavior for trial observers. The current version for Tokyo District Court translates as follows:

> The Following Are Prohibited in Court
>
> - Bringing guns, weapons, explosives or other dangerous items into court
> - Coercing employees for visits with prisoners
> - Protest actions, group meetings, and sit-ins
> - Singing, shouting, or making other disruptive sounds
> - Flags, vertical or horizontal banners, placards, megaphones, sound cars, or helmets
> - Wearing headbands, sign-vests, armbands, etc.
> - Bringing cameras or recording equipment to court
> - Anything else that disrupts administration of the court

While several of the rules might be found anywhere, such as prohibitions on guns, explosives, cameras, and recording equipment, fully half of the pro-hibitions relate to protest activities and protest paraphernalia. The helmets in question have nothing to do with motorcycles; they are part of the distinctive uniform of New Left student protest groups from the late 1960s and early 1970s. The prohibition on helmets in courtrooms stands as a historical marker, literally

1. Much of the research for this article was conducted under three Fulbright Senior Research Fel-lowships in Tokyo in 1982–83, 1990–91, and 1998–99, during which I was affiliated with the Institute of Social Science, University of Tokyo. I wish to thank both the Fulbright Commission and the Institute of Social Science for their support. Some segments of this paper have appeared previously in Steinhoff 1999a and are used here by permission.

cast in metal, of a particular kind of social movement activity that flourished as part of the New Left movement at that time, the trial support group (*shienkai* or *kyūenkai*).

Like the signs outside Japanese courtrooms, *shienkai* still exist today and have become an essential element of movements for social change in Japan. Sooner or later, anyone conducting research in Japan on a social movement that uses the courts to press its claims will probably stumble onto such a support group. I had been working in and around them for years as I followed various social movements, before I realized that these trial support groups were sociologically interesting in their own right. The reasons for their existence as a form of social movement activity, and the distinctive range of activities they perform, shed light on the routine practices of the Japanese legal system and the criminal justice system. More broadly, *shienkai* reveal how small, powerless groups of ordinary Japanese have learned to use the courts to contest state power.

This chapter will briefly review the history of *shienkai* and their reinvention as part of an escalating conflict between New Left protesters and the state in the late 1960s, followed by a summary account of the Japanese criminal justice system's procedures and how support groups interact with them. It will then examine the wide range of support activities that have developed over the past thirty-five years as the ramifications of one criminal trial involving a clandestine bombing group.

THE INVENTION AND REINVENTION OF TRIAL SUPPORT GROUPS

The concept of mobilizing outside support for political prisoners and politically significant legal cases is certainly not unique to Japan, as the French Dreyfuss Affair of the 1890s and the contemporary activities of Amnesty International attest. In these examples, however, the social movement generally operates at some remove from the principals in the case. Such groups publicize the case widely in order to mobilize public protest, but the closest the campaigns usually get to the participants in the case is to collect donations that may be used to cover expensive legal fees.

In contrast, the hallmark of the Japanese support groups of interest here is their intimate involvement with the legal case and its principals. They may also conduct some of the same kinds of publicity and fund-raising activities as other social movements concerned with the status of political prisoners, and they may also have a substantial number of passive supporters who only send monetary contributions. But their activities go well beyond such arm's-length support. The core support group members work directly with the lawyers handling the case to provide paralegal assistance, and they monitor the progress of the legal case closely. They also meet and communicate regularly with the criminal defendants or civil plaintiffs involved, and provide a wide range of personal support services to those individuals and their families. They care for, protect, and help the principals in unusually intimate ways.

The Origins of the Japanese Support Group System

These personalized support groups have developed and evolved in Japan out of a particular constellation of political, legal, and social conditions. The most basic element of that context is the heavy emphasis on confession and submission to state authority in the Japanese criminal justice system. For persons engaged in political activity, the coercive techniques used to induce confession are inextricably associated with the 1925 Peace Preservation Law and the subsequent pressure on persons arrested under that law to renounce their political beliefs through a practice known as *tenkō* (change of ideological direction) (Mitchell 1976; Mitchell 1992; Steinhoff 1991; Takizawa 1993). As a consequence of this historical legacy, the Japanese left is highly sensitive to the practices of the criminal justice system and has developed a repertoire of specific techniques for resisting them. Support groups form an essential element of that resistance, and their role has expanded in postwar Japan.

The Peace Preservation Law was struck down in 1945, and the postwar Japanese constitution gave new rights and protections to all citizens. The new constitution included specific protections for those accused of a crime, making it somewhat easier at least in theory to mount a vigorous defense or to challenge the state in court. These changes enabled the major political parties of the left to institutionalize the provision of legal assistance for individual cases whose cause they supported on ideological grounds. Despite the constitutional changes, both the continuing practices of the justice system and ordinary social expectations of compliance with authority have discouraged individuals from claiming their new rights or making direct challenges to authority. Hence, the cases taken up by the organized left often required not only legal assistance but also a broad range of social support to keep the challengers from giving up the fight.

The newly legal political parties of the left had the experience and the resources to provide legal support for their own party members and members of affiliated unions and issue organizations. The Japan Communist Party (JCP) in particular developed a model of trial support groups working with socially conscious lawyers as an integral function of a comprehensive adversarial political organization. As part of the party's mass political activity and social advocacy, it also provided institutional legal support for some politically significant cases outside the party's realm, through an organization called Kokumin Kyūenkai (The People's Support Group). This system was established early in the postwar era and continues to operate today. However, circumstances in the late 1960s revealed its limitations and led to a further expansion and reorientation of support groups under new political and social conditions.

The New Left Reinvents Support Groups

Although in the early postwar years student organizations were closely allied with the Japanese Communist Party, by the late 1950s a number of student organizations had broken with the parties of the Old Left to form a more radical and independent New Left, which was very active in the large, multifaceted protest wave of the late 1960s and early 1970s (Steinhoff 1999b; Takazawa and Takagi 1981). By 1967, New Left student protests began escalating into violent clashes with the riot police both on and off campuses, leading to injuries and arrests. In 1968 the state moved to control the rapidly escalating violence by criminalizing previously tolerated protest activities with mass arrests and indictments on felony charges. Over 6,000 students were arrested for protest activities in 1968, and 13,000 more were arrested in 1969. Late in 1968 the state also began holding arrested students in jail indefinitely, rather than releasing them after a day or two. The New Left student organizations encouraged nonaffiliated students to participate in their public protest activities, and on-campus protests under the banner of Zenkyōtō (all-campus student struggle organizations) in particular involved large numbers of students who were not formally affiliated with New Left organizations. Hence, both formal members of New Left organizations and unaffiliated students were caught in the crackdown and arrested indiscriminately.

The New Left's rhetoric was revolutionary, but its adherents also believed (along with a substantial minority of other Japanese) that both the causes they were fighting for and the means they were using were constitutional; from their perspective, the Japanese government was violating the constitution by its policies. They viewed the mass arrests and indefinite holding of students as analogous to the prewar arrests under the Peace Preservation Law because they aimed to suppress ideas and social movements that in postwar Japan were supposed to be constitutionally protected. If students were arrested for protest in the streets, they would take their resistance into the courts. To do so, however, they needed lawyers.

The major New Left student organizations, or "sects," operated under a formal structure adopted from that of the JCP. They had already established their own internal support organizations on the JCP model to provide support for their own arrested members, and they usually had their own lawyers on retainer. However, "non-sect" students who did not officially belong to these organizations did not have access to lawyers or organized support groups. The JCP strongly disapproved of the violent New Left students and refused to provide its lawyers and support system to them when they were arrested. Most other lawyers also refused to take on the student cases, which promised to be very time-consuming and unrewarding financially, as well as being politically and morally distasteful.

A small group of university professors and others who sympathized with the New Left students stepped into the breach and adapted the basic idea of the support group to address the emergency situation. Drawing upon the expertise of some sympathetic lawyers and activists with prior experience in support groups from earlier political cases, they created a new support system coordinated through a clearing house called Kyūen Renraku Sentā (hereafter Kyūen). In explicit reaction to the closed doors of the Old Left's support system, they declared themselves willing to support anyone who was being "oppressed by the state" without regard to ideology or affiliation. They created a loose, coordinating structure for independent groups, rather than a hierarchical central organization.

Kyūen trained a huge volunteer army of students, young workers, and housewives to provide support to the great majority of the 31,000 students arrested from 1968 to 1971 for what was called in government publications of the time "student group violence." Overall, the state's policy of controlling violent protest through mass arrests and the prosecution of students divided the mass protest movement and reduced the scale of street demonstrations, but it also pushed a small segment of the New Left underground, producing more extreme and less predictable violence throughout the 1970s (Zwerman and Steinhoff 2005; Zwerman, Steinhoff, and della Porta 2000). As they were arrested and accused of more serious crimes of violence, these suspects also called upon the Kyūen system for support. Some of these cases involved "frame-ups" in which innocent people were prosecuted and were only cleared after lengthy appeals, which reinforced Kyūen's view of the importance of providing strong legal and personal support to all suspects.

Through the extensive Kyūen network, thousands of people gained some experience with support activity during the late 1960s and early 1970s. Based on the number of students arrested and tried, I have estimated this number at 25,000 to 50,000 (Steinhoff 1999a). A much smaller number of volunteers have remained active in trial support groups through the 1980s and up to the present, supporting New Left defendants who were still in the criminal justice system. In these complex, long-running cases, the trial support group frequently became involved in civil lawsuits related to the same defendants, including suits over living conditions in unconvicted detention and support group members' access to the defendants. Some participants had joined a support group because of their personal affiliations with a defendant, while others were ready to participate wherever they were needed as an expression of their commitment to the movement. Over time, a substantial number of these volunteers developed support group "careers" in which they brought experience and specific skills to a succession of different support organizations.

THE SUPPORT SYSTEM AND CRIMINAL JUSTICE SYSTEM PRACTICES

The support system developed by Kyūen responded to specific practices of the Japanese criminal justice system, which in turn has devised more severe policies to circumvent the resistance of suspects and defendants who use the support system. This process can best be understood as a sustained conflict interaction between the two systems. Over the past three decades the Japanese criminal justice system has become steadily more punitive and no longer merits its image as benign and oriented to rehabilitation. The increasing severity of the criminal justice system can be viewed as an unintended negative consequence of the trial support system for New Left defendants. Certain criminal justice system practices first escalated in response to the activities of those who participated in trial support as a social movement activity. Later, those practices were extended to ordinary criminal defendants, until today they are routinely applied in a very punitive and overbearing way to any arrested person who refuses to cooperate fully with the criminal justice system authorities and instead tries to exercise his or her legal rights. In the face of this bureaucratic intransigence, participants in the trial support movement have been incredibly persistent and creative in finding new ways to support their particular prisoners. Thus, at one level this conflict can be regarded as a long-running continuation of the repression of the New Left movement in the 1960s and early 1970s; at another level it has led to criminal justice system practices that are widely regarded as out of step with international human rights standards and that violate the usual expectations of criminal justice procedures in democratic states. To anyone who is not familiar with these contemporary Japanese practices, they are shocking.

Emergency Support for Arrested Persons

As described in the introduction to this volume, the Japanese criminal justice system is heavily oriented to confession, although the confession must be corroborated with other evidence in order to obtain a conviction (Foote 1995). Miyazawa (1992) describes the system as "enabling" for police, since they may hold a suspect in a police station "substitute jail" (*daiyo kangoku*) for up to three weeks of interrogation, with no lawyer present and no outside contact, in order to induce the suspect to confess. The first element of Kyūen's support strategy is thus to try to keep the arrested person from succumbing to police pressure to confess, primarily by exercising the right to remain silent during the interrogation. Unfortunately, this strategy also virtually guarantees that the suspect will be held in jail for further interrogation. This form of support is triggered when an arrested suspect identifies the Kyūen official lawyer as his or her legal counsel. Arrested persons are not allowed to make their own phone calls, so they give a phone number to the police, who make the call for them. During the peak of the protests, tens of thousands of students memorized the mnemonic for the Kyūen hotline number, *Goku iri, imi ōi* (going to jail has much meaning) or 591-1301, and a surprising number of people from that generation can still reproduce the number today. Kyūen then sends a lawyer to the police jail to inform the person of his rights and how to protect them, and to collect basic information.

During the peak protest period Kyūen developed a system of volunteers assigned to particular local police stations. Kyūen would call a volunteer, who would then go to the police station and deliver basic supplies to the prisoner, who would be identified only by a booking number because he or she would be refusing to talk. In this way, Kyūen could meet the arrestee's initial needs for clean clothing, personal supplies, and supplemental food, all of which an unindicted suspect is entitled to receive from outside, but which can be manipulated by the police during the interrogation period if the person does not have strong outside support.

Trial Support and Support during Unconvicted Detention

Once the person has been indicted, with or without a confession, a team of lawyers is designated for the case, and a trial support group is formed from family members, friends, and other volunteers, often including "regulars" associated with Kyūen, who have the skills to organize and sustain a support group. All kinds of people participate in these groups as volunteers, for a wide variety of personal reasons. They include students, professors, housewives, retirees, and persons who work flexible hours and are available to attend court sessions or visit prisoners during the day, while others may only be able to contribute time in the evenings and on weekends. This group assists the lawyers with paralegal, investigative and secretarial support, provides personal support to the defendant for the duration of the trial and appeals, and publishes informational materials about the case, usually in the form of a regular newsletter. Political cases often involve multiple defendants, and a single support group normally supports all or most of the defendants in one case. Support group members meet each other during the monthly trial sessions, chat and share snacks during the breaks, and often hold a short meeting with the lawyers after the session adjourns. They may also hold other private organizational meetings and host public events, just as any social movement organization would.

New Left defendants who do not confess and do not accept the prosecution's statement of the case as presented in the indictment are invariably held in unconvicted detention (*miketsu shobun*) rather than being released on bail to a guarantor. Courts routinely authorize this form of preventive detention at the prosecutor's request. Although in the late 1960s and early 1970s such defendants were usually released as soon as the trial began, nowadays even for minor charges they are usually held until the prosecution has completed its case, and more often than not until the trial is completed and the sentence determined. Defense lawyers routinely and repeatedly seek to have their clients released on bail, but the prosecution always objects and the court goes along with the prosecutors. The reasons presented for denying bail follow the conditions included in the law: that the person might damage evidence, interfere with witnesses, or is a flight risk. Even if the decision is appealed, the courts stand firm and the person remains in unconvicted detention, sometimes serving more time before the trial ends than the maximum sentence permitted for the charges.

Japanese trials are not continuous, and usually meet for one or two half-day sessions a month. A trial in which the defendant contests the prosecution's case is likely to last from several months to several years, and even longer if the initial decision is appealed. Political offenders who have mounted a strong defense routinely appeal any decision that includes a prison sentence, because doing so maintains the small communications privileges of being held in unconvicted detention. Technically, Japanese courts regard the appeals process as part of the determination of whether the person is guilty, so defendants who appeal continue to be held in unconvicted detention during the appeal, but that time counts as part of the final sentence. Although it is incomprehensible by American standards, these individuals spend extended periods of time—often years or even decades—in unconvicted detention under very harsh conditions. The personal attention provided by support group members is essential to the prisoner's survival during this long period of isolation.

Persons in unconvicted detention are held in a special prison for this purpose, but since they have not yet been convicted of any crime, they enjoy some privileges that convicted felons serving sentences in regular prisons do not have. They are held day and night in solid walled isolation cells and let out of the cell only for a short period of exercise or a bath once or twice a week. Meals are delivered to their cells through a small slot in the steel door. They are not supposed to speak to other prisoners (ostensibly to keep first-time offenders from being contaminated by hardened criminals), but they wear their own clothing and are permitted to receive *sashi-ire* (items sent in from outside). *Sashi-ire* may include books, magazines, and clothing, as well as food and flowers purchased from special stores in or near the prison. If they have money, the prisoners may purchase items from these stores themselves. Since persons in unconvicted detention do not perform prison work and thus have no regular source of income, they are also dependent on the support group's donations in order to purchase small items such as stamps, postcards, and packaged food items from the prison store. There is a strict limit on how many items of clothing and bedding a prisoner may keep in the cell, and there is no facility for doing laundry inside the prison, other than washing small items by hand in the cell's washbasin. Support group members help with the seasonal exchange of clothing, and frequently take out the prisoner's dirty laundry and return it clean. They may also provide new clothing for long-term residents.

Under normal circumstances, prisoners held in unconvicted detention are permitted one twenty minute visit per day and may send and receive letters and telegrams through the regular postal service, although both incoming and outgoing mail passes through a censor. Support groups try to maintain as much communication as possible to keep up the defendant's spirits during the trial and to prevent or alleviate detention disease (*kōkin-byō*), a recognized syndrome of mental and physical symptoms brought on by the prolonged and severe isolation of unconvicted detention. For some prisoners, however, the isolation is even more severe.

While it is fairly routine for police and prosecutors to obtain a court order restricting a suspect's communications (*sekken kinshi*) during the initial phase of the interrogation prior to indictment, in certain cases from as early as 1970, and routinely since the late 1980s, political defendants have been held incommunicado until midway through their trial when the prosecution has completed the presentation of its case. The ostensible rationale for such a prolonged restriction of communications is to prevent the defendant from interfering with witnesses or destroying evidence, the same justifications used for denying prisoners release on bail. In addition to restricting the defendant's legitimate efforts to assist in his own defense, this puts additional pressure on anyone who resists the prosecution's version of the case. These conditions for persons not yet convicted of a crime are unimaginable in the American criminal justice system or in most other industrialized democracies, but they bear an uncomfortable resemblance to the conditions of prisoners being held by the United States as "enemy combatants" at Guantanamo Naval Base.

In recent years, court orders have extended incommunicado status through the end of the first trial for certain defendants. In fact, Japanese Red Army leader Shigenobu Fusako was held incommunicado long after the conclusion of her first trial, except for visits from her daughter. The incommunicado order was only lifted after her final questioning and statement before the appeals court, which was in effect the last time she would appear in public prior to final sentencing. Since the prison fears that this severe isolation increases the risk that the prisoner will commit suicide, persons being held incommunicado in unconvicted detention are placed in special suicide watch cells that are smaller than ordinary isolation cells, with sealed windows, and are monitored 24 hours a day by a security camera.

During the period of communications restrictions the support group members cannot visit the prisoner in unconvicted detention or communicate by mail, but can usually send in *sashi-ire* items such as flowers and food to let the prisoner know that people outside are still paying attention. All communications with the prisoner must take place through the lawyers, whose visits to prisoners in unconvicted detention cannot be prohibited even when other communications are barred.

Persons Awaiting the Death Penalty

Persons whose death sentence has been confirmed by the Supreme Court also continue to be held in the special prisons for persons in unconvicted detention, often on the same corridor. Until the mid-1980s they were treated essentially as persons in unconvicted detention, but since then they have been kept under severe communications restrictions that amount to permanent and total incommunicado status, except for designated family members who are permitted to visit, write, and send in some *sashi-ire*. The new restrictions on prisoners awaiting the death penalty were instituted shortly after several persons who had received death penalty sentences for ordinary criminal offenses won new trials after many years and were subsequently found not guilty. These persons were convicted of nonpolitical criminal offenses but had attracted support groups through their tireless insistence on their innocence and the presence of serious questions regarding the evidence used to convict them (Foote 1992; Foote 1993). Perhaps coincidentally, the new restrictions also were put in place shortly before the death sentences were confirmed for four prominent New Left political defendants who already had active support groups.

The formal rationale for the restrictions, as set forth in a 1963 administrative order that was not enforced until twenty years later, is that prisoners awaiting the death penalty are supposed to be "calming their spirits" in preparation for death. But because the severe isolation causes other psychological effects, the prison also puts them in suicide watch cells. Normally the death penalty is not carried out while any legal proceedings are pending. Since a variety of civil suits and petitions for a new trial may still be filed, prisoners may remain in this status for many years awaiting the death penalty in near-total isolation. They become increasingly withdrawn and angry, sometimes taking out their frustration against the family members who provide their only contact with the outside world.

Support for Civil Actions

The support system devised by Kyūen was designed to address conditions in the Japanese criminal justice system that affected arrested social movement activists, and participating in support groups also became a form of social movement activity. As the protest wave receded, New Left activists moved into a wide range of new social movements, including the women's movement, antipollution movements, the antinuclear movement, minority rights movements, and consumer movements. Kurita (1993) has shown that the generation of Japanese who were students during the protest wave of the late 1960s and early 1970s still maintains a distinctive attitude toward politics and society, and that those who protested as students have remained much more involved in social and political movements subsequently. A significant subset of that activist generation had personal experience not only of participating in protest activities, but also of involvement in trial support groups for arrested students.

In addition to the more general organizational, publishing, and fundraising skills they learned through participation in an active student protest movement, support group participants acquired specific skills and attitudes that reflect the intertwined components of legal support and personal support. New Left support group participants developed a detailed understanding of how the Japanese legal system and the criminal justice bureaucracies work in practice. One aspect of this is an understanding of legal procedures and how to utilize them to achieve small gains through patience and persistence. Another is an acute awareness of the difficulties faced by any individual in Japan who wants to insist on his or her rights, or wants to reverse arbitrary bureaucratic decisions. In addition, people with this experience are not afraid of using the legal system and confronting the bureaucracy to right an injustice, even as they understand the pressures in Japanese society that prevent others from doing so easily. Their expertise, their tenacity, and their fearlessness are all resources they can contribute to various social movements, by providing the direct personal and legal support that enables the victim of an injustice to pursue some form of redress.

These skills have been applied to a wide range of civil lawsuits and administrative procedures, as a form of social movement activity aimed at bringing about social change. Support groups assist the plaintiffs in a civil lawsuit, or help press claims against employers, corporations, or government agencies through administrative procedures. This broad category of support group activity encompasses preexisting social movement organizations that turn to the courts and administrative proceedings to pursue their collective goals, social movement organizations that solicit potential legal cases through hotlines or other channels and then develop and support the cases, support groups initiated by advocacy lawyers to help them pursue certain kinds of cases, and support groups that pursue civil lawsuits arising out of what are initially criminal cases.

My research concentrates on support groups and the criminal justice system; however, the support provided to the East Asia Anti-Japanese Armed Front bombing group illustrates both criminal and civil support group activity over more than thirty years. We now turn to examine the network of support groups that have worked with and for the small underground group. This account has been constructed from a variety of primary and secondary materials published by the group's members and supporters; interviews with support group members, Kyūen staff, lawyers involved in the case, and several prison interviews with one member; participant observation of support group meetings and trial sessions; and material published in the newspaper *Kyūen* and the journal *Impaction*.

PROVIDING SUPPORT FOR THE HANNICHI BOMBERS

After the main wave of New Left protest had subsided in the early 1970s, a few small groups went underground to begin new campaigns of clandestine violence. In 1974 and 1975 a previously unknown group called the East Asia Anti-Japanese Armed Front (Higashi Asia Hannichi Busō Sensen, nicknamed Hannichi) claimed credit for a series of bombings. Their targets were companies that had been implicated in the Japanese mistreatment of Asian laborers during the Second World War. Most of the bombings took place at night when the company site was unoccupied. In the most devastating incident, two time bombs left in a shopping bag at the entrance of Mitsubishi Heavy Industries headquarters in the Marunouchi district of Tokyo exploded during the lunch hour, raining glass shards down on the narrow street crowded with people going to lunch. Eight people were killed and over two hundred injured. As the bombings continued and police were unable to find the perpetrators, they became the object of a massive nationwide search and were arguably the most feared and hated persons in Japan.

None of the members were known to the police, because prior to beginning their underground bombing campaign they had done little more than participate in the Zenkyōtō movement on their own university campuses and in other fairly innocuous protest movements. The central figures had come together as a study group interested in Japan's colonial and wartime behavior in Asia and its treatment of internal minorities, turning to direct action only after most other groups had given it up. Their approach, developed as a direct critique of the Red Army's flamboyant public style, was to keep their regular jobs and carry on ordinary lives, while secretly carrying out a symbolic bombing campaign against the Japanese companies whose wartime activities they had researched. They were almost completely unknown even within the New Left, since their writings were limited to cryptic communiqués issued after their bombing attacks and a small pamphlet series called *Hara Hara Tokei* (The Ticking Clock). The second issue of the pamphlet series was a bomb manual and how-to book on conducting clandestine revolutionary activity that invited others to form their own underground cells. It was not widely circulated, and possessing a copy was cause for arrest in the tense mid-1970s.

Believing they were the only active revolutionaries left in Japan, they viewed arrest nihilistically as the death of their revolutionary movement, and they carried cyanide capsules so they could commit suicide when the police caught up with them. As fringe participants in the protest movements of the time, they were aware of the Kyūen support system but did not think it was relevant to their situation. They never imagined that they would be captured alive and would have to stand trial for their bombing campaign, or that they could continue to resist the state after they were arrested. When the police did arrest nearly all of them in a coordinated sweep on 19 May 1975, only one member was able to swallow his cyanide before the police discovered and removed the capsules.

Activating the Support Network

Alerted by news reports that one of the arrested suspects had committed suicide, Kyūen immediately sent a team of medical and legal specialists to investigate the death. As calls came into the hotline from family members, Kyūen arranged for a local affiliate to provide emergency support at the six different police stations where the seven surviving arrestees were being held. Kyūen dispatched lawyers to meet with them and explain the concept of continuing resistance through the legal system (*Kyūen* #74, p. 1). Kyūen also organized a support group of family members, and by July it had expanded into a broader trial support group that was holding public meetings and soliciting funds and supporters. Because of the heavy mass media and police pressure on everyone remotely connected to the case, the support group's public statements carefully noted that they did not support Hannichi's policies and actions, but were providing support to the defendants as a form of resistance against state oppression. The expression they used, *Nittei no chian dan'atsu ni taisuru tatakai*, literally "the fight against imperial Japan's oppression of public peace," evokes strong connections to prewar Japan and the Peace Preservation Law (Chian Iji Hō) (*Kyūen* #75, p. 3). It took a great deal of courage and commitment even to participate in the support group in the face of strong public hostility toward the defendants that carried over to anyone who appeared sympathetic to them.

Meanwhile, the Hannichi defendants were held completely incommunicado in police station jails and interrogated daily for long periods, while being rearrested and indicted several times on new charges. The initial arrest warrants were for their most recent bombing and included charges of destruction of a building and violation of the Explosives Control Law (Bakuhatsubutsu Torishimari Hō), a Meiji era (1868–1911) statute originally directed against anarchists, which carries the death penalty. The group was composed of three different cells that sometimes acted independently. As more evidence was developed, the charges were expanded to cover the whole bombing campaign. Murder charges were added for some defendants as a result of the Mitsubishi Heavy Industries bombing, and attempted murder for other defendants in connection with a different bombing in which a watchman was injured. However, they were all potentially liable for the death penalty from the outset under the Explosives Control Law.

They were eventually moved to Tokyo House of Detention, where they continued to be held in unconvicted detention, incommunicado and in suicide watch cells. Although some members had talked to interrogators immediately after their arrest, they proved to be quick studies in the art of prison resistance. The three women in the group in particular established a reputation for militant resistance. Their hunger strikes, refusal to comply with prison regulations, and loud defiance (a violation of the rule of silence maintained within the prison) aroused so much internal support among other women prisoners that they were eventually transferred out of the women's section of the prison and onto a vacant floor of the men's quarters to isolate them. The defendants remained in incommunicado status for two years and three months, allowed only limited communication with their lawyers. Even after the communications ban was formally lifted by the court, they were not permitted to have regular visiting privileges because they remained under nearly continuous punishment restrictions for their resistance to prison authority and regulations.

Most remarkable was the resistance of a woman named Arai Mariko, who had simply been a friend of some of the other defendants and had not participated in any of the bombings, although she may have shared her expertise as a pharmacist. She was also the younger sister of a woman who had been very marginally involved in the group, and who committed suicide shortly after the other members were arrested. Their parents became central members of the support group and helped sustain the other parents.

Since the defendants were being held incommunicado, there was little that a support group could do for them except help the lawyers and send in flowers. They did not publish a regular support group newsletter, but supporters attended the trial sessions and sometimes participated in trial disruptions. Both the events in court and the defendants' resistance in prison were reported regularly in the Kyūen newspaper. The support group also published several pamphlets containing legal documents and other communications that the lawyers had received from the defendants. In addition, the defendants received considerable moral support from other prisoners who were involved in political resistance and had organized an informal prisoners' union with assistance from supporters outside, by utilizing their mail and visit privileges. Just three months after the arrest of the Hannichi bombers, the Japanese Red Army staged a high profile international hostage-taking incident in Kuala Lumpur and won the release of several prisoners from Japanese custody, including one male Hannichi defendant, Sasaki Norio. As trial preparations began for the remaining six Hannichi defendants, three women and three men, the court announced that they would be split into three groups to stand trial separately based on the specific charges against them, a common court tactic at the time for New Left defendants. The lawyers and defendants objected and the defendants began a hunger strike, while both lawyers and defendants boycotted the split trial. The court then relented and agreed to try all six defendants in a single trial.

Support for Hannichi Broadens

During this period, news leaked out that the time bombs used to such deadly effect in the Mitsubishi Heavy Industries bombing had actually been recycled and re-deployed after a failed attempt to blow up the emperor's train as it crossed a railway bridge. The group had seriously underestimated both the power of the bombs and the effect they would have on the glass facade of the high rise building. They had made a warning telephone call to get people out of the building, but the call was not taken seriously. While these facts did not mitigate their responsibility for the human toll of the explosion, they generated some sympathy among Japanese opposed to the emperor system. The new information sparked historical comparisons to the 1911 High Treason trial of Kotoku Shusui and his associates and the 1925 High Treason trial against Korean anarchist Pak Yol (Boku Retsu) and his partner Kaneko Fumiko. Although the crimes of High Treason and Lèse Majesté giving special protection to the emperor were abolished in 1947, both High Treason trials had also involved violation of the same Explosives Control Law with which the Hannichi defendants were charged.

There were several more sideshows, legal and otherwise, as the trial went on. This account is taken largely from a detailed chronology published in a special issue of *Impaction* magazine (1985) and cross-checked with articles in *Kyūen*. In March 1976, the defendants and lawyers sued the state for damages because the prosecutors had lied to the defendants and slandered their lawyers during the investigation. A month later, the lawyers filed a complaint against two jailors for having physically tortured and injured Arai Mariko after she was moved into the men's section of the prison. A few months later a lawyer and a court observer were given contempt of court sentences for protesting the violent treatment of the defendants, and the defendants themselves received several days of punishment for the same offense, whereupon they refused to attend the next court session in protest.

At the end of 1976, the judge announced that he was speeding up the court schedule to the unusual pace of four sessions per month. The defendants and lawyers boycotted the next court session in protest. When the judge enforced his ruling and held court in their absence, the entire legal team resigned, saying they could not properly defend their clients under those conditions. After the Tokyo Bar Association's committee in charge of selecting court-appointed lawyers also weighed in with the opinion that holding court four times a month was an interference with the defendants' right to legal representation, the judge relented and the original legal team returned to duty. Court sessions resumed in late August 1976, after a seven-month hiatus, but just a month later two of the three remaining female defendants, Daidōji Ayako and Ekita Yukiko, were released to the Japanese Red Army as the result of an airplane hijacking in Dacca, Bangladesh. One of the hijackers was alleged to be Sasaki Norio, the Hannichi member who had been released to the Japanese Red Army two years earlier.

The following winter Arai Mariko, the one woman from Hannichi left in the men's section of the prison, was again subjected to violence by guards. This incident led to a coordinated campaign in which prisoners at all of the detention prisons in Japan sent official protests to the Tokyo prosecutors' office. Meanwhile, one of the male defendants, Kurokawa Yoshimasa, began suffering severe asthma attacks from spending nearly three years in a dank suicide prevention cell with no air circulation, but neither the court nor the prison responded to the lawyers' pleas for medical relief.

As the first trial drew to an end in 1979, there were several police searches of the support group's offices on various pretexts. Four people were arrested for pasting support group stickers on telephone poles in San'ya, the day laborer district of Tokyo where some of the defendants had previously worked. By then the Hannichi case was attracting much broader attention because the prosecution had called for the death sentence for the two men involved in the Mitsubishi Heavy Industries bombing, Daidōji Masashi and Kataoka Toshiaki, and a life sentence for Kurokawa.

On the day the decision was to be announced, all other court sessions at Tokyo District Court were dismissed, and the three judges in the case were placed under round the clock VIP security. General security in the vicinity of the court was heavy, and everyone entering the court was searched, questioned individually, and required to show identification. The three male defendants received the anticipated sentences, and Arai Mariko received an eight-year prison sentence for her "spiritual support" of the group.

Providing Support for Prisoners on Death Row

The severity of the sentences, and particularly the first death sentences handed down for political offenses in postwar Japan, aroused even broader support. A Christian group began a petition campaign to protest the sentences, and a number of rallies were held as the defendants prepared to appeal. By early 1981, several church groups and anti-death penalty organizations and a number of prominent intellectuals had joined the original support group, which was reconstituted as an association of support groups with a very long name, Higashi Asia Hannichi Busō Sensen e no Shikei, Jūkei Kōgi Funsai, Kōsō Shin o Tatakau Shien Renraku Kaigi (Support Coordinating Group to Fight the Appeal and Destroy the Death Penalty and Heavy Sentence Attack on East Asia Anti-Japanese Armed Front). This was quickly contracted to the nickname Shienren, which just means "support coordinating group."

Shienren became a national social movement organization with various local groups carrying out semi-independent activities that are loosely coordinated by Kyūen. During the two appeal trials, Shienren conducted a continuing series of public lectures and discussion sessions that attracted quite large audiences. Shienren remains active to this day, publishing a monthly newsletter called *Shienren Nyūsu*, managing a variety of support activities on behalf of the Hannichi prisoners, working for new trials for three of them, and maintaining a website. Shienren organizes several public meetings each year and is financially solvent. Its members are also involved in other social movement organizations pursuing related issues, including the anti-death penalty movement.

During the early 1980s, while their sentences were being appealed and the defendants remained in unconvicted detention, they could receive visitors and also began writing books about their life experiences and their ideas. They became minor celebrities in the left, attracting supporters for their personal qualities as well as their political ideas. While their lawyers and supporters fought hard to have their sentences reduced, no one had any illusions that it would actually happen. However, since codefendants of the two people with death sentences remained at large in exile, with their trials incomplete, the general assumption of lawyers and supporters has been that the death sentences would not be carried out for some time. In anticipation of the severe isolation they would face once the death sentences had been confirmed by the Supreme Court, the two death penalty defendants and their supporters began making arrangements to maintain external contact and support. The measures they took illustrate the lengths to which Japanese support group members go to provide personal support for "their" prisoners. Since only immediate family members can maintain contact with prisoners awaiting the death sentence, their strategy was to create family relationships, primarily by marriage and by using the Japanese practice of family adoption. Since both marriage and adoption are formalized legally in Japan by entering the name of the new member into a person's family register and removing it from its former location in a different family register, this can be done even when a person is in prison, if other family members agree to change the family registers involved.

Initially, Kataoka Toshiaki married a woman supporter. His elderly parents were unable to visit him, so with the cooperation of his parents, another older woman supporter named Masunaga adopted him into her family as her son. The adoption was carried out with the full support of Mrs. Masunaga's own daughter, who was also an active member of his support group, and her grandson. After Kataoka's death sentence was confirmed, all four (the wife, the adoptive mother and her daughter and grandson) applied for visitation rights as family members. The prison, well aware that all of them were highly political supporters, rejected all four.

The second Hannichi person with a death sentence, Daidōji Masashi, was the adopted only son of a frail, elderly widow. His wife, Daidōji Ayako, who was

33

originally a codefendant in the case, was released to the Japanese Red Army in a hostage exchange in 1977. Since she remains in exile, he cannot marry another supporter, so with his widowed mother's cooperation, three female supporters were adopted into his family as his sisters during the 1980s. By the time his death sentence was confirmed, one was visiting him less regularly and a second was living in a distant prefecture, but the third had just quit her job and moved to Tokyo in order to be able to visit him regularly.

Initially, the prison certified Daidōji's mother as a family visitor but refused to recognize any of the three legally adopted sisters. The one who had moved to Tokyo appealed vigorously through a variety of channels and eventually the prison felt pressured to respond. In order to treat codefendants equally, they asked both Kataoka and Daidōji to choose only one of their supporters to be certified as a family visitor. Daidōji chose the woman who had pursued the case most vigorously, but the prison only permits her to write letters and to visit him twice a month, rather than the daily visits that family members are normally allowed. She has legally taken his family name and is known by it in the Tokyo support group, where she has been an active member. She puts out a newsletter based on the letters he sends out, which are written with that public purpose in mind. In 2004 Daidoji's mother died, so this woman and a cousin who was later certified became his only regular link to the outside world until the relaxation of the restrictions on death row visitors in late 2009. However, other members of his wide support network handle his legal and financial affairs and are pursuing the possibility of a new trial.

Forced to choose only one of his four family members, Kataoka chose the wife, but after some years the relationship weakened and she divorced him. The prison initially rejected the petition of his adoptive mother Mrs. Masunaga and her family to visit him but allowed him to correspond with his natural parents. With their cooperation, the adoptive family puts out a newsletter based on letters he sends to his parents. His adoptive mother, Mrs. Masunaga, continues to be an active support group member who is always introduced as his mother at public functions. In support group circles and publications the prisoner is known by his adoptive family's name, Masunaga Toshiaki, although the court and prison continue to use his original name, Kataoka. After the prisoner's wife divorced him, the Masunaga family sued the prison to obtain visiting rights. The prison permitted Mrs. Masunaga to have restricted rights, but denied the other members of the adoptive family. However, in 2007 after several years of petitioning, Mrs. Masunaga's daughter was allowed to take over the visits because of her mother's advancing age and residence far from Tokyo.

All of these family adoptions, as well as Kataoka's marriage, were carried out by members of the support group explicitly in order to provide continuing support to a prisoner awaiting the death penalty, and they entail no traditional obligations to other family members. Although they are legal adoptions under the Japanese system, the prison does not recognize them and has in fact explicitly rewritten its regulations to exclude adopted family members.

Adapting to New Emergencies

At the time the death penalties were confirmed there were three Hannichi members in exile with the Japanese Red Army: Daidōji's wife Ayako, Sasaki Norio, and Ekita Yukiko. The Hannichi support system was further complicated in 1994 when Ekita was arrested in Romania and deported back to Japan, whereupon her trial for the Hannichi bombings picked up where it had left off. Ekita's return posed an unusual problem because although she had originally been a member of Hannichi, after her release in 1977 she had become a member of the Japanese Red Army in exile. She was therefore a candidate for support also from a separate support group that was formed in the late 1980s to handle assistance for a series of persons who were on international wanted lists because of their connections to the Japanese Red Army in the Middle East but who had been arrested upon re-entering the country (usually after being found abroad and deported to Japan under guard by Japanese officials). This group, Kikokusha no Saiban o Kangaeru Kai (Organization to Consider the Trials of Returnees to Japan) and nicknamed Kikokusha, put out a newsletter called *Za Pasupōto* (The Passport).

The two support groups met and agreed to handle Ekita's support jointly. They formed a new group nicknamed Yuki Q, which put out a separate newsletter called *Yuki Rin Rin*. However, news of Ekita's trial and her letters from jail were also published regularly in both *Shienren Nyūsu* and *Za Pasupōto*. Ekita's support group was initially composed of members of the Shienren and Kikokusha groups, but it attracted some new participants in part because of Ekita's lively and outgoing personality. After Ekita's return she was held incommunicado for over a year. Once her visitor privileges were restored, she was visited nearly every day by a support group member until she began serving her twenty-year prison sentence in 2004. As is customary, a member of the support group handled Ekita's visit calendar to ensure that someone went to see her every day except when her lawyers were scheduled to visit, and that supporters did not make the trip out to the prison only to find that they could not see her because someone else had already taken her one visit for the day. The support groups continue to publish her letters from prison in their newsletters.

An even larger problem for this little cluster of support groups arose in 1996, when another Japanese Red Army member, Yoshimura Kazue, was arrested in Peru and immediately deported to Japan. It turned out that she had been raising Ekita's fourteen-year-old son in Peru under an assumed name. He had been stranded there by her sudden arrest and deportation and was in the custody of Peruvian child welfare authorities. As the son of two exiled Japanese Red Army members, who had been born and raised overseas in unusual circumstances, the boy was stateless. However, he had a claim to Japanese citizenship if his parentage could be established. Kyūen Renraku Sentā staff and the lawyers for both women worked with the Japanese Foreign Ministry to obtain temporary papers for the boy and bring him to Japan, while the combined support groups tried to figure out what to do after he arrived—and how to pay for it. Since both his natural mother and the woman who had been raising him were in jail and his unidentified father was still in exile, they had to find a home for him and arrange for his care and schooling. The head of the Kikokusha support group took him into his home and became his guardian, in yet another demonstration of the extent to which these social movement groups are willing to meet the personal needs of the prisoners they support.

Meanwhile, Ekita's trial picked up where it had left off in 1977, with some additional minor charges stemming from her years in exile. Her lawyer had taken the case explicitly in order to contest the formidable wall of isolation that the prison system erects around persons awaiting the death penalty. Since both Daidōji and Masunaga are technically Ekita's codefendants, they could legitimately be called as witnesses in her trial, and the lawyer wanted to capitalize on this situation to test the prison's regulations. As it turned out, the prosecution called the two men as witnesses in the fall of 1998, but when the judge ordered them to appear in court, the prison refused to allow them to leave the prison and offered instead to hold closed sessions of the trial at the prison. The prosecution then advanced the prison's arguments that it was too dangerous to let Daidōji travel to Tokyo District Court because he had an active support group involved in the anti-death penalty movement that might cause court disruptions, the Japanese Red Army might kidnap him on his way to and from court, and allowing him to appear in court would disturb his spiritual preparation for death. Ekita's lawyer argued that closing the trial sessions was a violation of Article 82 of the Constitution, which mandates that in political cases there is an absolute requirement for trials to be held in open court, and that the usual exceptions do not apply.

The judge ruled in the prosecution and the prison's favor, with the noncommittal observation that closing individual sessions did not constitute closing the trial. Ekita's lawyer immediately appealed directly to the Supreme Court for a ruling, but the Supreme Court declined to act. The lawyer then tried unsuccessfully to get permission for the press and/or a limited number of official observers to be present. These requests were rejected, and the court met in several closed sessions at Tokyo House of Detention to hear the testimony and cross-examination of Daidōji and Masunaga (Kataoka). New material also came out in this trial that was subsequently used to seek a new trial for Daidōji and Masunaga, since testimony in their original trial had been limited by the departure of three of the codefendants. Ekita wrote about these closed trial sessions in her letters to the newsletters, where they served not only as accounts of her own trial, but as reports to the support groups on the current condition of the two isolated men on death row.

Innovative Efforts to Reduce Isolation of Death Row Inmates

In addition to this attempt to utilize Ekita's trial to crack the wall of silence surrounding prisoners awaiting the death penalty, their supporters have used other inventive tactics to maintain contact. Since Shienren is actually a loose confederation of several groups with an interest in supporting the case, different groups of people have pursued various tactics independently. These separate activities are reported in *Shienren Nyūsu* and at national meetings of Shienren. In connection with the 1999 publication of a book of Daidōji's letters, for example, the person handling the legal and financial aspects of the publication persuaded the prison that certain tax matters required direct contact with Daidōji. The prison thereupon permitted a young female tax accountant (carefully selected by the supporter) to have several direct visits with Daidōji in order to explain the royalty and tax documents and get his signature on them, but they would not permit the support group member to attend these meetings.

The most ambitious of these efforts to contest the isolation of persons awaiting the death sentence is a series of civil lawsuits known as the T-shirt trials. Shortly before the two death sentences for Daidōji and Masunaga were upheld by the Supreme Court, when the prisoners were still entitled to receive *sashi-ire* from anyone, a group of supporters in a Kyushu group called Umi no Kai (The Sea Club) sent Daidōji and Masunaga a small amount of cash, two small handmade dolls embroidered with their names, and white T-shirts on which they had signed their names and written messages of support. Tokyo House of Detention rejected the *sashi-ire* gifts and sent them back to the supporters, whereupon Umi no Kai sued the prison authorities and the Japanese government.

By the time the lawsuit was filed, the defendants' death sentences had been confirmed and the Tokyo prison authorities would no longer permit them to participate directly in civil lawsuits, although it is quite common for supporters and lawyers to file and conduct lawsuits on behalf of such prisoners. However, this sophisticated group of supporters wanted to challenge the prison's authority to prohibit the prisoners from speaking on their own behalf in such lawsuits. They therefore filed a suit in which they and the prisoners were co-plaintiffs, and they insisted on trying the case themselves without benefit of legal counsel. Their strategy was intended both to highlight the fact that prisoners awaiting the death penalty were not being permitted by the prison authorities to communicate directly with the court in their own lawsuits, and to create a situation in which the supporters, as co-plaintiffs acting without formal legal counsel, would have to be allowed to communicate with their co-plaintiffs in prison.

After considerable effort, they were able to persuade a sympathetic judge in Kyushu District Court to let them try the case without a lawyer. The judge's sympathy was reinforced by the prison's intransigent refusal to obey the judge's orders to permit a court session to be held inside the prison for a civil case, even after direct mediation from the Justice Ministry in Tokyo. Under the judge's orders, arrangements were finally made for court documents and other materials concerning the trial to be transferred back and forth between the co-plaintiffs as long as they went through the Kyushu District Court. In defending against the suit, the prison and state argued that receiving the *sashi-ire* items would disrupt the prisoners' spiritual preparation for death, and also that the supporters had sent in the money for the purpose of filing a political lawsuit. By the time the case was concluded, the original judge had moved on to a different post and was not involved in writing the decision, but his successor found partially in the plaintiffs' favor, ruling that it was illegal for the prison to prohibit gifts of money sent in to prisoners and awarding the plaintiffs the token sum of ¥3,000 each (about $30 at the time).

The state, on behalf of the prison, immediately appealed the decision, largely reiterating its original arguments about the special status of persons awaiting the death penalty and the political purpose of the senders of the rejected money. Ironically, the same judge who originally allowed the Kyushu support group to pursue their lawsuit as co-plaintiffs without a lawyer had returned to the Kyushu High Court and presided over the appeal, which was legal because he had not been involved in the initial trial decision. In addition to reiterating their earlier arguments, the Umi no Kai plaintiffs brought in a law professor to testify that the severe Japanese restrictions on persons awaiting the death sentence were a violation of the International Covenant on Human Rights that the Japanese government had signed and was therefore required to uphold under international law, an argument that was also being made in other cases at the time.

The appeal decision handed down in December 1999 upheld the original decision in favor of the plaintiffs, but in even stronger language (*Kyūen* #369, p. 3). It rejected the state's argument that the special status of prisoners awaiting the death penalty conferred on the prison the absolute authority to restrict their contacts with the outside, noting that such restrictions could not exceed reasonable limits. It also held quite firmly that it was unlawful for the prison to restrict gifts of money to either defendants or prisoners serving sentences (including those awaiting the death sentence), regardless of the purpose for which the money was sent. This expands the outside contact of prisoners awaiting the death sentence and restricts the prison's ability to reject *sashi-ire* from politically motivated supporters.

The only area in which the plaintiffs did not succeed was in their attempt to invoke international human rights doctrine. The appeal decision cited a 1999 Supreme Court decision to the effect that international human rights law did not apply to the rights of people in prison and therefore could not serve as a basis for arguing that the prison's actions were illegal. Since in the first decision the court appeared to leave to the prison officials themselves the final judgment of whether prison regulations were reasonable, the appeals court's reiteration that restrictions on gifts of money did not meet the definition of reasonableness, and were therefore illegal, appears to establish the court as the final arbiter of the standard.

Meanwhile, because they had only won a partial victory in the first T-shirt trial over the right to send money to prisoners, Umi no Kai had already filed a second lawsuit, with thirty co-plaintiffs including Daidōji and Masunaga, over the prison's rejection of the T-shirts and dolls, the withholding of court documents, and restrictions on visits to death penalty inmates. That suit, known as the Second T-Shirt Trial, concluded in 2004 with reconfirmation of the right to send money into the prison, a partial victory on documents that had been withheld, and an award of ¥10,000 to each of the two imprisoned plaintiffs. Twenty-four plaintiffs including the two prisoners immediately filed a third T-shirt lawsuit over the prison's refusal to hand over other items they had sent in such as stamps and newspaper clippings, the restrictions on visits to death penalty inmates, and the prison's refusal to let the outside co-plaintiffs participate in trial sessions held within the prison. This suit concluded in 2008 with a decision that small items such as stamps could be sent in by anyone to any prisoner, including those awaiting the death penalty. Shienren immediately began a coordinated campaign of sending in sheets of stamps to the prisoners on death row, reporting in the newsletter when the prisoners received them.

Meanwhile, new revised prison regulations went into effect in June 2007 that are supposed to broaden the range of persons who are permitted to correspond with and visit persons awaiting the death sentence to include nonfamily members with legitimate business ([Nagai] Jin 2007). Although the authorities would never admit it, it seems highly probable that the vigorous efforts of the Hannichi support groups to contest the prison's restrictions on death row inmates through repeated civil lawsuits, along with repeated international criticism, have contributed to the change. Initially Tokyo House of Detention dragged its feet on implementing the new rules, except to reduce the length of time for regular visits to persons in unconvicted detention to eight minutes (later expanded to fifteen minutes) on the grounds that they were going to be handling so many more visits. Various groups in the trial support and anti-death penalty movements have been monitoring the application of the new rules for correspondence and visits with persons serving prison terms as well as those on death row. They have reported very uneven results, as the prison system grudgingly relaxed some rules only to suddenly tighten others, and rejected virtually all requests to visit persons on death row.

With the change of government in August 2009, the anti-death penalty movement was able to use its access to a long-time Diet member and supporter who became a Cabinet member to raise some questions about apparent systematic violations of the new rules. They learned that application of the rules was being left to the discretion of the administration at each prison, and that Tokyo House of Detention was limiting requests for visits to three persons per prisoner awaiting the death penalty, on the old grounds that visits would disturb the prisoners' spiritual preparations for death. Then, in October 2009 the prison suddenly lifted all limits on the number of people who could apply for permission to visit persons awaiting the death penalty. Shienren responded with a new campaign for its members to seek permission to visit the two prisoners on death row. Forty supporters and old friends immediately applied to visit Daidoji, and thirty-two applied to visit Masunaga. Only two of the seventy-two persons were given permission for visits, one for each prisoner, but some of the others received permission to correspond with them. The reports of the first two visits to the death row inmates after twenty-three years of nearly total isolation were published in the January 2010 issue of *Shienren Nyūsu*, and visits are now reported regularly in each issue.

With two more codefendants still in exile and with legal efforts to obtain a new trial for Daidōji and Masunaga, the Hannichi support groups are likely to be in business for some time. Both of the codefendants in exile participated in the Mitsubishi Heavy Industries bombing, and therefore would also face the possibility of a death sentence if they were returned to Japan and their trials resumed. New trials for the two prisoners currently awaiting the death sentence and for a third serving a life sentence remain possible, albeit unlikely. Both of the death penalty prisoners are now suffering from severe, chronic medical conditions, so the support groups have turned their attention to getting better medical care for prisoners. They continue, however, to seek ways to use the Hannichi case to reduce the isolation of all persons awaiting the death penalty.

THE HANNICHI CASE AND TRIAL SUPPORT IN CONTEMPORARY JAPAN

This complex and long-running case illustrates the wide range of functions performed by trial support groups in Japan as a form of social movement activity. At its inception this was a standard case for the Kyūen system of support, noteworthy only for the extreme nature of the crimes and the general public hostility toward the defendants, which made participation in the support group itself an act of strong political commitment. The initial small support group did all of the standard things support groups do: helped the lawyers, attended trial sessions, published reports on the case, and provided personal support to the defendants.

The severity of the sentences handed down in the first trial, plus greater familiarity with the ideas, personalities, and prison behavior of the defendants, attracted much broader support for Hannichi in the early 1980s. Through the formation of Shienren, support for the Hannichi defendants became part of the anti-death penalty movement and the anti-emperor movement, and more broadly, began to resonate with the left's critique of Japan's colonial and wartime behavior in Asia and the treatment of minorities within Japan. Although these movements are small and far removed from the mainstream of Japanese society, they do enjoy considerable currency within the left. Shienren itself is widely known in New Left circles, and its efforts on behalf of death row prisoners are reported regularly in *Kyūen*, the monthly newspaper of Kyūen Renraku Sentā that maintains a fairly wide circulation.

Hannichi supporters clearly view their involvement as an expression of their political commitment and a form of social movement activity, yet they provide a powerful illustration of the level of intimate personal support that characterizes Japanese trial support groups. By tracing the origins of the Kyūen support system as a direct response to the routine practices of the Japanese criminal justice system, I have tried to show that such personal support is fundamentally a strategy for sustaining political resistance to overwhelming state power. While the power of the state is exercised most directly when individuals confront the criminal justice system, it is also manifested indirectly in generalized demands for social conformity and the power of social opinion in Japanese society. Consequently, for a broad array of social movement causes that have nothing to do with the criminal justice system but seek to change Japan through legal challenges mounted by individuals and small groups, trial support groups have become an essential component of social movement activity. Understanding how and why they act as they do provides a new perspective on both social movements and the legal system in contemporary Japan. In a recent comparative study, Gilda Zwerman and I have found that quite similar forms of direct personal involvement also characterized the legal support system for Americans facing criminal charges for their New Left political activity in the late 1960s and early 1970s, although there are still variations because of the quite different legal systems and legal cultures of the two countries (Zwerman and Steinhoff 2012)

At an even broader level, the Hannichi political defendants fall within contemporary definitions of terrorists, although their original acts were committed in the 1970s and the term was not applied to them at the time. In both Japan and the United States, the term "terrorist" was applied retroactively to criminal defendants from the New Left in the 1980s (Zwerman and Steinhoff 2012). Moreover, from the perspective of the post-9/11 world, the practices that the Japanese criminal justice system applies to such defendants bear striking similarities to the extraordinary procedures the United States has been applying to persons it defines as "enemy combatants." Thus, although the Kyūen trial support system arose as a response to specific practices that the Japanese criminal justice system applies in political cases, some of the practices themselves cannot be considered uniquely Japanese. On the other hand, the nature of the support system and the way it addresses the needs of the principals in legal cases resonates with particular characteristics of its Japanese context.

REFERENCES

1985. Higashi Asia Hannichi Busō Sensen: Tatakai no Kiseki. *Impaction*: 46–82.

Foote, Daniel. (1992). From Japan's Death Row to Freedom. *Pacific Rim Law & Policy Journal* 1: 11–103.

Foote, Daniel. (1993). "The Door That Never Opens"?: Capital Punishment and Post-Conviction Review of Death Sentences in the United States and Japan. *Brooks Journal of International Law* 19: 367–521.

Foote, Daniel. (1995). Confessions and the Right to Silence in Japan. *Georgia Journal of International and Comparative Law* 21: 415–88.

Kurita Nobuyoshi. (1993). *Shakai Undo no Keiryo Shakaigakuteki Bunseki: Naze Kogisuru noka* [A Quantitative Sociological Analysis of Social Movements: Why Do They Protest]. Tokyo, Nihon Hyōronsha.

Mitchell, Richard H. (1976). *Thought Control in Prewar Japan*. Ithaca, NY and London, Cornell University Press.

Mitchell, Richard H. (1992). *Janus-Faced Justice: Political Criminals in Imperial Japan*. Honolulu, University of Hawaii Press.

Miyazawa, Setsuo. (1992). *Policing in Japan: A Study on Making Crime*, ed. G. Geis and D. J. Newman. Trans. F. G. Bennett, Jr. and J. O. Haley. Albany, NY, State Universty of New York Press.

[Nagai] Jin. (2007). Kangoku Hō Zenmen Kaiseika no Shikei Kakuteishu Shogu Kitei [Regulations concerning the Treatment of Prisoners with Confirmed Death Penalty Sentences in the Overall Revision of the Prison Law]. *Shienren Nyūsu* (April 5, 2007): 8–9.

Steinhoff, Patricia G. (1991). *Tenko: Ideology and Societal Integration in Prewar Japan*. New York, Garland Publishing Company.

Steinhoff, Patricia G. (1999a). Doing the Defendant's Laundry: Support Groups as Social Movement Organizations in Contemporary Japan. *Japanstudien, Jahrbuch des Deutschen Instituts fur Japanstudien* 11.

Steinhoff, Patricia G. (1999b). Student Protest in the 1960s. *Social Science Japan*: 3–6.

Takazawa Koji and Takagi Masayuki. (1981). *Shinsayoku Nijunenshi* [A Twenty Year History of the New Left]. Tokyo, Shinchosha.

Takizawa Ichiro. (1993). *Nihon Sekishoku Kyūenkai Shi*. Tokyo, Nihon Hyōronsha.

Zwerman, Gilda, and Patricia G. Steinhoff. (2005). When Activists Ask for Trouble: State-Dissident Interactions and the New Left Cycle of Resistance in the United States and Japan. In *Repression and Mobilization, Social Move-*

ments, Protest, and Contention, vol. 21, ed. C. Davenport, H. Johnston, and C. Mueller, 85–107. Minneapolis, University of Minnesota Press.

Zwerman, Gilda, and Patricia G. Steinhoff. (2012). The Remains of the Movement: The Role of Legal Support Networks in Leaving Violence while Sustaining Movement Identity. *Mobilization: An International Journal* 17: 489–507.

Zwerman, Gilda, Patricia G. Steinhoff, and Donatella della Porta. (2000). Disappearing Social Movements: Clandestinity in the Cycle of New Left Protest in the United States, Japan, Germany, and Italy. *Mobilization: An International Journal* 5.

CHAPTER 2

Karōshi Activism and Recent Trends in Japanese Civil Society: Creating Credible Knowledge and Culture[1]

Scott North

> *Karōshi* is one concrete *manifestation* of the many paradoxes born in the course of Japan's abnormal economic growth. Your movement has great meaning, for, in considering those paradoxes, it aims to rectify the course of Japanese society.
>
> (*Mainichi Shinbun* reporter Fujita Satoru, in a letter to Hiraoka Chieko, plaintiff in a *karōshi* suit, November 16, 1993)

Understanding the social epidemiology of *karōshi* in Japan, that is, how the organization of work leads to overwork and the deaths of workers, requires some explanation. At the macrolevel it is useful to think along the lines of the French sociologist Emile Durkheim (1964), who postulated that increasingly frequent social interactions, stemming from the increasingly complex social division of labor, will give rise to regulatory law. Properly regulated, complementarity in social relations of production results in social solidarity and well-being. In a particularly well-governed state, the ever-finer grained division of labor might even lead to Adam Smith's "universal opulence." However, Durkheim also postulated that the speed of differentiation of functions could be so great that regulatory law would not be able to keep up. In such cases, pathological forms of the division of labor may emerge.

Such was arguably the case during Japan's era of high-speed economic growth. In the postwar rush to catch up with the West, powerful techniques for

---

1. The author is grateful to the International Agreements Fund of the University of Hawaii at Manoa for a fellowship that supported the initial fieldwork for this study. I also wish to thank the Japan Foundation and the Alfred P. Sloan Foundation's Berkeley Center for Working Families for fellowship support during the preparation of the article upon which this chapter is based. It was published in *Japanstudien, Jahrbuch des Deutschen Instituts für Japanstudien* 11 (1999).

getting the most out of labor and increasing production became diffused throughout Japanese industries. Microlevel analysis of the work process reveals how management's coordinated manipulation of an invented "traditional" family ideology emphasized the naturalness of hierarchical rather than horizontal alignments. The conflicts that Durkheim's theory predicts will lead to the development of enforceable regulation of the relations between capital and labor were thus suppressed.

Anti-*karōshi* activism aims to redress this manifest imbalance of power and Japanese workers' limited access to law. Defendants in criminal trials (Steinhoff), consumer groups (Maclachlan), and union members (Turner) share with *karōshi* activists many of the same institutional and practical obstacles to organizing and litigating in pursuit of their interests. As in these other cases, *karōshi* litigants are not so much reluctant to litigate as turned away by the difficulties, low rewards, and risks of doing so. One problem is plaintiffs' general ignorance of complex administrative and legal procedures, including how and where claims can be brought, who has legal standing to sue, and who can be sued. Another is a marked predisposition to avoid conflict, with a special reluctance to challenge social superordinates; most plaintiffs are wives whose social identities are a poor fit with aggressive social activism. Third, there is the fear that litigation may damage one's reputation. This is all the more frightening because the consequences may not be immediate or flow directly from the issue. Fourth, legal and administrative procedures are often vague, opaque, or subjective; disclosure and discovery rules are biased in favor of elite insiders and major social actors. Finally, there is the sheer length of administrative processes and trials and the costs associated with waging legal battles. Recent attempts to make trials speedier and more intensive notwithstanding, the infrequency and brevity of trial sessions in Japanese courts mean that claimants must bear protracted financial and emotional burdens while trials drag on year after year. Overcoming these obstacles to litigated solutions requires collective organization, as well as an inexhaustible supply of individual resolve and pluck.

This chapter argues that the long duration and difficulties inherent in fighting *karōshi* cases are, paradoxically, resources that give activists time to make facts and spur them to build civic movements that can support the plaintiffs, put pressure on bureaucrats and judges, and change the conventional wisdom of employers and employees regarding work and health.

ORIGINS AND OVERVIEW OF *KARŌSHI* ACTIVISM

Karōshi, directly rendered in English as death due to overwork, is a term coined by Dr. Uehata Tetsunojō (1978, 250). It describes the relationship he observed between work environments, stress, and the sudden deaths of Japanese workers. Movement activists do not elongate the "ro" of *karōshi* when using the term in English language documents. It is their stated intent to do what they can to have the term become part of the international lexicon (Karōshi Bengōdan Zenkoku Renrakukai 1990).[2] In a later work, Dr. Uehata (1990, 98) defines *karōshi* as a sociomedical phenomenon characterized by "a permanent disability or death brought on by worsening high blood pressure or arteriosclerosis resulting in diseases of the blood vessels in the brain such as cerebral hemorrhage, subarachnoid hemorrhage and cerebral infarction and acute heart failure and myocardial infarction induced by conditions such as ischemic heart disease." By coining the term *karōshi* and publishing widely on the links between work, stress, and death, Dr. Uehata, a specialist in occupational medicine and cardiovascular diseases and former head of the Adult Disease Department at the National Institute of Public Health, became one of the founding figures of the anti-*karōshi* movement.

Similar in organization to the health-related activism concerning pollution-caused mercury poisoning (*Minamata-byō*), cadmium poisoning (*Itai-itai-byō*), and PCB poisoning (*Kanemi yushō*), the anti-*karōshi* movement originated from the combined efforts of professionals in medicine, law, and academia. To a greater extent than in these famous environmental pollution cases, labor unions sometimes play prominent roles in *karōshi* cases. However, as in the environmental cases, no *karōshi* movement is possible without victims and their families. In the words of economist Morioka Koji (1993), a leading authority on Japanese working hours and *karōshi*, "To create a social problem in Japan, it is necessary to have a death and a trial with lawyers. This functions as a refuge (*kakekomidera*) for other sufferers."

Karōshi victims come from all walks of life, all classes, and all occupational categories. Most victims are men, although a few women have also succumbed. Enduring links between work and self-worth in the gender ideology of Japanese men make reducing work or taking time off tantamount to diminishing one's masculinity.

Company size does not predict the frequency of *karōshi*, nor does employment in the public sector provide protection. Many teachers, doctors, and nurses have been victims. The lead investigator in the notorious Wakayama Curry Incident died during the investigation of that nationally publicized case; his death was recognized as *karōshi,* and his family was awarded compensation. One of the overworked Ministry of Labor investigators I interviewed during my research made a point of showing me his day planner, in which he carefully noted the number of hours he worked each day so that his family might have this record to use as evidence in the event of his untimely passing.

Perhaps the most likely candidates for *karōshi* are middle-aged men from crowded metropolitan areas, who must endure long commutes to jobs in companies whose fortunes are often determined by sudden and unpredictable market shifts. Often they are subject to heavy work quotas, which rob them of occupational

---

2. Karoshi (without the macron) was added to the Oxford English Dictionary in 2002.

autonomy and require them to make unstinting efforts. *Karōshi* risk is greatest for those whose work deprives them of adequate sleep and nutrition, starves them of psychological satisfaction, and denies them opportunities for physical and spiritual renewal.

Guided by the lawyers of the National Defense Counsel for Victims of *Karōshi* (hereafter Karōshi Bengōdan) and supported by medical and other professionals, fellow sufferers, labor activists, and growing numbers of sympathetic citizens, the anti-*karōshi* movement has made some progress in winning relief for victims' families. Based ultimately on constitutional guarantees of equal protection and "minimum standards of wholesome and cultured living," civil litigation and administrative lawsuits have proven to be effective tools for persuading the Ministry of Labor to revise the standards for recognizing and compensating work-related illness and death. Because of these revisions, work-induced depression and suicides are now compensated, adding to the growing tally.

For example, only about 15 percent of the just over 500 applications for *karōshi* compensation filed in 1995 were approved. These 500 applications represented only 5 percent of the estimated 10,000 annual cases of *karōshi* in Japan at that time (Kawahito 1991, 150). Press coverage of these victories stimulated public attention. In an insurance company poll of 500 Tokyo office workers, 46 percent responded that *karōshi* was a possibility for them, with 9 percent saying the possibility was high (Keizai Kikaku Chō 1994, 8).

In contrast, 2006 saw 1,757 claims filed for circulatory disease, death, or major depression caused by overwork. That year 560 claims were approved, including 66 for suicide or attempted suicide, and 355 for circulatory ailments such as stroke and heart disease. Nearly all the recognized claims concerned men (94 percent). The majority of claims for psychological problems, including suicides, concerned men in their thirties. Recognized claims for psychological distress caused by work increased 61.4 percent over 2005 (*Nikkei Shinbun* 2007). Due to revisions in the standards for recognizing these claims and the large backlog of cases, we can expect to see further increases in the ratio of claims to compensated cases in the future. It is clear that the courts and the medical profession, as well as the general public, accept *karōshi* as a cause of death.

But despite the tide of increasing recognition that overwork is bad for health, many firms (and workers) remain in purposeful denial about overwork and the toll it takes. Attempts to survey corporate attitudes toward *karōshi* produce very low response rates. On the other hand, public awareness has increased. So much so that the Ministry of Health, Labor, and Welfare website devoted to overwork was overwhelmed and crashed when it first came online in 2003 (Morioka 2005, 2–3).

Anti-*karōshi* activism has increased the visibility of the problem, but the large and growing number of cases indicates that the movement still has a long way to go to reach its two goals of relief for all victims' families and the elimination of working conditions that cause *karōshi*. Still, in comparison with the United States, Japan has a well-articulated and relatively advanced concept of corporate responsibility for the relationship between work stress and illness.

In the United States, workaholism and its attendant diseases are not as clearly linked to inhumane corporate cultures and practices, nor are organized anti-overwork movements evident. Diana Fassel's (1990) book, *Working Ourselves to Death: the High Cost of Workaholism and the Rewards of Recovery,* equates overwork with addictions like alcohol abuse: an individual affliction, treatable through a twelve-step program. Death may be the ultimate result, but she does not try to establish epidemiological links or inspire either collective action or litigation. To my knowledge, there is no comparable development of a movement to name death from overwork, elaborate cause and effect, seek compensation for victims, pursue revision of labor laws, or demand corporate responsibility for worker exploitation and work illness in the United States.

Overwork in the United States is not generally seen as symptomatic of corporate malaise or skewed social priorities. Individual bosses, rather than the corporate system, get the blame. A website, bullybusters.org, which gives abused employees advice on how to deal with bullying bosses, has been receiving as many as 100,000 hit per month, and I have seen advertisements in which recovering workaholics testify to the benefits of counseling. On the other hand, social crusaders like Noam Chomsky and Ralph Nader, who, like their anti-*karōshi* activist Japanese counterparts, argue that unaccountable concentrations of corporate power are undermining individual freedom, ethics, the environment, and health, have been characterized as political extremists. A comparative investigation of why an anti-*karōshi* movement can exist in Japan but not in the United States is a tantalizing question for future research.

Karōshi *Activism and Japanese Civil Society*

The movement's limited progress toward its distant goal of eradicating *karōshi* notwithstanding, this paper argues that anti-*karōshi* protest is an example of two emergent trends representative of contemporary civil society. The first is common to most, if not all, the industrialized democracies. The second may have functional equivalents abroad; however, this paper will be concerned with a specific Japanese variant.

Elaborated by sociologist Steven Epstein (1995) and other theorists of "new" social movements, the first trend is the development of health-related social movements, or disease constituencies, in which diverse lay activists amass varied forms of credibility. With this credibility, they are able to take increasingly visible roles in fact making and the construction of scientific knowledge. Epstein's study of American AIDS activism argues that credibility is a system of political and cultural authority. This authority endows those who exercise it with power to "transform[ing] the very definition of what *counts* as credibility" and, consequently, to provide new moral ground for the organization of group identities (Epstein 1995, 409–10 [italics in original]).

Epstein's notion of credibility as authority is useful for understanding how collective action by lawyers, housewives, unionists, educators, reporters, doctors, and union members in *karōshi* cases has the power to compel Ministry of Labor bureaucrats and employers to acknowledge the perspectives of *karōshi* victims as credible knowledge. The central tenet of this knowledge is the necessity of seeing the work-stress relationship from the point of view of each worker and his or her individual abilities. From this follows new medical knowledge of the relationship between work, stress, and disease, new legal doctrines regarding the burden of responsibility for employee health, and moral claims with far-reaching implications for how a humane (*ningen rashii*) society should be organized.

The second trend, identified by Patricia G. Steinhoff (1999 and elsewhere in this volume), is a pattern of voluntary participation in Japanese civil society with direct antecedents in the student movement of the 1960s and other, earlier criminal trials of people on the Japanese left. According to Steinhoff, this form of social movement organization has fairly standardized practices and activities. It has been carried into the post-1970s by veterans of those student protests and become institutionalized as the vehicle for a variety of social movements that support individuals and groups fighting extended legal battles amid the terrific pressures of Japan's conformist cultural system.

Clearly a descendant of the same lineage, *karōshi* activism has inherited most of these same organizational characteristics. These include the use of hotlines, provision of free legal assistance, creation of volunteer support groups to help central figures weather lengthy trials, and reliance on litigation to bring about changes in social policy. It also displays some of the factionalism and conflicts particular to the contest for control of limited resources on the Japanese left.

The landmark *karōshi* case of Mr. Hiraoka Satoru and his family, which is described in detail below, illustrates the ways in which *karōshi* protest is a manifestation of the two trends sketched above. It was the first case in the nation recruited through the Karōshi Bengōdan's *"karōshi 110 ban"* emergency hotline, the first to be explicitly recognized as a case of death due to overwork, and the first to pursue corporate responsibility via a civil trial. It adds to our understanding of new institutions of Japanese civil society by illuminating the central role of lawyers and other professionals in directing the activities of the lay participants in citizens' movements. Finally, the Hiraoka case serves as an example of how the epidemiology of disease is socially constructed. It gives insights into the politics of scientific knowledge construction in the contentious arena of labor law and occupational health and reminds us that constitutional "guarantees" depend on an informed and active citizenry.

The Bureaucratic-Legal Context of Karōshi *Struggles*

A brief outline of Japan's labor and social welfare laws is a necessary prelude to understanding why *karōshi* cases require the support of a social movement. The following account is not a comprehensive overview of these laws, but deals only with those aspects relevant to *karōshi*. Since brevity carries the risk of over-simplification, interested readers may wish to consult additional sources, such as Upham (1987), Ueyanagi (1990), Hanami (1985), and Sugeno (1992). The Constitution of Japan (Articles 13, 25, and 27) establishes state responsibility for worker well-being. Through the Constitution, the state is charged with establishing laws to promote social welfare and public health, individual rights, and standards for wages and working hours. The most important of these laws are the Labor Standards Act of 1947 (Rōdō Kijun Hō), the Industrial Safety and Health Act of 1972 (Rōdō Anzen Eisei Hō), and a companion law that is the basis of the Workers' Compensation Insurance System (Rōsai Hoken Seidō).

The substance and enforcement provisions of both the Labor Standards Act and Industrial Safety and Health Act are weak. Capital and labor are to reach agreements regarding working hours, overtime, and work rules in each enterprise. These are then reported to the Labor Standards Office holding jurisdiction over particular geographic areas. Above them are regional Labor Standards Bureaus with even wider jurisdictions. The Ministry of Health, Labor, and Welfare in Tokyo has ultimate jurisdiction. Both the Labor Standards Office and the Labor Standards Bureau are understaffed. Due to heavy case loads, only the most serious and intentional violations can be investigated. Compliance with the standards established by the Labor Standards Act and Industrial Safety and Health Act is thus, in effect, voluntary. Furthermore, these standards only apply to firms with ten or more workers. Consequently a large minority (between 35 and 42 percent) of the private sector work force that works in small enterprises is not protected by these laws (Chalmers 1989, 102; Rebick 2005, 107). The Workers' Compensation Insurance System, however, covers all workers. Even if a worker reports a violation of the Labor Standards Act or Industrial Safety and Health Act to the Labor Standards Office, the Labor Standards Office cannot issue an injunction to stop illegal labor practices, but must refer the case to the overburdened public prosecutor. In cases where a conviction is obtained, punishment seldom exceeds exhortations to make greater efforts, or small fines.

In sum, the Labor Standards Act and Industrial Safety and Health Act are inadequate to protect workers from abusive employers or dangerous working conditions. The workers themselves must know the law and see that its provisions are carried out. However, in many companies, corporate culture or the pressure of hierarchical relations with supervisors thwart employee initiatives. Unions seldom make safety or working hours their top priorities, preferring to concentrate instead on job security and wages. The protections of the labor laws are most effective for workers in large firms.

When a worker is injured or killed on the job, he or she is eligible for Workers' Compensation Insurance payments. The compensation system is administered by the Ministry of Health, Labor, and Welfare through the Labor Standards Office and Labor Standards Bureau, which oversee the first two steps of the application process. The ministry itself sets the standards for compensation. The basic standard is a demonstrable cause and effect relationship between work and the death or injury of the worker. When this relationship is easily established, the system moves quickly to compensate the victim's immediate family, one of whom must file the claim. Unions and other groups may support such claims, but may not file them without the participation of the next of kin. Compensation is based on the severity of the injury. When a worker dies, compensation is based on salary at the time of the incident, the number of dependents, and the ages of any children. The average daily wage, exclusive of bonus, for the ninety days prior to death is multiplied by a number of days between 175 and 245 to get the basic compensation. This is paid monthly to the survivors and replaces the Survivor's Pension (only about ¥120,000 per month) awarded by the Welfare Insurance System. To this is added a bonus, calculated in similar fashion (about 20 percent of the basic compensation). A one-time special payment to survivors of ¥3 million and funeral expenses of ¥600,000 complete the compensation package.

When a cause and effect relationship is more difficult to establish, as in *karōshi* cases, simply applying for compensation may take years. Lawyers for *karōshi* victims say this is due to ministerial reluctance to recognize *karōshi* and its implied relationship between work stress and illness. The ministry has acknowledged issuing both public and internal sets of guidelines for determining compensation in *karōshi* cases. Courts have taken a harsh view of that duplicity, and the criteria are now freely available on the Ministry of Health, Labor, and Welfare website. Nevertheless, there are many obstacles to reaching the courts. The claimant must first apply for compensation at the Labor Standards Office having jurisdiction over the employer. Decisions at this level are based only on documentary evidence, which the plaintiff is not allowed to view. If compensation is denied, the plaintiff has sixty days to file an appeal for a review of the judgment with the Labor Standards Bureau having jurisdiction. At this stage, a Workers' Compensation Insurance investigator carries out an investigation based on the evidence submitted by both the claimant and the firm, sometimes including examination of the job site.

No time limit is stipulated for reaching these decisions. Two years or more may elapse at each stage of the application process. The ministry has tried to speed the handling of cases in response to charges that it purposely stalls them as a way of discouraging victims' families from filing *karōshi* claims. If the judgment at the Labor Standards Bureau is against the plaintiff, an appeal may be filed with the Central Workers' Compensation Insurance Board in Tokyo. At this third stage plaintiffs can at last see the evidence presented by the firm, as well as have a right to be heard. Nevertheless, rejection by the board is a near certainty. In 1996, Japan's Supreme Court ruled that plaintiffs may file a civil suit to have the judgment against compensation removed without first having to appeal to the Central Workers' Compensation Insurance Board. Although this ruling allows plaintiffs access to the judicial system sooner, claimants must still anticipate a struggle of several year's duration, as civil trials are often broken into brief and infrequent sessions.

Beyond these administrative hurdles, involvement in public disputes such as lawsuits imposes a significant stigma in Japan. The majority of survivors are bereaved widows who feel powerless in the face of their loss. Many refrain from filing claims for compensation because they are unfamiliar with and intimidated by bureaucrats and bureaucratic procedures; they do not wish to publicize their plight; they fear for their reputations if they complain; they are concerned that filing a claim will only prolong the suffering of their families; and they do not know that compensation is possible in *karōshi* cases. Moreover, companies tend to handle *karōshi* deaths as if the victim had merely retired. Wives seldom know that, in addition to their individual life insurance policies, their husbands have been enrolled in group life insurance through their employers; nor are they aware that the company collects on these policies because the firm rather than the family is the beneficiary. This practice is being contested in court. With this brief introduction to the social and legal difficulties of filing a claim, we can now turn to the story of Mr. Hiraoka.

From August 1993 through June 1994, I participated in several *karōshi*-related groups in the Kansai area. During this time, and in subsequent visits to Japan in June 1996 and again in 1998, I gathered documentary information on Tsubakimoto Seiko and the Hiraoka case. I attended sessions of the trial, observed meetings of the legal team, the Osaka Karōshi wo Kangaeru Kazoku no Kai (Osaka Association of Families Concerned with *Karôshi*), and the Zenkoku Karōshi wo Kangaeru Kazoku no Kai (National Association of Families Concerned with *Karôshi*), including negotiations at the Ministry of Labor in Tokyo. I had one formal, three-hour interview with Mrs. Hiraoka at her home on October 23, 1993, as well as many subsequent informal conversations and correspondence with her, her children, her lawyers, and other supporters. These conversations I recorded in my field notes. Movement participants sent me newspaper clippings, newsletters, magazines, and copies of books in which the case was reported when I was out of the country. In constructing this account of the case, I have drawn from my collection of both formally and informally published sources as well as my field notes. (Sources of direct quotes are identified in the text and References.)

THE WORK AND DEATH OF HIRAOKA SATORU

A native of Kagoshima Prefecture, Hiraoka Satoru first came to Osaka in 1959 at the age of nineteen. Fresh out of high school, he became a lineman for an electric company. He quit after six months because of bad working conditions, which he attributed to the firm's lack of a union. He then joined Tsubakimoto Seiko, remaining there for twenty-eight years. At the time of his death, at age 48, Mr. Hiraoka was a section chief in charge of approximately thirty workers at Tsubakimoto's S-2 factory in Nara. Employing a secret process, the plant produces very small, precision ball bearings, which are used in devices ranging from ballpoint pens to rockets to automobiles.

The S-2 factory came on line in 1985. It quickly became the most profitable section of the firm, and with its debut the company's stock began to rise. Throughout 1986 and 1987, the company stepped up production in preparation for entry into the first section of the Tokyo Stock Exchange. For workers in the S-2 plant, this meant an increased workload. Saturday holidays were abolished, and the plant was operated around the clock. However, to keep costs down, it was done with only two shifts of workers each putting in large amounts of overtime and holiday work. Meeting production quotas was difficult because of labor shortages and mechanical breakdowns. Section chiefs like Mr. Hiraoka bore especially heavy burdens. Seven of them performed the work of nine by each working a double shift once a week. Section chiefs trained new workers, supervised and evaluated their sections, oversaw quality control, made frequent repairs to the production line, and worked on the line themselves.

When he collapsed due to heart failure in the toilet of his home on February 23, 1988, his family was devastated. Mrs. Hiraoka was convinced that he had "been killed by the company." Several top company officials attended the funeral. They brought ritual sympathy and a small sum of cash. Afterward, Mrs. Hiraoka pressed the firm's personnel manager about why her husband had been working more than 3,500 hours a year. In a rare moment of candor, he confirmed her suspicions, saying, "Well, in truth, he was doing more than one job" (Ikeda 1997, 164) However, after Mrs. Hiraoka had filled an occupational death claim with the local Labor Standards Office, relations with the firm deteriorated. Tsubakimoto Seiko refused to support her application with time cards or other records. They claimed his death was due to "personal infirmity" and handled it as if Mr. Hiraoka had simply retired. After paying the family his accumulated ¥7 million retirement bonus, the company severed ties. His daughter, Tomoko, recalled, "At the funeral, they called him 'Hira-san, Hira-san,' but afterward they never even phoned to see how we were getting along" (Hiraoka Tomoko 1991, 4) Use of the diminutive form "Hira-san" was probably meant to indicate familiarity and close relations with the deceased, but, ironically, it can also be taken as a reference to "Mr. Ordinary," as in *hirashain* or ordinary worker.

Reconstructing the Facts

Facing corporate indifference, Mrs. Hiraoka and her children felt betrayed and frustrated. Then, in April 1988, they happened upon a small newspaper article announcing the advent of *"karōshi 110 ban."* This was a free, legal consultation hotline service offered by the Osaka Defense Counsel for Victims of *Karōshi* (Osaka Karōshi Mondai Renrakukai, hereafter Renrakukai). The organizers were Kansai (Osaka and Kobe) area labor lawyers. Lawyer Matsumaru Tadashi took Mrs. Hiraoka's call. As he hung up the phone and looked at the notes he made regarding her case, he mused incredulously, "Are there really still companies with working conditions like these?" (Ikeda 1997, 164). Soon thereafter, Mrs. Hiraoka participated in a seminar about *karōshi* compensation and met Mr. Matsumaru and the other lawyers in the Osaka group. Her case was the first one recruited via the hotline. The Renrakukai agreed to take her case *pro bono*.

The first step in applying for workers' compensation insurance benefits was to compose a portrait of Mr. Hiraoka's work environment. Her lawyers helped her put this information into chart and graph form that would demonstrate to the Labor Standards Office that a cause and effect relationship existed between her husband's work and his death. However, since the company would not provide her with the documents she requested, only Mrs. Hiraoka and her children, Tomoko (then 21) and Shōgō (17), could create the facts necessary to support that interpretation of Mr. Hiraoka's death.

The company union, Mr. Hiraoka's original reason for changing jobs, was uncooperative. Parroting the dominant discourse of Tsubakimoto's corporate culture, the union head answered Mrs. Hiraoka's request for support by saying, "If the firm doesn't profit, our salaries won't go up. Workers who can't accept that idea aren't needed. If the company won't support your application for workers' compensation, then we can't either" (Hiraoka Chieko 1993).

Sitting together around a calendar, the three remaining members of the family reconstructed Mr. Hiraoka's work schedule from January 4, 1988 to February 23, 1988, the day of his death. Although they had lived together, the process of recreating his schedule made the family acutely aware of how little he was with them. With his pay receipts, his datebook, and other documents found in his desk at home, as well as their memories of when he left for work and returned, mother and children established the number of days he worked, how many hours of overtime he put in, and how many hours of night work were involved. As directed by her lawyers, Mrs. Hiraoka visited or called each of his coworkers and asked for their assistance. One former employee provided details about the nature of the work in the plant and Mr. Hiraoka's duties, although he was unwilling to testify or be identified. When the schedule was done, it was discovered that Mr. Hiraoka had not had a single full day of rest in the fifty-one days prior to his collapse. In addition, nearly half of his working hours had been on the night shift, including two weeks of continuous night work just prior to his death.

Effects of Overwork on Family Life

The family had long been aware that Mr. Hiraoka's work kept him apart from family life. They recalled him coming home late, eating alone, and then falling asleep in his chair at the dinner table, too exhausted to make it to bed. They recalled the many times he was called in to work on his days off and how he refused when the family urged him to take time off, saying, "They will just call me in anyway," or, "I have to be there because there aren't enough workers" (Ikeda 1997, 165). Tomoko was angry with him for working so much that he did not even have enough energy to greet family members when he returned home. Growing up, there were weeks when she did not see his face. Once she had even complained to him that the house was devoid of signs of his presence. She was upset about his slovenly (*darashinai*) appearance. Shōgō, too, had few memories of his father, but he remembered offering to walk with him to the train station "to eat ice cream" when he had to work the night shift and that arguments with Tomoko about his working at night had grown heated. Mrs. Hiraoka thinks her son was trying, in his own way, to protect her husband from becoming isolated from the family. After reconstructing his father's working life, Shōgō had a political epiphany: "Little by little I came to see how society gives rise to *karōshi*. Ironically, I feel that it was only with his death that we came together to do something as a family for the first time. But now, as then, he isn't here" (Ikeda 1997, 165).

Calculating the Cause

Extending the reconstruction back to February 1987, a full year before death, Mrs. Hiraoka and her children found that Mr. Hiraoka had been required to spend more than 4,000 hours at the factory, of which only 3,550 were paid. The first two years at the S-2 plant had actually been worse. His compensated overtime in 1986 reached 1,650 hours, and in 1985 it was 1,715 hours (Morioka 1995, 5–6). Such a workload would have been taxing for a healthy, young man. Mr. Hiraoka was neither. In 1984 his annual company physical examination revealed that he had ischemic heart disease, a narrowing of the arteries that feed the heart muscle. He began taking medication and regularly saw a doctor in his neighborhood. He was still being treated when he died.

According to his wife, he complained of fatigue in these years. Especially after night work, his legs felt heavy:

> He would be so tired that he could not climb the stairs to the second floor or change his clothes. In the last two days he was having trouble talking. The company should have taken steps to protect him, knowing that he had heart trouble. His overtime should have been restricted, but they just kept calling him in to work. If he complained, they would have told him he could leave. He didn't want to aggravate his condition by arguing. Besides, where would he have gone? He would have been like a sumo wrestler [without a stable]. So, they could force him to work murderously long hours. (Hiraoka Chieko 1993)

APPLYING FOR WORKERS' COMPENSATION

Flanked by her lawyers and children, and recorded by the media, Mrs. Hiraoka filed her application for workers' compensation on July 7, 1988. In addition to the reconstructed schedule, she submitted depositions from Mr. Hiraoka's doctor and a specialist in occupational medicine, both of which made a clear, strong case for overwork as the reason for his heart problems and his death. During the next ten months, she went to the Labor Standards Office every other month to ask about the progress of the investigation. At the urging of her lawyers, she talked about her case with labor unions, students, and other victims' families. This helped her expand her network of supporters, garner publicity, and demonstrate the credibility of her interpretation and the sincerity of her intent.

Signing Up Support

On February 13, 1989, Mrs. Hiraoka, her lawyers, and about fifty other people gathered to hold the inaugural meeting of the Association to Consider Overwork Society and Support Recognition of Mr. Hiraoka's Workers' Compensation Claim (Hatarakisugi Shakai o Kangae Hiraoka-san no Rōsai Nintei o Shien Suru Kai). After being abandoned by her husband's union and shunned by his employer, this was a great encouragement to Mrs. Hiraoka. Aided by this group, in less than a month she got more than 2,000 individuals and another 200 groups, including labor unions and associations of victims of other occupational injuries, to sign petitions urging action on her claim. These she delivered to the Labor Standards Office officer in charge of her case. Henceforth, when she visited the Labor Standards Office, members of the support group came along to demonstrate that she and her children did not stand alone. A Socialist Party parliamentarian, sympathetic newspaper and magazine articles, and coverage of her case by NHK, the quasi-public broadcasting network, all supported her version of the facts.

Mrs. Hiraoka was unable to see copies of her husband's time cards before her application was filed. However, once this step had been taken, her lawyers finally succeeded in obtaining time cards and other documents from Tsubakimoto Seiko. Comparing them with the calendar that the Hiraokas assembled showed that the family's reconstruction of Mr. Hiraoka's last year of work was essentially accurate: hours of required attendance at the plant: 4,038; hours of actual work compensated: 3,663; hours of overtime worked: 1,399; hours of overtime compensated: 1,015. Work taken home was not included in these totals. The difference between paid and unpaid hours of both regular work and overtime was 759 recorded hours, or 2.07 hours per day of uncompensated "service overtime." In addition to Mr. Hiraoka's time cards, the Labor Standards Office considered his pay receipts, his physical examinations, the company's work rules, and its Article 36 overtime work limits exemption agreement with the union in reaching its decision.

Article 36 of the Labor Standards Act provides for agreements between capital and representatives of labor in firms of ten or more full-time employees. Filed with the local Labor Standards Office, these agreements permit companies to exceed the maximum working hours established in Article 32 of the Labor Standards Act without penalty or sanctions. Workers sometimes refer to these agreements as "blue sky" agreements, the inference being that there is no limit on the amount of overtime a firm can demand. Sugeno (1992, 233–38) provides a full discussion of these agreements. At Tsubakimoto Seiko, the agreement stipulated a daily maximum of five hours of overtime for male workers and a monthly maximum of 110 hours. In practice, however, the firm ignored even these limits, and a workday in excess of 24 hours was possible when, in the firm's judgment, it was necessary to "maintain the integrity of the production process."

Obstacles on the Road to Compensation

Mrs. Hiraoka worried that the Labor Standards Office would not take her seriously. She learned from her lawyers that she had to insist that her husband's death was *karōshi*. However, despite her conviction that his company had killed him, it was hard to take such a determined stand. She received unsigned letters in which Tsubakimoto employees or their wives criticized her campaign as self-serving and potentially damaging to the other workers. One told her she should be grateful for having been supported by the firm for twenty-eight years. Neither Mrs. Hiraoka's parents nor her in-laws backed her efforts. The former did not wish to be associated with a public complaint. The latter claimed that sending Tomoko to a private music college contributed to their son's need to work overtime.

When Mrs. Hiraoka first began to inquire about the progress of the investigation, the Labor Standards Office officer in charge of the case made vague statements that seemed to indicate that her application would be rejected. "Hiraoka-san did not have the longest working hours at the plant. . . . Tsubakimoto's work environment is not the worst in Nara Prefecture" (Ikeda 1997, 166). The Ministry of Labor had, in October 1987, just revised the standards for recognizing death due to work-related circulatory diseases to include the week before, rather than just one day before, the onset of symptoms. However, the tone of the officer's statements gave Mrs. Hiraoka the impression that her case was being judged by the old standards in which it was necessary to prove that some calamity or accident immediately presaged the onset of symptoms.[3]

The Result: Rōsai *Recognized*

It was with some surprise, then, that Mrs. Hiraoka and her children received a call from the Labor Standards Office in May 1989 asking them to come and receive the decision in person. Normally the result—a single sentence, with no explanation—is sent by mail. In a decision that the lawyers felt was "epoch-making," the Labor Standards Office ruled that in comparison with official working hours, Mr. Hiraoka's workload had been excessive enough to cause his collapse. The Labor Standards Office cited three points: (1) three days before the onset of symptoms, he worked 16 hours despite it being a holiday; (2) Mr. Hiraoka worked almost twice the normal hours in the week prior to his death; and (3) he worked 19 and 12 hours, respectively, on a holiday and a scheduled day off eleven and twelve days prior to dying. In addition, the Labor Standards Office decision noted that Mr. Hiraoka was being treated for a mild heart ailment prior to his death and that his excessive workload could be seen to have caused the condition to worsen rapidly. Mrs. Hiraoka (1993) recalled, "When I heard the decision, I thought, 'At last he is free of that place. He is mine again and doesn't belong to them anymore.'" The practical result was that the Workers' Compensation Insurance System would pay Mrs. Hiraoka and her children a package of compensation consisting of a pension, funeral expenses, and a special, one-time, lump-sum payment of ¥3,000,000. The pension would replace the much smaller Welfare Insurance System's survivor pension she had been receiving. Details of how such pensions are calculated can be found in Osaka Karōshi Mondai Renrakukai (1989, 64–65) and Sugeno (1992, 328–32).

3. A description of both older and newer standards can be found in Osaka Karōshi Mondai Renraku-kai (1989, 44–55). The standards continue to be challenged as too strict and not in keeping with either the medical understanding of the relationship between work, accumulated stress, and health, or the public sense of what the standards for compensation ought to be. Further revisions were made in 1994.

Despite the favorable outcome, the lawyers were dismayed that the Labor Standards Office decision did not mention the effects of night work and irregular shift rotation, which Mrs. Hiraoka felt had as much impact on her husband as his excessive hours. Even more dismaying were Tsubakimoto's public comments, which betrayed the firm's unrepentant attitude. In response, Mrs. Hiraoka and her children filed a civil suit against the firm.

CREATING CREDIBILITY THROUGH LITIGATION: INTERPRETING *KARŌSHI* IN COURT

Tsubakimoto Seiko rejected the Labor Standards Office implied criticism of the firm's work practices in its decision. "Seven others do the same work as Mr. Hiraoka," said the personnel manager in a statement to the press. "Mr. Hiraoka's devotion to his work was an extreme example and was not forced by the company. Our interpretation is that he overworked of his own volition" (Hiraoka Tomoko 1991, 3).

Mrs. Hiraoka was angry that Tsubakimoto could ignore even the judgment of the government. The company's attitude was an insult to her husband's years of unstinting hard work, and she was determined that they should apologize and pay a price for their callous disregard for his health, his memory, and the feelings of herself and her children. She declared herself committed to the goal of a *karōshi*-free society for the next generation.

Mrs. Hiraoka and her children together filed suit in Osaka District Court, in May 1990. In her opening statement, she made it clear that she was taking this action on behalf of her husband's coworkers at Tsubakimoto, as well as her dead husband. The suit alleged negligence on the part of Tsubakimoto Seiko with regard to its legal obligations to abide by its own work rules and agreements with workers regarding overtime work and rest days. Furthermore, the plaintiffs alleged that Tsubakimoto should have been able to foresee that its work practices would be harmful to a 48-year-old man with heart problems. They argued that the firm was negligent in its duty to show concern for Mr. Hiraoka's well-being, that it ordered him to work beyond all reasonable limits, and that this made his death their responsibility. The plaintiffs demanded that Tsubakimoto Seiko publicly acknowledge responsibility in the Hiraoka case and pay a total of ¥55 million to Mrs. Hiraoka and her children, as well as funeral expenses of ¥1 million, the costs of the trial, and lost wages estimated at over ¥66 million (Hiraoka Chieko 1990).

Shortly after she filed the suit, lawyers for Tsubakimoto Seiko offered Mrs. Hiraoka ¥12 million to settle out of court. She explained to them that her prime objectives were contrition and an apology. No amount of money would entice her to give up these goals. Unwilling to admit responsibility, the firm's representatives departed. For their part, Tsubakimoto expressed regret that there would be a trial in spite of its sincere efforts to gain the understanding of the family. However, they also said they welcomed the trial as an opportunity to make the facts of the case clear (Uchihashi 1990, 20).

The defense strategy was based on the concept of labor performed at the worker's initiative (*sossen rōdō*). Tsubakimoto's attorneys insisted that Mr. Hiraoka needed extra money to meet his living expenses. He therefore elected to work many hours of overtime on his own. Furthermore, they said his work was supervisory and did not entail physical hardship.

Making the Legal Case: Why Had Mr. Hiraoka Worked So Much?

Since the case was without precedent, Mrs. Hiraoka's lawyers had doubts about being able to prove corporate responsibility for Mr. Hiraoka's *karōshi*. The key point would be demonstrating that Tsubakimoto should have been able to foresee that its illegal labor practices would have adverse consequences for Mr. Hiraoka. In twenty-four trial sessions over the course of the next four years, the lawyers worked to expose coercion hidden within the organizational structure of Tsubakimoto Seiko. Although no rank and file worker from within the factory testified for either side, skillful use of documentary evidence and questioning of hostile management witnesses established that there were good reasons to doubt the defense notion that Mr. Hiraoka had worked so much at his own initiative.

Using time cards and pay receipts, the plaintiffs established that Mr. Hiraoka's working hours were abnormally long and violated the company's work rules. Operating the factory 24 hours a day, 365 days a year with only two shifts was illegal. Tsubakimoto had been previously warned about this by the Labor Standards Office, but had done nothing to rectify it. According to the firm's work rules, the day shift should have been from 8 a.m. to 5 p.m. with an hour for lunch. Similarly, the night shift was to start at 8 p.m. and go to 5 a.m. with a 90-minute break for food and rest. In reality, to meet quality and quantity quotas set by management, four hours of overtime was automatically added to the end of each shift. This filled the gap between shifts and enabled the plant to run without interruption. But it also meant that workers seldom got the rest to which they were entitled. Mrs. Hiraoka testified that her husband told her the factory manager roamed the plant and used his rank and threatening glare to force workers to stay beyond quitting time, to work unpaid overtime, or to prevent them from taking full lunch breaks or sleeping during the 90-minute break on the night shift.

To avoid having to shut down the line during meals and other breaks, the company also insisted that half the workers take over the whole line for half the break, changing places with the other half during the second half of the break. Although the workers were paid the standard 25 percent premium for this work, the practice is illegal. The Labor Standards Office cited Tsubakimoto for this violation and cautioned it to make improvements at the time that it recognized Mrs.

Hiraoka's workers' compensation claim. Motivation at Tsubakimoto was by intimidation rather than rewards.

Frequent mechanical breakdowns and other difficulties with the production process, as well as a shortage of trained manpower and management's unreasonable production targets, made long hours necessary. In theory, workers were to alternate between the day and the night shifts on a weekly basis. All Sundays and thirteen Saturdays each year were to be designated by the firm as days off. Public holidays and 20 days each year of paid leave in Mr. Hiraoka's case, rounded out the vacation schedule.

Nevertheless, Mr. Hiraoka did not have a single 24-hour period off between January 4, 1989 and his collapse on February 23. According to his pay receipts, compensated overtime in the last three months of his life averaged 150 hours a month, which exceeded the 110-hour limit imposed by the firm's Article 36 agreement with the company union. If money was his aim, why was he working an average of more than two hours of *unpaid* overtime daily?

In a notebook begun nine months before his death and entered into evidence at the trial, Mr. Hiraoka recorded his own view. As he saw it, it was impossible to keep enough good workers in the factory when the working conditions were so severe. "The real problem is to get 48 hours a week down to 40. But right now 60 or more is the norm. No one is able to take any of their paid holidays. I want the union to negotiate with management for a reduction to 48 hours in 1988" (Hiraoka Satoru 1994, 6–7). In addition, his diary expressed personal disappointment when workers he had trained quit because of the harsh working conditions.

Mrs. Hiraoka testified that her husband as a man who was proud of his abilities and the role he played in Tsubakimoto's success. From a firm of 120 employees when he joined, it grew to have more than 900 and, at the time of his death, was the second largest manufacturer of ball bearings in Japan. She said that his sense of responsibility for his subordinates and his professional pride were strong, but the real reason for his overwork was not any abstract loyalty to the company but his manager's cruel exploitation of his uncomplaining nature.

Ignorance Is No Defense

Mr. Hiraoka's immediate supervisor provided the key testimony. Under intense questioning, he had to admit that foremen at Tsubakimoto were forced by quotas, understaffing, and rigged employee evaluations to both work on the production line and supervise their crews. A copy of the firm's secret overtime plan, bearing the supervisor's personal seal (the Japanese equivalent of a signature), was found by Mrs. Hiraoka on Mr. Hiraoka's desk at home. When confronted with the document in court, the supervisor blurted out, "Where did you get that?" but then conceded that even leaving out work done on holidays, the firm's schedule called for

322 hours more overtime work than authorized in the Article 36 agreement with the union. "We couldn't meet the targets," he sighed. He tried to deny knowing about Mr. Hiraoka's heart problem, although his seal was also on the copy of the physical examination results that he personally handed to Mr. Hiraoka.

Other company officials also claimed ignorance of Mr. Hiraoka's continuing heart problem. They testified that his health was his responsibility. Because he did not mention it to them, they assumed he had no problem. They also asserted darkly that he smoked and drank to excess, although the executives who testified had to admit that they seldom socialized with him. Their protestations of ignorance in regard to other matters, such as their firm's work rules, labor laws, the legal requirement to have a physician trained in occupational medicine conduct regular inspections of the plant, and even the date of Mr. Hiraoka's death, caused the judge to wonder aloud from the bench how a firm with such managers could stay in business. Indeed, Tsubakimoto Seiko was unable to remain independent, and in 1996 it was forced to merge with Nakashima Seisakusho. Today the company is known as Tsubaki-Nakashima.

Credible Legal Doctrine

Attorneys for the plaintiffs in the case argued that a proper legal notion of employee responsibility for health maintenance must be based on the worker's right to considerate treatment by the firm as established by various provisions of the Labor Standards Act of 1947 and the Industrial Safety and Health Act of 1972. They reasoned that if a company has no system for reassigning workers to jobs commensurate with their individual physical abilities, the employer rather than the worker bears the legal obligation to protect the worker's health. Forcing workers to announce their infirmities under such circumstances would give management carte blanche to dismiss older or handicapped workers.

This interpretation impressed the court. Moreover, Tsubakimoto's refusal to allow inspection of the S-2 factory and failure to put any rank and file workers on the stand to support their case created a strong suspicion that they were hiding something. However, rather than issue a judgment, the court proposed a face-saving compromise settlement, which the parties accepted. Tsubakimoto would make a public apology and pay Mrs. Hiraoka and her children ¥50 million. In return, the Hiraoka family would drop their other demands. Each side would bear its own share of the costs of the trial. The plaintiffs regarded this outcome as a victorious settlement (*shōri wakai*).

The Hiraoka case might have had more of a precedent-setting impact if Mrs. Hiraoka had rejected the settlement and forced the court to issue a judgment. Her most cherished goal, however, was an apology, for an apology that recognized the firm's negligence in her husband's death would restore his good reputation and validate his hard work. When Tsubakimoto agreed to publicly apologize, Mrs. Hiraoka would have lost face by not accepting. She would have seemed more concerned with money or revenge than honor. Moreover, forcing the case to judgment would remove the social obligation for the firm to apologize. Nor did her legal team think a judgment would lead to a significantly greater monetary award. By concluding the case in this way, both sides could appear magnanimous. For the lawyers, the Hiraoka case broke new ground in establishing credible legal strategies for pursuing *karōshi* claims against employers and demonstrated how those strategies could contribute to redress of larger social issues as well as individual problems. Avoiding the appearance of vindictiveness was important for growing the credibility of the movement as a whole.

SOCIAL MOVEMENT ACTORS, ACTIVITIES, AND MOTIVES

As a pioneer case, the Hiraoka *Karōshi* Saiban became a rallying point for a variety of groups and individuals concerned with labor and quality of working life issues in the Kansai area. Mr. Hiraoka's death and a trial with lawyers proved to be the key ingredients in the founding of the anti-*karōshi* movement in Osaka.

Mrs. Hiraoka's earliest and most important supporters were the lawyers who recruited her case through the hotline. All seven of her lawyers were members of the Japan Labor Lawyers Association (Nihon Rōdō Bengōdan). The leader of her legal team, Matsumaru Tadashi, is the *de facto* head of the Osaka Defense Counsel for Victims of *Karōshi* (Osaka Karōshi Mondai Renrakukai), which holds its monthly meetings at the office of the Osaka Democratic Law Association (Minshû Hōritsu Kyōkai). Matsumaru was the college classmate of Kawahito Hiroshi, head of the National Defense Counsel for Victims of *Karōshi*. Both men graduated from the Faculty of Economics at Tokyo University before becoming lawyers. Matsumaru says "widow's tears" are behind his *pro bono karōshi* work. He is also a central figure in the Stockholder's Ombudsman (Kabunushi Omubutsuman), a watchdog group that has been filing suits to make corporations accountable to their stockholders. Other lawyers on the team share Matsumaru's zeal for using litigation to reconfigure the institutions of society to produce a more level playing field. Above all, the lawyers' concern is the protection of the human rights guaranteed by the Constitution of Japan.

Frequent attendees at the monthly Renrakukai meetings also included Professor Morioka Koji and doctors specializing in occupational medicine. One of them, Tajiri Junichirō, was the specialist whose deposition helped win Labor Standards Office recognition for Mrs. Hiraoka. This group was the central nervous system of the movement. It directed overall strategy and planned events. The lawyers examined potential cases carefully and took those that they felt would help them boost their winning percentage and enhance the movement's success.

The Renrakukai members, according to their individual political and philosophical inclinations, have diverse connections to other groups such as Occupational Disease Countermeasures Council (Shokugyōbyō Taisaku Renrakukai), the Communist Party-affiliated labor union federation Zenrōren, the Kansai Laborers' Education Cooperative (Kansai Kinrōsha Kyōiku Kyōkai), and others.

Although Mrs. Hiraoka had Japan Socialist Party support for her workers' compensation application, they backed away when she decided to sue for negligence. Only Communist Party supporters seemed willing to join her confrontation with Tsubakimoto management in the civil trial. Chief among these were members of the dock, chemical, and metal workers unions. Owing to the inherent dangers of working in these industries, members of these unions had a keen interest in workplace safety issues as well as a strong tradition of union activism. I was told that their history of confrontation, with management and underworld competitors, gave their solidarity a hardened edge. As the Hiraoka case went on, these unionists came to play a larger role in supporting her case. The class-struggle-oriented agenda of these unionists was broader and more militant than either Mrs. Hiraoka or her lawyers. At times they seemed to relish making the Hiraoka case an outlet for their anger.

Early in the trial, the factory manager testified that he was unable to recall the date Mr. Hiraoka died. More than anything else, for Mrs. Hiraoka this symbolized Tsubakimoto's lack of care and concern for their employees. She and her supporters choose to use the 23rd of each month to hand out leaflets in front of the factory as a way to remind the factory manager of the date when Mr. Hiraoka died. The leaflets described in detail the progress of the trial, including some of the highlights of the testimony of company officials. The Hiraokas and their lawyers hoped that workers inside the plant might be encouraged to come forward and tell what they knew. They passed out the leaflets to workers as they walked from the nearby train station to the gates of the factory for the morning shift. Other supporters with bullhorns explained why the trial was being held and appealed to the workers for support.

Tsubakimoto's management at first tolerated the leaflets, and the workers were cordial. However, some months later, after thirty or so of Mrs. Hiraoka's more militant unionist supporters forced an acrimonious meeting with top management, workers were ordered by the firm not to take the leaflets. For the remainder of the trial, the firm photographed the leafleting. Telephoto lenses could be seen peeking between the blinds of the factory office, and the number of workers who accepted the handbills fell to near zero.

For the unions, who sent members to accompany Mrs. Hiraoka thereafter, the trial provided an opportunity to attack Tsubakimoto's poor reputation and score points for unionism. They became progressively more aggressive, thrusting the leaflets into the mid-sections of the workers and telling them to get a union that would fight for their rights and not let the company tell them who they could talk to or what they could read. Likewise, the unionists attended the trial sessions and could be counted on to mutter and grunt derisively in response to the statements of defense witnesses. When the judge asked why the court could not examine the S-2 factory, the defense attorney's explanation was followed by cries of, "What are you hiding?!" Mrs. Hiraoka's lawyers thought that this peanut gallery behavior had a beneficial effect on the judges as long as it was kept within reason.

Many of Mrs. Hiraoka's personal supporters became associated with other *karōshi* plaintiffs through mutual friends in the Renrakukai, or through the Association of Families Concerned with *Karōshi* (Osaka Karōshi o Kangaeru Kazoku no Kai), a survivors' mutual support group. As the attorneys recruited additional cases from around the Kansai area, they enrolled the plaintiffs in this mutual aid association. Here, Mrs. Hiraoka played the role of guide. Each new recruit had to be educated about how to file for compensation, how to approach doctors for depositions and expert testimony, how to gather signatures on petitions, and how to cope with the stress of bereavement and the long ordeal of being a plaintiff waiting for a bureaucratic decision. Mrs. Hiraoka symbolized the possibility of eventual success for this group. As *karōshi* numbers have increased, the Kazoku no Kai has grown. It is now a national organization, with lawyer-led chapters in every prefecture in Japan.

KARŌSHI AS MORAL CULTURE
AND THE STRUGGLE OVER THE MOVEMENT'S IDENTITY

In June of 1991, Mrs. Hiraoka's case became even more central to the *karōshi* movement. A Nagoya labor drama group called Aspiration Theater (Kikyūza) had learned of the trial through the media. They approached Mrs. Hiraoka and asked if they could base a play on her family's experiences. The group's leader and playwright, Koguma Hitoshi, thought her case the perfect way to take up the *karōshi* problem, and he wanted to make it the first in a series of new productions about the impact of corporate society on the lives of workers and their families. He sent Mrs. Hiraoka a draft of the script and a tape of the proposed theme song. Mrs. Hiraoka was deeply moved to find her family's plight rendered with such sensitivity and feeling.

The following year, the play was performed four times in Nagoya to packed houses. Called *The Sudden Tomorrow* (*Totsuzen no Ashita*), it is the story of the causes and consequences of a *karōshi* death. A factory supervisor is overworked, despite having a heart condition known to the company. A snarling factory manager pushes the workers unmercifully to meet ever-increasing quotas, but he refuses to take on extra staff. One worker is forced out when he thinks to file a complaint. The company's feckless union, afraid to make working conditions an issue, refuses to come to his aid. After the unfortunate supervisor dies, his wife, an unsophisticated woman of gentle character, and her two children find the courage to collect evidence and pursue a workers' compensation claim. Their claim is eventually recognized thanks to evidence provided by an older worker who decides that gaining a clear conscience is worth sacrificing his retirement pension. He comes forward to tell the truth about the firm's illegal and heartless methods. His testimony subsequently results in the widow and her children filing a civil suit against the firm, and in the dismissal of the greedy factory manager.

Totsuzen no Ashita is a powerful representation of the *karōshi* movement's central themes. It mobilizes images of protection, mutual care, and love and insists that compassion and familial relations are the essential foundation of both a good society and a good business. With the aid of jurisprudence, rendered in the play as a booming voice from above, the dead worker's family is reconstructed as a site of courageous resistance and source of moral value.

The play represented a cultural resource for the movement, and there was a small struggle over who would perform it in Osaka. A representative from the Communist Party-affiliated Osaka labor drama group Kizugawa asked that his group be given permission to perform the play in Osaka in December. Other movement participants wanted Kikyūza to bring the production to Osaka. Both groups worried about saturating the market. This was the same problem plaintiffs who followed Mrs. Hiraoka faced: the limited number of groups willing and able to support *karōshi* cases meant competition between plaintiffs that could fragment the movement. Iwaki Yutaka, one of Mrs. Hiraoka's lawyers with close ties to various groups, brokered a win-win compromise. Kikyūza would perform the play in August, and Kizugawa would perform it in December. The two groups would work together and form the *Totsuzen no Ashita* Osaka Performances Promotion Association (*Totsuzen no Ashita* Osaka Kōen o Miru Kai). Kizugawa would help stage the August performances, and a joint committee to carry out both sets of performances was formed. This committee gathered staff members and established the Miru Kai, printed a newsletter, publicized the play, handled ticket sales and distribution, and arranged liaison between the two drama groups. The two key organizers were volunteers with strong Communist Party ties. At the event, both sets of performances played to full houses. Over ¥200,000 in donations was raised, and the funds were given to the Kazoku no Kai. The two Miru Kai organizers subsequently became the secretariat of that organization, too. Building on their success, the following year the Miru Kai published a volume of reflections and opinions about the play and the *karōshi* movement entitled No More *Karōshi* (Nō Moa Karōshi).

As with the play, these two skilled organizers tried to use the Kazoku no Kai and its members to create additional cultural resources and political meaning

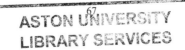

for the movement. Their success was limited. Over 200 people turned out for a November 1993 evening of music, education, and fellowship that featured several plaintiffs in performing roles. However, the members of the Kazoku no Kai were reluctant to be used as mascots for the broad array of social causes implied by some of the speakers that evening. Their interest was less about social change and strengthening the labor movement than about gathering support for their individual cases. They resented being used as propaganda tools. After a subsequent concert with professional singers failed to generate much interest, the secretariat concentrated on returning the Kazoku no Kai to its original mission of mutual self-help for its members. Mrs. Hiraoka, who did not like the way some of her communist supporters sometimes tried to use her case as a vehicle for union organizing and JCP politics, withdrew from the Kazoku no Kai in 1996. However, she remains grateful to and friendly with them as individuals for the assistance they rendered, and she is still working for a *karōshi*-free future.

CONCLUDING REMARKS

While the Hiraoka case typified the social movement strategies and practices generally employed by *karōshi* activists, it was atypical in the ease and speed with which workers' compensation insurance payments were granted. It was also atypical in pursuing corporate responsibility in a civil suit. In the years since her case was settled, however, it has become common for claimants who win Ministry of Health, Labor, and Welfare recognition of their cases to sue companies for additional damages. Lawyer Matsumaru says that official recognition of a *karōshi* case enables an easy victory over the firm.

Karōshi activists base the credibility of their claims on facts created by their own research into the work environment and its relationship to workers' health. This is exactly what the investigators from the Labor Standards Office do. However, where once the opinions of victims' families took a back seat to documentary evidence supplied (or not supplied) by firms, today facts discovered by the plaintiff can acquire a most potent credibility. In this, Mrs. Hiraoka was exceptionally fortunate. Her husband's overtime schedules, medical records, and other documents were found on his desk at home. Since these became the key evidence in the civil trial, in this sense she and her children were lucky that Mr. Hiraoka was so overworked that he had to bring work home. The documents corroborated his family's recollections of his working hours and demonstrated that the firm was willfully negligent in its failure to care for Mr. Hiraoka and provide him with a safe working environment.

Many other families have followed in the wake of Mrs. Hiraoka's success. In Osaka, they are often led by the same lawyers who worked on the Hiraoka case. In Tokyo and other cities, her case is known through its portrayal in books written by those lawyers. Subsequent successful cases received similar treatment. In addition to creating a growing body of legal doctrine, the approximately 300 lawyers in the National Defense Counsel for Victims of *Karōshi* across Japan have been instrumental in the creation of a national *karōshi* discourse. They have publicized the concept of *karōshi*, shown how it occurs, explained how to prevent it, and how to gain compensation when it happens. In league with their medical colleagues, these lawyers are primarily responsible for making *karōshi* a social problem. Their guidance and suggestions teach plaintiffs the accepted conventions of credible fact making, give rise to support groups, and help plaintiffs construct their own personal discourses for use in public appearances, in petitions, or in visits to the Labor Standards Office. They also try to engineer a balanced distribution of resources among the various plaintiffs who are fighting *karōshi* cases at any given time.

Over time, the volume of critical judicial opinions generated by Karōshi Bengōdan activities has influenced the Ministry of Labor. Since 1987 the standards for recognizing *karōshi* have been relaxed three times, an example of litigation encouraging regulatory law to catch up to social realities. Recently, compensation has even been extended to victims of suicide due to work-induced stress (*karōjisatsu*). The concept of *karōshi* and the understanding of its epidemiology have become widespread in Japan. Many, though by no means all, Japanese can now identify with victims such as Mr. Hiraoka. There is a growing consensus that Japanese men have focused too much on work at the expense of family life and personal growth.

Changes in Japanese workplaces and employment practices due to the collapse of the late 1980s bubble economy and ensuing stagnation, however, are intensifying the competition for corporate survival. Pillars of social stability, such as lifetime employment and seniority wages, are being replaced by flexible, fixed-term employment and results-based compensation schemes. Revisions to the Labor Standards Act in April 1999 made women subject to the same overtime provisions as men. In the absence of strong unions, it is widely believed that these revisions, carried out in the name of gender equality, will put women in the same unprotected position as men. Business leaders have recently introduced proposals that would exempt many white-collar workers from limits on working hours and free employers from having to pay them overtime premiums (North and Weathers 2007). Mrs. Hiraoka says that while the gains of the anti-*karōshi* movement are not insignificant, there is little reason to be optimistic about eliminating *karōshi* anytime soon.

In the face of business efforts to water down or eliminate many provisions of the Labor Standards Act and Industrial Safety and Health Act, the success of *karōshi* plaintiffs such as Mrs. Hiraoka points to the impact that ordinary Japanese citizens can have when their energies and knowledge are mobilized within the organizational framework and practices of a social movement led by dedicated professionals. With this guidance and expertise, victims and their families can generate credibility sufficient to activate the potential for protection and redress inherent in the law and thus, in some measure, confront and successfully battle both the manifest power differences between capital and labor and bureaucratic inertia and indifference. The tactics and strategies of the anti-*karōshi* movement— using the courts and raising a public fuss about a private problem—while perhaps distasteful to many Japanese, are a viable alternative to capitulation and quietism. They contain the potential for individuals to exercise the power of the law in a way that calls attention to the common interests of workers, using litigation and the threat of litigation as a means to the enactment of policies that ultimately benefit them all.

REFERENCES

Chalmers, Norma J. (1989). *Industrial Relations in Japan: The Peripheral Workforce.* New York, Routledge.

Durkheim, Emile. (1964). *The Division of Labor.* Glencoe, Il, The Free Press.

Epstein, Steven. (1995). The Construction of Lay Expertise: AIDS Activism and the Forging of Credibility in the Reform of Clinical Trials. In *Science, Technology, and Human Values* 20.4: 408–37.

Fassel, Diane. (1990). *Working Ourselves to Death: The High Cost of Workaholism and the Rewards of Recovery.* San Francisco, Harper Collins.

Fujita Satoru. (1993). Letter to Hiraoka Chieko, plaintiff in a *karōshi* suit. November 16.

Hanami, Tadashi. (1985). *Labor Law and Industrial Relations in Japan,* 2nd ed. Boston, Kluwer Law and Taxation.

Hiraoka Chieko. (1990). Iken chinjutsu sho [Plaintiff's Opening Statement]. Osaka District Court, July 12. Reprinted in *Karōshi o Kangaeru: Yutakasa tte Nani?* [Thinking about *Karōshi*: What is Affluence?], 3–4. Osaka, Hiraoka Karōshi Saiban o Shien Suru Kai, 1994.

Hiraoka Chieko. (1993). Interview by author, Fujidera City, September 23.

Hiraoka Chieko, Hiraoka Tomoko, and Hiraoka Shōgō. (1990). Hiraoka v. Tsubakimoto Seiko K.K. Complaint filed in Osaka District Court, May 19.

Hiraoka Satoru. (1994). Hiraoka Satoru shi no techō yori [From Mr. Hiraoka Satoru's Notebook]. In *Karōshi no nai ashita no tame ni* [For a *Karōshi*-Free Future], 6–7. Osaka, Hiraoka Karōshi Saiban o Shien Suru Kai.

Hiraoka Tomoko. (1991). Otōsan no shi o muda shitakunai [I Don't Want My Father's Death To Be in Vain]. In *Karōshi o Kangaeru: Yutakasa tte Nani?* [Thinking about *Karōshi*: What is Affluence?], 4. Osaka, Hiraoka Karōshi

Saiban o Shien Suru Kai.

Ikeda Naoki. (1997). Otōsan, kaisha ga ayamatta yo [Father, the Company Has Apologized]. In *Rōdōsha no Kenri: Gendai Kigyō Shakai to Rōdōsha no Kenri* [Workers' Rights: Modern Corporate Society and Workers' Rights] 220.7 (Summer): 164–70.

Karōshi Bengōdan Zenkoku Renrakukai, eds. (1990). *Karōshi: When the Corporate Warrior Dies*. International edition. Tokyo, Mado-sha.

Kawahito, Hiroshi. (1991). Death and the Corporate Warrior. *Japan Quarterly* 38 (April–June): 149–57.

Keizai Kikaku Chō. (1994). *Hataraki sugi to kenkō shōgai* [Overwork and Health Problems]. Tokyo, Government of Japan.

Morioka Koji. (1993). Interview by author. Osaka, November 15.

Morioka Koji. (1995). *Gekiron! Kigyō shakai: karōshi to hataraki kata o kangeru* [Debate about Corporate Society: Considering *Karōshi* and How We Work]. Iwanami Booklet no. 383. Tokyo, Iwanami Shoten.

Morioka Koji. (2005). *Hatarakisugi no jidai* [The Age of Overwork]. Tokyo, Iwanami Shoten.

Nikkei Shinbun. (2007). Karo de jisatsu saita no 66 nin [Suicides from Overwork Reach New Peak of 66 People]. May 5, p. 39.

North, Scott, and Charles Weathers. (2007). The End of Overtime Pay: More Production or Just More Work for Japan's White Collar Workers? http://japanfocus.org/products/details/2320

Osaka Karōshi Mondai Renrakukai. (1989). *Karōshi 110 Ban: Otto ga taoretara, taorenai tame ni* [Dial 110 for *Karōshi*: If Your Husband Collapses, or To Prevent His Collapse]. Tokyo, Gōdō Shuppan.

Rebick, Marcus. (2005). *The Japanese Employment System*. Oxford, Oxford University Press.

Steinhoff, Patricia G. (1999). Doing the Defendant's Laundry: Support Groups as Social Movement Organizations in Contemporary Japan. In *Japanstudien. Jahrbuch des Deutschen Instituts für Japanstudien* 11: 55–78.

Sugeno, Kazuo. (1992). *Japanese Labor Law*. Seattle, University of Washington Press.

Uchihashi Katsuto. (1990). Nihon kaibō [Dissecting Japan]. *Shûkan Gendai,* July 7. Reprinted in *Karōshi o Kangaeru: Yutakasa tte Nani?* [Thinking about *Karōshi*: What is Affluence?], 20–22. Osaka, Hiraoka Karōshi Saiban o Shien Suru Kai.

Uehata Tetsunojō. (1978). Karōshi ni kansuru kenkyû, dai 1 po: shokushû no kotonaru 17 kêsu de no kentō [First Report on Research concerning *Karōshi*: Consideration of 17 Cases in Different Occupations]. In *Dai 51 kai Nihon Sangyō Eisei Gakkai Kōenshû* [Collected Speeches of the 51st Japan Industrial Health Association Meeting], 250–51.

Uehata Tetsunojo. (1990). A Medical Study of *Karōshi*. In *Karōshi: When the Corporate Warrior Dies,* ed. National Defense Counsel for Victims of *Karōshi*, 98–102. Tokyo, Mado-sha.

Uehata Tetsunojō. (1993). Hon to hito: karōshi no kenkyû [Review of *Research on Karōshi*]. *Mainichi Shinbun*, August 23, 1993.

Ueyanagi, Toshiro (1990): Laws Concerning *Karōshi*. In *Karōshi: When the Corporate Warrior Dies,* ed. National Defense Counsel for Victims of *Karōshi*, 84–97. Tokyo, Mado-sha.

Upham, Frank K. (1987). *Law and Social Change in Postwar Japan.* Cambridge, MA, Harvard University Press.

CHAPTER 3

Courting Justice, Contesting "Bureaucratic Informality": The Sayama Case and the Evolution of Buraku Liberation Politics[1]

John H. Davis, Jr.

Under normal circumstances a signed confession would hardly seem like a sound basis for seeking reversal of a criminal conviction. However, the legal team representing Ishikawa Kazuo and the thousands of supporters who have rallied around him for more than five decades point to his signed confession and the circumstances surrounding its elicitation by authorities as compelling evidence proving his innocence. On July 9, 1963 at the Urawa District Court, prosecutors indicted twenty-four-year-old Ishikawa for the abduction and murder of sixteen-year-old Nakata Yoshie in Sayama City, located northwest of Tokyo in neighboring Saitama Prefecture. Although initially maintaining his innocence for the first month following his arrest on May 23, 1963, by June 20 Ishikawa confessed to being one of three perpetrators who acted in concert to commit the crime. Three days later the story would change again as Ishikawa claimed sole responsibility.

1. This research would not have been possible without the assistance of countless people in Japan. First, I want to express my gratitude to the residents of Saiwaichiku, the pseudonym I have given the community where the initial research was conducted between 1997 and 1999. For more than two years they proved to be remarkably welcoming and patient despite the intrusive presence and persistent queries of an American anthropologist. I would also like to extend a special thank-you for the valuable help provided by Mr. Tomonaga Kenzo, Director of the Buraku Liberation and Human Rights Research Institute in Osaka. Without his support the research upon which this essay is based would not have been possible. Likewise, I benefited from the gracious assistance of Mr. Yasuda Satoshi of the Buraku Liberation League Headquarters in Tokyo who provided me with an eye-opening tour of the *genba*, Sayama City. I thank him for sharing his valuable insight into the Sayama incident. I am eternally grateful to the following entities that provided the financial support to make various phases of this research possible: U.S. Department of Education Fulbright Program, Abe Fellowship Program, MMUF-WW Junior Faculty Career Enhancement Fellowship Program, The Institute for the Study of World Politics, and Stanford University's Institute for International Studies. Finally, I would like to express my sincere thanks to Dr. Sato Yoshimichi and Dr. Numazaki Ichiro for providing a superb environment for reflection and writing at Tohoku University's fabulous Center for the Study of Social Stratification and Inequality.

Various aspects of the Sayama case, as it is widely known, seem to violate Japanese criminal law. First, police employed an illegal practice known as *bekken taiho* whereby an individual is arrested on charges unrelated to the crime for which that individual is being investigated. Ishikawa was originally taken into custody on suspicion of larceny, assault, and attempted extortion. When dressed in the technical terminology used in official documents, such as arrest warrants, the charges sound quite serious, but the evidence on which they are based is highly dubious. For example, police alleged that Ishikawa stole the work uniform of Takahashi Ryohei. Takahashi, however, was a longtime friend of Ishikawa and seemed fully cognizant that Ishikawa was borrowing the uniform since Takahashi asked him to "wash it before you return it." The assault charge seems equally peculiar. It claims that Ishikawa roughed up a young man who caused a fender bender in February 1963. While Ishikawa was involved in a minor traffic accident, a police officer called to the scene helped mediate an out-of-court settlement between the parties involved. In other words, Ishikawa was being arrested for involvement in an incident that had already been resolved. The third and final crime listed on the arrest warrant, attempted extortion, alleges that Ishikawa delivered a ransom note to the Nakata residence seeking money for the missing girl's safe return. It is a far more serious allegation than the previous two, yet the public prosecutor could find no basis to prosecute Ishikawa for this particular crime. However, the prosecutor did decide to bring formal charges for the other two crimes on June 13. Four days later, on June 17, Ishikawa was released on bail. Yet before he could leave the police station, police served him with another arrest warrant naming him as a suspect in the killing of young Yoshie.

Rather than being reunited with his family members after nearly four weeks in police custody, Ishikawa found himself being subjected to yet another round of intense questioning. A 2005 episode of "The Scoop" included a segment on the Sayama case as part of a special zeroing in on the problem of false accusation in the Japanese criminal justice system. Broadcast nationally on Asahi TV, the news program opened by giving viewers an intimate look at what transpires during police questioning. Speaking from a studio set built to replicate a typical interrogation room, co-host Torigoe Shuntaro describes how a suspect sits alone on one side of a small table in a tiny room that measures roughly fifty square feet while taking questions from a police officer seated directly in front of him on the other side of the table. Handwritten notes of the proceedings are taken by another officer seated at a second table. While these notes do not become part of the official court record, they may inform the separate statements crafted by police and prosecutors and offered as evidence. Unlike in the American judicial system, there is no right for the defendant to have legal counsel present during interrogation. Nor is audio or visual recording of the session permitted at that time. Thus, there is no impartial account of what is said or done at the time of questioning when a defendant is essentially cut off from the outside world. The host of the program notes that it is an environment ripe for potential abuse by authorities, resulting in incidents of "false accusation" or *enzai*.

Although defendants are not allowed to have an attorney present during questioning by authorities, Article 39 (1) of the Code of Criminal Procedure does allow them to confer privately with their attorneys during incarceration. However, during the time that he was in police custody, Ishikawa had this legally protected right severely constrained, if not outright violated. On the day of his re-arrest, Ishikawa was not allowed to meet with his lawyers. The following day, he met with his counsel for only twenty minutes. The day after that, their consultation time dwindled to just five minutes. He would spend another five minutes with his lawyer on June 20 before entering a five-day period where he did not meet with anyone. Given that he was taken into custody as a murder suspect, one wonders why Ishikawa seemed so disinterested in meeting with his attorneys. During part of his televised interview with Torigoe, Ishikawa explains his unwillingness to speak with his lawyers by stating that the police told him not to talk to them. Reluctant to violate a directive given by his jailers, he says, "Even when my lawyers did come, I would have them leave after two or three minutes." By his thirty-second consecutive day in police custody (counting since the day of his initial arrest), Ishikawa's story changed from a denial to a confession. On June 23 he accepted sole responsibility for the kidnapping and murder by signing a confession written not by Ishikawa himself but, as is standard practice in Japan, by his jailers/interrogators.

Ishikawa had declared his innocence from the time he was arrested on charges unrelated to the murder. From the very beginning authorities were asking him about the death of Nakata Yoshie; they subjected him to polygraph tests and started asking him about the case shortly after taking him into custody on May 23. Despite the polygraph tests and having his hair pulled repeatedly during long hours of questioning late into the night while handcuffed, Ishikawa had been steadfast in denying any involvement with or knowledge of the disappearance and murder of Yoshie.

What happened to convince or compel him to reverse his testimony and confess to murder? Ishikawa described how investigators presented him with evidence linking his older brother to the crime. He was told that a footprint recovered from the crime scene matched that of his sibling. Unaware that this was a total fabrication by police, Ishikawa agreed to accept responsibility for the murder to spare his brother, the family's principal bread winner at the time, from incarceration and thus to save his family from economic hardship. Police reassured him that if he confessed, they would not seek to prosecute his brother. What's more, they told him he would only have to serve a ten-year sentence. At the opening of the trial on September 4, 1963 Ishikawa pleaded guilty. Roughly six months later on March 11, 1964 the Urawa District Court sentenced him to death.

The television special did a fantastic job of highlighting trouble spots within Japan's criminal justice system by pointing to some of the systemic problems that enable law enforcement to exert extraordinary pressure on individuals in order to extract confessions that then become the primary basis for conviction. Many of these systemic deficiencies were evident in the way that authorities conducted their investigation in the Sayama case: arrest on unrelated charges, interrogation under duress, and restricted access to defense. The program notes a startling statistic that makes it clear that coerced confession and the specter of abuse of authority by law enforcement officials is more common than one might think. A confession was part of the evidence marshaled against defendants in 84 percent (42 out of 50) of the confirmed *enzai* cases between 1945 and 1991 in which a conviction was later overturned. In other words, those wrongly convicted were coerced into confessing to a crime it was later proven they did not commit. As I will discuss shortly, Ishikawa and his supporters are convinced his case would be added to this tally of overturned cases were the courts to do an impartial analysis of the facts of the case.

There is another wrinkle to Ishikawa's story that received only a brief mention at the very end of Scoop's segment on the Sayama case. Torigoe notes that Ishikawa is from a community that historically has been subject to discrimination and prejudice: he is a *burakumin*. As a result, Torigoe chastises his media counterparts for failing to give the story adequate attention and for neglecting to scrutinize the actions of investigators and the court. It must be encouraging to Ishikawa and his supporters to see some journalists accepting a measure of responsibility for what happened to him and start to give the Sayama case more attention now. But in addition to explaining why journalists shied away from this story, I discuss in this chapter how Ishikawa's link to Japan's *burakumin* is a critical element for understanding what the Sayama case means to a core group of supporters numbering in the thousands, who have worked tirelessly for decades using a variety of tactics and strategies to influence what was happening in the courts.

Even though Ishikawa was released on parole in 1994, twice each year supporters from all over the country gather in Tokyo and rally in support of him. They then take to the streets to march in protest against his arrest and conviction and, with this public show of outrage, to pressure the courts to revisit his case. Thousands more still work toward a reversal of the guilty verdict by writing letters and cards demanding a retrial and by sponsoring local public awareness initiatives to educate people about the dubious facts surrounding Ishikawa's conviction.

Ishikawa and his supporters have sought to exert ever-increasing pressure on the judiciary by expanding the base of supporters from a predominantly *burakumin* constituency to include Japanese citizens in general as well as those from the international community, using leverage from members of the United Nations

Human Rights Committee to pressure the Japanese government. In examining why Ishikawa and his supporters keep going to court and pursuing his case, I hope to illustrate how people in Japan are no less interested than people elsewhere in working through and on the courts to resolve conflict and bring about social change.

I use the Sayama case as a lens for reexamining the current trajectory of the Buraku Liberation League (Buraku Kaihō Dōmei), a group of activists arguably best known for confronting discrimination head-on outside of the courts using confrontational tactics such as denunciation sessions (*kyūdankai*). I challenge this prevailing image of the organization; I argue that both the long history of protest activities concerning the Sayama case and the nature of some of the more recent forms the protest has taken make it clear that working through the judicial system has become an increasingly important part of the political repertoire of those engaged in the Buraku Liberation Movement (BLM). As I show below, through these activities the Buraku Liberation League (BLL) has been influential in leveling some degree of external pressure (*gaiatsu*) on the state, even if it has yet to significantly alter the functioning of specific state institutions such as the judiciary. Critiques concerning the state's handling of the Sayama case now include specific reference to government statements in official reports submitted to international human rights entities like the United Nations Human Rights Committee. This is no minor accomplishment because it works as a critically important counterbalance to "bureaucratic informality."

Frank Upham (1987) coined the term "bureaucratic informality" to describe the way that elite bureaucrats within Japanese society seek to maintain the social and political status quo by manipulating the legal framework to "control the pace and course, if not substance, of social change" (p. 17). In other words, by taking an aggressive and central role in mediating disputes that could fundamentally alter the power structure, bureaucratic elites controlling the machinery of the state are able to make the changes necessary to resolve the potential crisis in a manner that ultimately maintains the status quo by preferring informal mechanisms to formal ones. According to this particular model, in the legal sphere the judiciary plays a rather limited role because, as Upham argues, "informality means most of all legal informality" (p. 22). This limited capacity of the judiciary to act to resolve disputes is essential to maintaining the power structure because the judicial process has the ability to make transparent, and thereby expose for public consideration and debate, fundamental issues that could potentially threaten the current balance of power.

Marshaling support for his argument, Upham presents several case studies of which the Buraku issue is one example. In his estimation, the various efforts of the government, specifically the wide range of programs created with the adoption of the Law on Special Measures for Dōwa Projects in 1969, have effectively contained the potentially catalytic effect of the grassroots movement for Buraku liberation by limiting the ability of activists supporting this cause to expand their base of support to the wider community. He observes that Buraku liberation activists "have not been able to universalize their complaints or gain the political support that would enable the movement to begin to bring [them] into the mainstream of employment and society" (p. 24). Upham provides an excellent model for charting the political dynamics limiting the ability of social movements that have taken root within a particular constituency to expand beyond their traditional political base of support and make inroads within the wider society. In this essay I consider how the BLL is responding to this challenge.

The attempt here to (re)assess the character of BLL activities as well as gauge their efficacy in terms of Upham's model engages the central problematic at the heart of this volume—revisiting the all too common notion that people in Japan are presumably less interested than their Western counterparts in pursuing legal means to resolve conflict. In the case of the BLL the trope of the reluctant litigant is coupled with an equally intransigent image of Buraku liberation activists as intimidation brokers who choose deliberately to operate outside of the legal sphere in order to protect their prerogative of using high-pressure persuasion to achieve short-term compensation, if not long-term justice.

The exemplar par excellence of this style of persuasion is the denunciation session. The denunciation tactic was inherited from the National Levelers Society (Zenkoku Suiheisha), the first national political organization representing the interests of residents of Buraku areas. Denunciation essentially consists of BLL members confronting those who have allegedly engaged in some sort of behavior prejudicial against Buraku residents. This form of protest was radical when initially adopted because it publicly challenged the idea that Buraku residents were legitimate targets of discrimination because of their low social status. There have been times in the past when this confrontational approach resulted in violence of some sort (see Rohlen 1976; Upham 1987, 87–103). These days, however, outbreaks of violence are exceedingly rare. Denunciation sessions are preceded by small-scale fact-finding meetings (*kakuninkai*) between the parties involved. During the denunciation sessions that I witnessed involving companies believed to be practicing employment discrimination and rejecting applicants from Buraku districts, representatives of the local government were also present to witness the proceedings.

However, the Sayama case demonstrates that the goal of having a significant impact on the judiciary has inspired Buraku liberation activities for more than four decades. Despite its long history as a cornerstone of the Buraku Liberation Movement, the special significance of the Sayama case for those participating in the movement has not been examined thoroughly. By situating part of my analysis in the context of experiences accumulated during my fieldwork within a specific

Osaka Buraku, I hope to illuminate some of the activities that *burakumin* engage in outside of the court in an effort to influence what happens within the court. This is vital if we are to understand the uptick in activity following Ishikawa's release on parole. The extent to which the Sayama case continues to be a focal point of the BLM addresses the question of why Ishikawa and his supporters keep going to court. The case is a potent mobilizing force for the movement and a constant reminder of the continuing victimization of *burakumin*.

BRIEF OVERVIEW OF THE BURAKU ISSUE

The Buraku issue can be understood partly as an anachronistic vestige from an earlier historical period characterized by gross disparities in status and power. The word *buraku* literally means "hamlet" or "village." The term *hisabetsu buraku* (discriminated-against *buraku*) refers to those communities whose roots can be traced back to outcaste groups during the Tokugawa period (1609–1867). During this time a calcification of status disparities tethered individuals to one of several groups that were ordered hierarchically. Society was divided into the following rank-ordered statuses: warriors followed by farmers, artisans, and merchants, each of which had to dress and live according to detailed regulations that made their status visible to all. Outside of the status hierarchy altogether (or rather at its very bottom) was the *eta-hinin* class. *Eta* translates roughly into "abundant filth," and *hinin* means "nonhuman." Both terms are extremely pejorative and are no longer considered acceptable to use. As these terms indicate, *eta-hinin* were subjected to intense prejudice and social control. They were required to marry others of their status, reside in *eta-hinin* villages, and wear clothing and hairstyles that readily communicated their status (Ninomiya 1933, 97–98).

Outcasts were officially liberated in 1871 when the Emancipation Proclamation issued by the Meiji Government declared all outcasts to be "new commoners." The change in legal status did little, however, to improve their plight. If anything, the situation may have worsened as many in the general population bristled at the notion that they now occupied the same rung of the social hierarchy as the "former *eta*," a phrase used in records and documents intermittently with "new commoner" to keep track of outcast households and individuals long after the status system was officially abandoned.

During the postwar years, much of Japan experienced improvements as the country went through a period of rapid economic growth. Those in Buraku areas, however, did not progress as rapidly as the rest of society. National surveys revealed significant gaps between the general population and Buraku residents, who experienced higher levels of poverty exacerbated by high unemployment and low educational attainment (Buraku Kaihō Kenkyūsho 1997; Sōmuchō 1995). Moreover, social prejudice against those residing in Buraku districts manifests itself in areas such as marriage and employment discrimination. Private investigators would be hired by companies and individuals alike to conduct background checks on potential spouses or prospective employees to see if they had any ties to a Buraku. One need only gain access to an individual's family register (*koseki*) to obtain information about his or her hometown. In 1976 the national law was amended to curtail discriminatory background checks by eliminating unfettered public access to family registers. An address alone, however, might provide investigators sufficient information if they are willing to travel in person to examine the neighborhood and talk with locals to determine whether or not an individual is *burakumin*. Of course if one had access to one of the comprehensive Buraku lists with the names and locations of more than 5,300 Buraku communities across the country, travel would not be necessary (Tomonaga 2006).

Over the years a number of organizations have formed to deal with the range of economic and social challenges confronting Buraku residents. The largest of these is the BLL, which dates back to 1946.[2] The organization resumed the work of its organizational predecessor, the National Levelers Association (Zenkoku Suiheisha) founded in 1922. One of the distinctive features of the National Levelers Association was its use of direct confrontation to deal with instances of discrimination against Buraku residents as a way of reaffirming the human dignity of *burakumin* while also challenging the prevailing social norms of the day. The BLL inherited this tradition of confronting and correcting various manifestations of discrimination experienced by Buraku residents including everything from social prejudice to material needs such as adequate and affordable housing.

The cause of Buraku liberation received a huge boost in 1969 when the government passed the Law on Special Measures for Dōwa Projects, which designated public funds for community improvement projects in designated Buraku. Buraku communities that received money are referred to in government documents as *dōwa* districts. The last such law expired in March 2002. During the thirty-three years of legislative initiatives, funds were allocated to pave roads, to construct housing with adequate plumbing and sewage facilities, and to establish youth and senior citizen centers that provided important services. The economic position of many Buraku households was improved thanks to programs such as housing subsidies, employment assistance, and a scholarship program

---

2. Initially the organization was named the National Committee for Buraku Liberation as individuals with a diverse range of political views joined in collaboration to restart the Buraku Liberation Movement. The organization changed its name to the Buraku Liberation League in August 1955. The diversity of opinions eventually led to the splintering of the organization a few years after the Special Measures Legislation went into effect in 1969. Members favorable to the general approach taken by the Communist Party, which preferred to address the Buraku issue as part of the larger social and economic challenges confronting society at large opted to break away from the Buraku Liberation League and form their own organization in 1976, named Zenkoku Buraku Kaihō Undō Rengōkai (National Buraku Liberation Association).

for youth designed to boost education levels and thus facilitate a transition into better paying jobs. Human rights education programs in schools and companies, denunciation sessions by the BLL, and mass protests have all helped curtail blatant acts of discrimination. Nonetheless, discrimination persists (Central Executive Committee for the Establishment of Buraku Liberation and Human Rights Policies 2008; *New York Times* 2009).

HISTORICAL BACKGROUND OF THE SAYAMA CASE[3]

May 1, 1963 in Sayama City—this day should have been a happy one for Nakata Yoshie because it marked her sixteenth birthday. However, it became a day of tragedy when she never returned home from school. According to Yoshie's classmates, she departed school around 3:30 p.m. When she had not returned home by early evening, her family began to worry. Her brother, Kenji, searched for Yoshie in the general vicinity of her high school and the local train station. His search was fruitless. He returned home at 7:30 p.m. Although deeply concerned, the family members commenced to have dinner. During dinner, Kenji noticed a white envelope lodged in the glass door of the main entrance. The envelope contained a ransom note addressed to the father. This was the start of the Sayama incident.

In the letter the kidnapper demanded that on the following night ¥200,000 be brought to the gate of Sanoya, a general store located about one kilometer west of the Nakata residence. Not wanting to jeopardize Yoshie's welfare, the family complied, but not before consulting with police. It was decided that Yoshie's older sister would deliver counterfeit money in accordance with the instructions contained in the ransom letter. At 11:50 p.m. she traveled to the designated location with an envelope of fake bills in hand. She was not alone. Approximately forty police officers waited surreptitiously for the kidnapper to appear to collect the money. The officers came not only from the local police station but also from the Saitama Prefectural Police Headquarters.

Twenty minutes passed before the abductor arrived. Calling out from a tea field located next to the store, he asked warily, "Hey! Hey! Are you here?" The older sister acknowledged that she was there with the money. The culprit, possibly suspecting that he may have been walking into a trap, did not come out to get the money immediately. Instead, he continued the conversation for another

---

3. The particulars of the Sayama case presented here are taken from Buraku Liberation League Headquarters (1994, 1998), Buraku Liberation Research Institute (1989, 71–76, 187–200), and Hinamoto (1994), plus the voluminous compilation of Noma Hiroshi (1997) that totals nearly two thousand pages. This three-volume set contains articles Noma wrote for the magazine *Sekai* over a sixteen-year period from February 1975 to April 1991. Pages 27–74 of the introduction to this volume contain an illuminating roundtable discussion in which the lead attorney for Ishikawa's legal team, Nakayama Taketoshi, participates.

ten minutes or so. Suddenly, things went awry. The kidnapper yelled, "You told the police, didn't you! I can see two of them over there. Since I can't pick up the money, I am going home." Upon hearing this, police officers sounded their whistles and rushed into the field to apprehend the kidnapper. Their efforts were to no avail, however. The kidnapper successfully managed to escape though the field.

Several consequences followed from not apprehending the kidnapper on that night. First, the outcome most likely contributed to the murder of Yoshie, whose corpse was found on May 4, just two days after the botched arrest attempt. Second, the Saitama Prefectural Police became the target of intense public scrutiny. Their competence was being questioned publicly in major newspapers and even within the Diet because one month earlier police in neighboring Tokyo had failed to apprehend a kidnapper in the abduction case of a young boy. This initial failure had done much to undermine public trust in the competence of police. Predictably, that trust further eroded when news spread of police committing the same kind of mishap again within one month's time. Prime Minister Ikeda Hayato stood in the Diet and implored the police to "take every necessary step to see to it that such a thing never happens again." With the discovery of young Yoshie's body, it seemed that public opinion placed a great deal of responsibility, if not outright culpability, on the police.

In an effort to rehabilitate their tarnished image and regain the public trust, police stepped up efforts to find the kidnapper/killer in the Sayama case. Their investigation quickly led them to focus on 120 young men residing in Buraku areas, from whom they collected alibis and handwriting samples to compare with the writing style of the person who penned the ransom note. Some were asked to provide biological samples, which were used to compare their blood type to that of the murderer. Ishikawa was one of the individuals targeted by the police investigation. The way the investigation was conducted, with authorities collecting information from such a large group of people with nothing in common other than their Buraku roots, seems to indicate that police had no specific information leading them to a particular individual. Rather, the investigations looks like a fishing expedition that smacks of residential profiling. I use "residential profiling" in a similar sense as the better known "racial profiling" in order to highlight the significance of the Buraku as a place, both in terms of identifying *burakumin* as a group and also in order to highlight the special attention given to location in the way that the police investigation unfolded.

SABETSU SAIBAN (DISCRIMINATION TRIAL)

News of a judgment in the Sayama case in March 1964 spread around the country. Mainstream media outlets would report that the Sayama incident had come to an end as the man convicted of killing Tanaka Yoshie would pay with his own life. This death sentence, which most likely signaled to the general public a just resolution to an emotionally wrenching case, signaled something quite different to many Buraku residents across the country. They saw the verdict issued in the Sayama case as a clear example of a Buraku resident being made a scapegoat. Ishikawa's arrest, conviction, and sentence were deemed to be grossly unjust acts that needed to be contested and overturned so that justice might ultimately be done.

There are several points of contention noted by Ishikawa's supporters. First and foremost are the facts surrounding the ransom note. Buraku liberation activists have argued that the author of the ransom note was clearly someone who had attained a literacy level higher than that of Ishikawa, who, like many Buraku residents during the time, had to forego formal education beyond primary school so that he could earn money to help his family make a living. As is evident from the writing sample obtained prior to arrest, Ishikawa had a limited knowledge of *kanji* (Chinese characters) corresponding roughly to the number of *kanji* learned during the first three years of elementary school. Moreover, he seemed unable to use punctuation marks appropriately. He frequently failed to use any punctuation at all, producing a sequence of run-on sentences. Unaccustomed to writing, his characters were blockish. All of these characteristics of his writing style stand in stark contrast to those of the author of the ransom note. Punctuation and *kanji* are used freely, and the penmanship has a measure of originality stemming from the use of characters with curvature. Critics of the Sayama case adduce this difference in writing ability and writing style to argue that Ishikawa could not be the one who wrote the ransom note. This objection, however, carried very little weight with the trial judges. In rejecting Ishikawa's request for a retrial, the court acknowledged the difference in writing styles of the ransom note and the samples of Ishikawa's writing, but asserted that an individual's handwriting can be influenced both by external factors, such as the environment, and internal factors, such as state of mind. Therefore, according to the rationale offered by the bench, just because the writing style is different it does not necessarily mean the same person did not write it.

Another suspicious piece of evidence upon which Mr. Ishikawa's conviction was based is a pink fountain pen allegedly belonging to the victim. The pen was not discovered at the Ishikawa residence until three days after his confession. It took three officers 24 minutes to locate this item on June 26, 1963. Critics point not only to the timeliness of this discovery but also to the fact that police had failed to discover the pen on two previous searches. The initial search of the Ishikawa home by twelve officers took place on May 23, the same day that he was first arrested on unrelated charges, and lasted for two hours and seventeen minutes. Fourteen officers conducted a second search on June 18 for two hours and eight minutes. Neither of these searches turned up any physical evidence linking Ishikawa to the crime. Most importantly, however, an officer who was part of the first investigation for evidence inside the home is on record as saying he was "surprised" when he heard a pen was found above a doorframe of the Ishikawa residence because he had previously searched that specific place thoroughly and found nothing.

Aside from the timing of its discovery, questions arose as to whether the pen that was found was actually the one that belonged to Yoshie. Her school notebook contained writing in blue ink only. However, the pen discovered at the Ishikawa home was filled with black ink. The court discounted this by maintaining that one cannot rule out the possibility that Ishikawa might have stopped at a post office or somewhere and purchased new ink for the pen. Since prosecutors presented no evidence to this effect, many are puzzled (and frustrated) at the unwillingness of the court judges to acknowledge inconsistencies such as this, which raise important doubts about the discovery of the pen and whether in fact this was actually the writing instrument used by the victim. A final point concerning this one piece of evidence, the only piece of evidence used by prosecutors to establish a direct link between the victim and the alleged murderer, is the fact that Ishikawa's fingerprints were not found on it. For that matter, his fingerprints were not found on any items recovered by the police during their investigation, including the ransom note and the envelope within which it was placed.

Such questionable circumstances regarding evidentiary items have supported a general belief among many Buraku residents, and increasingly the general public, that the Sayama case is a clear example of *enzai* or "false accusation." This view is strengthened all the more by a general sense that the choice in the very beginning to arbitrarily target Buraku residents smacks of prejudice. In addition to this initial decision to focus on youth residing in Buraku areas, there is a feeling that the consistency with which the judicial system has turned a blind eye to the dubious veracity of the evidence in the Sayama case is also the product of discrimination against Buraku communities. For these reasons the Sayama case is referred to most often by Buraku liberation activists as a *sabetsu saiban* or "discrimination trial."

SIGNIFICANCE OF THE SAYAMA CASE

As a cornerstone of the BLM, the Sayama case provides a unique perspective on subtle but significant shifts in the political mobilization efforts of those with ties to Japan's Buraku areas. It also gives a vantage point from which to critique a dominant image in Japanese society of Buraku residents as political extortionists who rely on tactics like denunciation sessions to achieve their ends. Denunciation sessions continue to be one of several means employed by the BLL in parts of Japan. However, the Sayama struggle makes it clear that the organization employs more conventional means too. Through a combined use of domestic courts, human rights discourse, and international organizations, the BLL has reframed its movement as a universal one aimed at protecting the fundamental rights of the individual against the state.

The Sayama case provides a superb opportunity to gauge the shifting political trajectory of the BLM. During my fieldwork in Osaka from July 1997 to August 1999, it became apparent that the case was a focal point of postwar politics concerning the Buraku issue. First, it is one of but three issues printed on the yellow protest vests often worn by members of the BLL during official events such as negotiation sessions with the local government, denunciation sessions, and public demonstrations like the protest marches held in Tokyo to condemn verdicts rendered in the Sayama case and demand a retrial. The Sayama case dominates one entire side of the protest vest upon which the following is written: "We Denounce the Sayama Discrimination Trial" (*Sayama Sabetsu Saiban Kyūdan*) and "We Demand a Retrial" (*Saishin Yōkyū*). The other side of the vest calls for the establishment of a Fundamental Law of Buraku Liberation and denounces the Buraku Lists Incident, which refers to the discovery in 1975 of several books listing the names and locations of Buraku areas that were found in the possession of several large companies that used them to weed out job applicants from Buraku districts (see Tomonaga 2006).

The second thing that impressed upon me the significance attributed to the Sayama case was my discovery one day of a bas-relief in an obscure spot in Saiwaichiku (pseudonym), the Buraku in western Japan where I conducted the bulk of my research. The right side of the bas-relief shows riot police wearing helmets and wielding shields as they stand at the entrance of the Supreme Court. Foregrounded on the same side of the sculpture is a group of BLL protesters identifiable by a flag held in the air by the leader of the group. The flag being hoisted is none other than the *Keikanki*, the official flag of the Buraku Liberation League, which features the symbolic mark inherited from the National Levelers Association: a red crown of thorns against a black backdrop. Within the sculpture one can discern protesters of various ages showing expressions of frustration, outrage, and determination as they mobilize against what they believe to be a miscarriage of justice. One can also make out in the background school-age children distributing leaflets to passersby. When asked who created this piece of work, residents answered that it was a joint effort by "everyone" in the community. While there are certainly those that played no part in the creation of the sculpture, the sentiment expressed about the broad support for the Sayama case was largely confirmed by my own observations. The Sayama case received considerable support from the overwhelming majority of the community. It did not have the kind of polarizing effect other issues sometimes had. Thus, the sculpture exceeds being a representation of communal solidarity and becomes its very manifestation.

Notably, this politically inspired artwork also represents a divide between Saiwaichiku and the local government. This symbol of support for Ishikawa is located on a second floor balcony on the back side of the Youth Center, a location that renders it invisible to anyone except those standing on the balcony. This less than ideal location was picked because local officials disapproved of placing it in a more prominent location, given that Ishikawa had been convicted of murder. There were two other artistic works authorities did not contest, and they were prominently displayed. Perched atop the Human Rights Culture Center, for example, is a statue named Ogari. It portrays a mother protecting two of her children from a looming threat by shielding them with her body as she stretches out her right arm in what appears to be an attempt to keep some sort of peril at bay. Likewise, running along the side of the Youth Center that faces a park area, there is another piece of community-crafted art showing individuals of various ages wearing expressions of pain and agony. The trio of artistic works was part of a joint venture meant to represent different elements of the community and the BLM—the emotional toll taken on those subjected to discrimination, the determination to meet any challenge, and the resolve to mobilize en mass to challenge injustice.

The third and final indication of the importance of the Sayama case within the movement was the fact that it was routinely on the agenda of local, regional, and national meetings of the BLL. During larger gatherings the topic of Sayama was often addressed within the context of a thematic session devoted to disseminating the latest information regarding the status of the push for a retrial. Occasionally, lawyers representing Ishikawa would be in attendance to answer detailed questions regarding the legal intricacies of the case. It was not unusual for Ishikawa himself to make a personal appearance, as he did at the national meeting of the women's branch of the BLL in 1997. His presence alone sent a spark through the room; his soft-spoken manner and frequent expressions of gratitude for the unwavering support he has received from core members of the organization seemed to strengthen the resolve of those listening to him speak. Since being paroled on December 21, 1994, he has become a living legend within Buraku communities throughout the country. His apology to the group of activists assembled from all corners of the country for not being able to entertain all of the requests for a personal visit underscored just how significant the cause he symbolizes continues to be within the contemporary movement for Buraku liberation.

I had the opportunity to meet him during the national meeting of the women's branch, when I was introduced to him by a resident of Saiwaichiku who had personal ties to his wife. My impression at the time was that he was not altogether comfortable with the central role he has come to play. He struck me as a reticent man who would just as soon not be caught in the limelight. I noticed during the afternoon's session (and on one other occasion as the Ishikawa couple addressed a crowd of thousands during one of the Tokyo demonstrations) that Mrs. Ishikawa bore a considerable share of the weight of her husband's celebrity by appearing in public with him and following his usually concise public statements with her own comments. Her well-chosen words, charisma, and apparent comfort before large crowds made her especially effective at communicating gratitude to long-time supporters. Her outgoing personality made her the perfect person to act as a buffer between her somewhat subdued husband and the multitudes of people who look to him as a source of inspiration, something which has become arguably a critically important function as the BLL grapples with changing circumstances. Long before they got married in 1996, Mrs. Ishikawa was a Buraku liberation activist who campaigned tirelessly with others demanding a retrial of the Sayama case. It is hard to imagine anyone better suited to help Mr. Ishikawa make the transition back into society after thirty-one years and seven months of incarceration. Ishikawa struck me as a totally different person when I saw him at a 2005 Citizens' Meeting Demanding a Retrial of the Sayama Case held for the first time in the city of Sayama. When he addressed the crowd of roughly 4,000 supporters, he spoke with a confidence and determination I did not see in 1997. To the extent that this was due to the overwhelming support network he had both in public and private, one can only wonder how others embroiled in suspected as well as confirmed *enzai* cases cope with life post-prison. See Steinhoff (this volume) for more on the significance of support groups.

Sayama had a firm place not only within the national meetings of the BLL but also within small-scale gatherings that took place in communities like Saiwaichi-ku. During one of the regular neighborhood meetings, for example, everyone was encouraged to write postcards to be sent to the Supreme Court expressing disapproval with the handling of the Sayama case. Pens and postcards were prepared in advance. They were distributed along with several succinct examples of how one might express dissatisfaction with the reluctance of the courts to overturn Mr. Ishikawa's guilty verdict or retry his case. One reason sample statements supporting Ishikawa were distributed is that many among the older generations in Buraku areas received little formal education. In general, senior residents of Saiwaichiku were much more active in local affairs, and they were well represented at this meeting. Of course, having a model at hand also made it much easier to complete the task, thereby increasing the odds of widespread participation.

Whether at formal sessions within larger national meetings or more informal gatherings within particular Buraku communities like Saiwaichiku, it was not uncommon to bring things to a close with a rendition of what might be called the Sayama theme song: "Sabetsu Saiban Uchikudakō" (Let's Shatter the Discrimination Trial).

Declaring innocence from West to East
We march beneath our flag of a crown of thorns

Let's shatter the discrimination trial
Let's shatter the discrimination trial

Against the Sayama discrimination trial
We must fight resolutely
Let's take back young Ishikawa
Let's take back young Ishikawa

We declare his innocence
As a group of three million brothers
Let's shatter the discrimination trial
Let's shatter the discrimination trial

The lyrics clearly are a call for sustained engagement with the courts in the fight against the verdict rendered in the Sayama case. The only way to shatter the trial is to work through and on the courts to achieve the ultimate aim of proving Ishikawa's innocence and, in so doing, win this particular round in the ongoing battle against discrimination.

DEVELOPMENT OF THE SAYAMA PROTESTS

The Sayama case had a catalytic effect among the various branches and members of the BLL. The organization quickly began to rally around the fate of Ishikawa. Public pronouncements of support for him would in a short time give rise to large-scale demonstrations numbering in the thousands. At its twentieth national meeting on October 5, 1965, just a year and a half after his conviction, the BLL officially took the position that he was in fact innocent, and it called for a new public trial to exonerate him. Four years later it would begin protest activities demanding Ishikawa's release. In 1970 a massive demonstration was organized against the "discrimination trial." A procession traveled across the country protesting his conviction and continued incarceration.

Mr. Ishikawa's death sentence was commuted to life imprisonment by the Tokyo High Court on October 31, 1974. Although likely relieved to some degree to see that his life was no longer on the line, those protesting against the Sayama case were enraged by this verdict because, in their eyes, an innocent man was still being held accountable for a crime he did not commit. Despite revelations such as glaring inconsistencies between the confession Ishikawa gave the police and the facts established in the case, the judge disregarded these discrepancies as insignificant and attributed them to the defendant's tendency to mix fact with fiction (Buraku Kaihō Kenkyūsho 1989, 3:134). Upon hearing the news that the original conviction was upheld by the courts, thirteen thousand people took to the streets of Tokyo in protest over the ruling that, in effect, reaffirmed Ishikawa's culpability.

This verdict, which seemed indifferent to the appeals of the thousands organizing in support of Ishikawa, sparked another phase of protests. A couple of demonstrations that stand out in particular were those staged by youth living in Buraku areas. Simultaneously with the submission of an appeal to the Supreme Court by Ishikawa's lawyers on January 28, 1976, approximately ten thousand elementary and junior high school students in Nara and Osaka participated in the Sayama *dōmei kyūkō* and refused to attend classes in protest (World Human Rights Research Center 1999, 190). This number increased tenfold on May 22 of the same year when one hundred thousand school children from 1,500 schools across the country boycotted classes in a day of protest (Buraku Kaihō Kenkyūsho 1989, 3:187). Of course the young age of the participants in both cases raises questions about whether they were acting on their own volition. It is unlikely that they would be able to execute such a well-coordinated act of protest without the guidance and permission of their parents and other adults in the community. Nonetheless, one can argue that these two protests are indicative of just how galvanized Buraku communities and the families living within them were during this time. Even children were encouraged to take part in the mass protests.

Saiwaichiku was also abuzz with political activities criticizing the handling of the Sayama case. According to local residents, the roots of the national Sayama campaign can be traced back to this very community. "At a time when other *shibu* [BLL branch offices] were preoccupied with *machizukuri* [community improvement projects], we pressed the importance of the campaign against the Sayama verdict because it was literally a matter of life and death." These words were spoken by the head of the Saiwaichiku branch of the BLL as he showed me pictures of local residents in protest dating back more than twenty years. The pictures depicted scenes of an entire community that stood together: a photograph of hundreds of men, women, and children crowded in the local gymnasium (the only space available at the time for public meetings of this magnitude) during a community forum to discuss the Sayama case; a picture of community residents marching through the local streets carrying signs denouncing the verdict; and snapshots of groups of residents distributing informational fliers clarifying the facts surrounding the Sayama trial to people at train stations, shopping centers, and other public venues.

The extent to which the community mobilized around the Sayama case is reflected in an original form of protest carried out by five young men from Saiwaichiku. Protesting the handling of the Sayama case in particular and discrimination against Buraku residents in general, these five individuals walked roughly 700 kilometers from Osaka to Tokyo. It took the better part of one month for them to reach their destination. The extended journey helped galvanize and solidify Buraku communities across the country as the group made several stops along the way for food and lodging, enlisting the support of several Buraku areas located between Osaka and the nation's capital. The documentary of the protest march, "Sayama: 700 Kilometers from Osaka to Tokyo," which is preserved in the library of the Human Rights Cultural Center in Saiwaichiku, contains ample footage of the five men being cheered on by local BLL members and Ishikawa supporters in whatever region of the country they were passing through on that particular day. Many who came out to voice their support wore yellow protest vests nearly identical to the ones donned by the marchers. Against the yellow background of the vest, the text of the slogans, written in bold red characters denouncing the Sayama verdict and calling for a retrial, seemed to jump off the chests of the marching protestors and their supporters.

Mass protests were part of a comprehensive effort to respond to what was transpiring within the judicial system and to put pressure on the state to overturn Ishikawa's conviction. In addition to these types of mass demonstrations, there have been a dizzying amount of legal actions pursued to spur the reversal of court decisions. Yet at every turn prosecutors have presented a rebuttal deemed more compelling in the opinion of the bench. The courts have consistently ruled against legal challenges mounted by Ishikawa. Following his original conviction and sentencing by the Urawa District Court on March 11, 1964, Ishikawa's lawyers filed an appeal with the Tokyo High Court on the very next day. Though the sentence was downgraded to a life sentence with hard labor, the conviction was upheld on October 31, 1974. This decision too was challenged with an appeal to the Supreme Court, which was ultimately dismissed by the Second Petty Bench of the Supreme Court on August 9, 1977. Just two days later Ishikawa's lawyers filed an objection with the Supreme Court over the ruling, but the Court rejected this challenge four days later on August 15. On August 30, attorneys for Ishikawa filed papers seeking a retrial with the Tokyo High Court. The Fourth Criminal Division of the High Court ruled against the retrial request on February 7, 1980. Ishikawa's legal team filed a formal protest with the Tokyo High Court on February 12 on the grounds that the Court failed to consider new evidence germane to the case, but this action was also denied on March 25, 1981. Five days later a special appeal was filed with the Supreme Court. Like in the past, this proved to be unsuccessful when rejected by the Supreme Court's Second Petty Bench on May 28, 1985.

The following year on August 21, legal proceedings were initiated at the Tokyo High Court requesting, for a second time, a new trial. More than thirteen years would pass before Judge Takagi Toshio ruled against the request on July 9, 1999. Ishikawa's legal team wasted no time as they filed a complaint over the decision with the Tokyo High Court on July 12. Judge Takahashi Shogo dismissed the complaint on January 23, 2002, setting the stage for another round of legal actions at the highest court. On January 29, Ishikawa filed a special appeal with the First Petty Bench of the Supreme Court. Yet again the Court would rule against him in the decision rendered by Supreme Court First Petty Bench Judge Shimada

Niro on March 16, 2005. On the day marking the forty-third year since his arrest, May 23, 2006, Ishikawa commenced proceedings demanding for the third time that the Tokyo High Court grant him a retrial.

The BLL has helped coordinate Ishikawa's legal team, most of whom work at greatly reduced rates. Money to pay legal bills and other expenses is raised partly through donations routinely collected as part of the mass demonstrations in Tokyo. Additional funds are raised through selling literature relating to the Sayama case, including one monthly serial titled *Sayama Sabetsu Saiban* (The Sayama Discrimination Trial), which has been published since February 21, 1974. A nongovernment organization started by the BLL in 1988, the International Movement Against All Forms of Discrimination and Racism, has helped extend support for the Sayama struggle beyond the borders of Japan. For decades the BLL has played a critical role by providing the political, economic, and emotional support to help Ishikawa sustain his legal battle for exoneration. Perhaps because the base of support has expanded considerably and the audience it hopes to reach with its message has grown too, one can discern a subtle shift in the tenor of recent Buraku liberation activities.

Evolving Struggle

The changing character of the Sayama struggle was evident during one of the mass demonstrations I attended in Tokyo in October 1998 to denounce the 1974 upholding of Ishikawa's conviction by Justice Terao Shōji of the Tokyo High Court. The event attracted thousands of participants, the majority of whom seemed to be close to Ishikawa's own generation. As was true with the delegation from Saiwaichiku, young faces were present but scarce. Predictably, the bulk of the audience was affiliated with a Buraku community that could be identified by the flag each delegation carried. However, I saw several banners designating non-BLL groups, such as labor organizations and religious coalitions, that were on hand to show their support.

Still more unexpected were the citizens groups present to express their support for reconsidering the Sayama case. There were about forty such groups at the rally, each hailing from a different part of the country. These groups were called Sayama Jiken o Kangaeru Jyūmin no Kai (Association of Citizens for Contemplating the Sayama Case).[4] Most of these citizens wore makeshift vests with slogans calling for a reexamination of the Sayama case or demanding all the evidentiary material be disclosed. These slogans were in line with most of the demands

---

4. As of 2001 the number of such groups jumped to 103 (Buraku Liberation and Human Rights Research Institute 2002, 184), and the number increased to 125 by February 2005 (http://www.bll. gr.jp/sayama/jumin.html).

written on the large banners that were draped over the stage.

- We demand that Justice Takagi have the prosecution make the entire evidentiary record available!
- The Tokyo prosecutor's office should comply with the United Nations and make all evidence available!
- We demand that the Tokyo prosecutor's office immediately make available a list of all evidentiary items!
- Let's encourage a democratic revolution within the judiciary through a broad-based citizen's movement!

The above slogans approach the Sayama case as a matter of protecting the individual from abusive state power. It is interesting to note the slight tension between this particular framing of the Sayama case and the way it was presented in some of the other banners:

- Ishikawa Kazuo is innocent! We denounce the Sayama discrimination trial!
- We denounce the 36th year of the false arrest of Ishikawa Kazuo and the illegal use of state authority rooted in Buraku discrimination!
- We demand that the Tokyo High Court immediately conduct an investigation into the true facts and hold a retrial!
- Let's bring about an investigation into the true facts, open up access to the evidentiary record, and win a retrial and a not-guilty verdict!
- Let's create a "Citizens Group for Contemplating the Sayama Case" in every region of the country!

The sentiments expressed through these banners are more politically charged than the others. Likewise, they call for more drastic action than both the first set of banners and the types of slogans espoused by the citizens groups. In fact, the slogan of the final banner explicitly identifies growing the number of such civic groups scrutinizing the criminal justice system's handling of the Sayama incident as a key organizational aim of the BLL. The other banners assert Ishikawa's innocence, question the veracity of the Supreme Court proceedings, list securing a not-guilty verdict as the endgame, and subordinate the issue of excessive use of state authority to a theme of Buraku discrimination.

A close look at the messages on the banners revealed that the Sayama demonstration drew its support from two different sources. This was suggested not only by the particular concerns written on the banners but also by their spatial arrangement. The first four slogans were listed on the left side of the stage area, and the remaining five were listed on the right side. The right side banners clearly situated the Sayama case within the long history of political activism of Buraku residents and their attempts to liberate Buraku districts through their own efforts, a goal first articulated by the National Levelers Association (Zenkoku Suiheisha) in the 1920s. The demands listed on the left, however, drew on more general themes that present the Sayama case as a fundamental problem resulting from infringements by the state. These different bases for critiquing the Sayama case were manifest among the participants in the slogans they chanted as well as those they displayed on their chests as they marched through the streets of Tokyo. Despite attending the event to express solidarity, the call from citizens groups to think about or consider the breakdown of the judicial process in the Sayama case and the fundamental human rights concerns it embodies were considerably more measured in tone than the unqualified assertions of Ishikawa's innocence and charges of anti-Buraku discrimination coming from the various BLL delegations.

An equilibrium of sorts seems to have been reached, judging from more recent protests. The number of banners at some meetings, for example, has been reduced to a single one overhanging the stage area. In other protests where multiple banners are featured, the same banner is reproduced multiple times. Judging from photographs of the many different events held across the country in support of Ishikawa, the emphasis seems to have shifted to framing the Sayama case as an example of false accusation (*enzai*). Casting the Sayama incident primarily as an *enzai* matter spurs greater awareness of the problem of false accusation in the criminal justice system as well as greater awareness of troubling aspects of police investigations and court proceedings that increase the risk of *enzai*. This way of framing the Sayama case also allows the BLL to synchronize it with international human rights discourse and seek assistance from external bodies like the United Nations Human Rights Committee, which has consistently pressed the Japanese state to make reforms such as full disclosure of all evidence gathered during investigations so that defendants have access to material that might exonerate them. The continuous expansion of the community of potential supporters through the superimposition of gradually broader frames—Buraku discrimination, denial of due process guaranteed by the Japanese Constitution, human rights violation—reflects a concerted effort to universalize the problem and expand the limited options available through bureaucratic informality.

Discursive Duality and Political Mobilization

The Sayama case continues to be a focal point of the political activities within Buraku communities across Japan. It still has the support of thousands of members of the BLL. It is also attracting new supporters because it illustrates a concrete problem concerning the rules of evidence within the judicial system. Attorneys representing Ishikawa maintain that one reason they were not able to mount a suitable defense was because the prosecution was under no obligation to share evidence they were not going to use during trial. Until very recently, there was no rule of discovery obliging the prosecution to share all evidence regardless of whether it strengthens or weakens their case. There is a strong feeling among many that there is evidence in the possession of the state that may help prove the innocence of Ishikawa.

This argument has been used to broaden the base of support well beyond Buraku residents. Ordinary citizens are politically mobilized as partners in protest by pointing out that the Sayama case illustrates how the fundamental human rights of *all* Japanese citizens are imperiled within the current judicial system. Thus, the banners and slogans of the non-BLL members participating in the demonstration advocate thinking broadly about the Sayama case as something of significance for every citizen of Japan. Among the mainstream citizens protesting Ishikawa's arrest, there are fewer slogans denouncing the ruling of Justice Terao of the Tokyo High Court or asserting Ishikawa's innocence. This is in stark contrast to BLL protesters for whom the demonstration is a massive denunciation of nearly every aspect of the Sayama case.

The legalities concerning evidentiary proceedings have also been used as a basis for constructing the Sayama case as a gross human rights violation before members of the United Nations Human Rights Committee. The BLL has worked hard to promote knowledge of the Buraku issue in general and the Sayama case in particular outside of Japan. Although the committee does not mention Ishikawa or the Sayama case by name, there are unmistakable echoes of Sayama resonating in the words of criticism the Human Rights Committee directed at the Japanese government in response to the Fourth Periodic Report submitted in 1997:

> The Committee is concerned that under the criminal law, there is no obligation on the prosecution to disclose evidence it may have gathered in the course of the investigation other than that which it intends to produce at the trial, and that the defense has no general right to ask for the disclosure of that material at any stage of the proceedings. The Committee recommends that, in accordance with the guarantees provided for in article 14, paragraph 3, of the Covenant, the State party ensure that its law and practice enable the defense to have access to all relevant material in order that the right of defense is not hampered.[5]

5. The Committee's full response to Japan's Fourth Periodic Report can be found on the website of the United Nations at the following web address: http://www.unhchr.ch/tbs/doc.nsf/(Symbol)/CCPR.C.79.Add.102.En?Opendocument. One can also locate the Human Rights Committee's response to Japan's Fifth Periodic Report submitted in December 2006. The committee expressed frustration that most of its recommendations were not acted upon sufficiently. See Repeta 2009.

The committee's words are perfectly in synch with one of the rallying cries of the demonstration: Make all evidence available! The words of the committee are also a testament to the success of the BLL in courting justice domestically by enlisting the support of international organizations and institutions.

Ishikawa himself made a plea in person to members of the United Nations Human Rights Committee on October 15, 2008. Having obtained special permission to leave the country and travel to Geneva, Switzerland despite his status as a parolee convicted of murder, he appealed to members of the committee to help him gain access to the evidentiary materials not disclosed by the prosecution. New evidence is the primary factor considered by the courts to determine whether or not to grant an appeal to retry a case. Ishikawa and his legal team continue to press for full disclosure of all evidence gathered by investigators during the Sayama case in order to be able to determine what evidence not introduced by the prosecution during the trial could be presented to the courts in an effort to win a retrial. Although recent changes in the legal system permit more discovery if the defense asks for it, the revisions do not apply to cases tried under the old rules. Thus, pressing for full disclosure is of paramount importance to the success of Ishikawa's quest for exoneration. In his brief statement to the committee, Ishikawa, then sixty-nine years old, expressed his desire to clear his name while he still walks this earth. With the exception of the following three lines from the very beginning and the very end of his address, his presentation was in Japanese: "Dear Members of the Committee, my name is Kazuo Ishikawa. . . . Dear Members, I am innocent. . . . Thank you for your attention."[6]

CONCLUSION

The mass protests organized around the Sayama case give us a glimpse into how Buraku liberation activists creatively reframe their struggle, combining two separate bodies of discourse to amplify the appeal and the power of their movement. They have managed to accomplish several things. First, by modifying the discursive framework within which they articulate concerns about the Sayama case, they transform a subject typically avoided by most people and still considered somewhat of a taboo, the Buraku issue, into something less threatening. Second, they have managed to enlist the support of influential human rights institutions to help them pressure the Japanese government in an effort to influence the judiciary. Again, by stressing the improper use of state power over the individual and framing it as a fundamental human rights issue, they are able to win the cooperation of people outside of the Buraku and outside of the country. At the same time, by linking the Sayama case to broader concerns for judicial reform, the BLM is able to

6. For the full text of his speech see http://www.sayama-jiken.com/ki/top/ki2002.htm.

contribute to and benefit from a growing public concern with some of the tenets of the legal system. The numbers of people concerned is likely to continue to grow, as is the legal IQ of the general public as more individuals experience judicial proceedings firsthand as jury members. The reintroduction of the jury system last year has made the courthouse a hot topic of the mass media and spurred a mix of curiosity and anxiety among a general public somewhat uneasy about how best to execute this new civic duty.

The push for a retrial now enters its third phase. On March 16, 2005 the Supreme Court ruled against Ishikawa's second bid for a retrial (*Asahi Shinbun*, online edition, March 17, 2005). Justice Shimada Niro of the First Petty Bench of the Supreme Court downplayed the significance of arguments contained in the appeal. Ishikawa's counsel based the appeal on the discrepancies within the evidentiary record. For example, they provided a new handwriting analysis that confirmed what now has become common knowledge among many BLL activists supporting Ishikawa—he could not have written the ransom note. Three reasons given to substantiate this claim are the distinct differences between Ishikawa's handwriting style and the style in which the ransom note was written, the likelihood that the author of the ransom note possessed a literacy level exceeding Ishikawa's level of formal education, and traces of fountain pen ink were discovered on the envelope containing the ransom note despite the fact that Ishikawa confessed to writing it using a ballpoint pen.

In response to the issues raised by the lawyers, the First Petty Bench ruled that whatever differences might exist between the ransom note and the confession that Ishikawa wrote in 1964, "there are many similar characteristics." With respect to the point concerning Ishikawa's level of literacy at the time, the judge dismissed the argument that he was only able to write a composition equivalent to that of a young primary school student on the basis that the confession makes clear that he was accurately able to communicate his intentions and emotions. Finally, the court opined that there was a high probability that Ishikawa possessed a fountain pen and a bottle of ink at the time of the crime and ruled that the issue of whether there were traces of fountain pen ink on the ransom note envelope has no bearing on his guilt or innocence.

Despite this setback, the Sayama struggle seems to be gaining momentum of a particular sort. The month before Japan's highest court made its determination, information about the Sayama case was broadcast in homes throughout the entire country during the special episode of the program "The Scoop" discussed above. The following year the popular weekly news magazine *AERA* published by the *Asahi Shinbun* featured a humanizing article profiling Ishikawa that also noted dubious aspects of the case and the broader backdrop of discrimination against *burakumin*. In the article Emori Ryōko, the *Asahi Shinbun* journalist who was present to cover Ishikawa's arrest at 4:30 a.m. on May 23, 1963, says, "I was certain it was a case of *enzai* (false accusation). Since the day that [he] was arrested, and to this day, I am ashamed. I feel ashamed because I was one of the reporters who continued to report the case from the vantage point of the police rather than the point of view of a person police were underhandedly making into a murderer just because he was from a *hisabestu buraku*" (Kitanokuchi 2006, 72). The recent publication of a book on the Sayama *jiken* by renowned investigative journalist and author Kamata Satoshi (2004) is just one additional example of how a fifty-one-year-old case is being infused with the voices of those bringing new perspectives and generating a new wave of interest in both the Sayama case and the judicial system. Intellectuals, literary figures, journalists, and entertainers as well as legal scholars and practitioners have joined the steady core of activists raising awareness about the Sayama case and demanding modifications to the administration of criminal justice.

The Sayama case remains a centerpiece of the BLM. To the extent that this is true and the struggle to prove Ishikawa's innocence continues, working both on and through the courts will continue to be a central focus of Buraku liberation activists and newcomers to the struggle. Their efforts have finally borne fruits. In December 2009 the Tokyo High Court recommended that additional evidentiary material be made available to the defense. On May 13, 2010 the Tokyo High Prosecutor's Office signaled its intention to release an additional thirty-six pieces of evidence.[7] Not included, however, is evidence deemed by the defense to be of inestimable value in terms of establishing key elements of the case and exonerating their client. Such items include a range of video and photographic evidence gathered during the investigation as well as evidence that might potentially shed light on the circumstances surrounding Ishikawa's questioning by authorities. Even these missing items signal an important shift in the dynamic between the parties involved. The High Prosecutor's Office cited its inability to locate some of the material sought by the defense, rather than denying the existence of such evidence outright as it did in previous exchanges with Ishikawa's lawyers.

Suguya Toshikazu's appearance on stage in support of Ishikawa at the May 12, 2010 rally held at Tokyo's Hibiya Park is yet another indication that the call to reexamine the Sayama case is continuing to gain momentum. Sugaya was convicted of murder in 1990, but his conviction was overturned after a reanalysis of DNA evidence. Sugaya emerged victorious in a retrial that concluded a couple of months prior to the rally and produced not only an innocent verdict but also an apology from the bench. During the retrial audiotapes were played of the grueling interrogation that extracted the false confession that helped seal Sugaya's fate.

---

7. The recent information relayed in this section is taken from an article in the May 2010 issue of *Connect*, the newsletter for the human rights non-government organization International Movement against All Forms of Discrimination and Racism (IMADR).

Following his acquittal, images of Sugaya wearing a dark suit and gleefully raising a banner declaring himself "absolutely innocent" appeared in newspapers and
on television screens across the country. The image of him standing on stage in
solidarity with Ishikawa, I argue, symbolizes the burgeoning support for Ishikawa
coming from an increasingly broad spectrum of groups and individuals.

Although the BLL and other supporters of Ishikawa have yet to achieve the
stated goal of gaining access to all of the evidence pertaining to the case and proving Ishikawa's innocence, if recent events are any indication, they have been able
to find ways to counter the effects of bureaucratic informality, and they have begun to integrate into the Buraku issue universal themes that have started to attract
widespread interest and backing from a broader constituency.

REFERENCES

Asahi Shinbun. (2005). Sayama jiken: Dainiji saishin yōkyū no tokubetsu kōkoku
o kikyaku saikōsai [Sayama Jiken: Supreme Court Rejects Special Appeal
Containing Second Request for Retrial]. Online ed., March 17 and 18. http://
www.asahi.com/national/update/0317/ TKY200503170216.html.

Buraku Liberation and Human Rights Research Institute. (2002). *Buraku kaihō
jinken nenkan* [Buraku Liberation and Human Rights Almanac]. Osaka,
Kaihō Shuppansha.

Buraku Liberation and Human Rights Research Institute. (1998). *Discrimination
in Japan from the Perspective of the International Covenant on Civil and Political Rights: Counter-Report to the Fourth Periodic Report.* Osaka, Kaihō
Shuppansha.

Buraku Liberation League Headquarters, ed. (1971). *Sayama sabetsu saiban*
[Sayama Discrimination Trial]. Osaka, Buraku Kaihō Chūō Shuppankyoku.
Originally published 1970.

Buraku Liberation League Headquarters and Sayama Struggle Central Headquarters. (1998). *Shitte imasu ka? Sayama jiken ichi mon ittō* [Do You Know
about the Sayama *jiken*? Questions and Answers]. Osaka, Kaihō Shuppansha.
Originally published 1994.

Buraku Liberation League Headquarters and Sayama Struggle Central Headquar-
ters. (1993). *Subete no chikara o hitotsu ni: ansorojī Sayama jiken sanjyūnen*
[Combining All Effort into One: A Thirty-year Anthology of the Sayama
Case]. Osaka, Kaihō Shuppansha.

Buraku Kaihō Kenkyūsho. (1989). *Buraku kaihōshi* [History of Buraku Libera-
tion], 3 vols. Osaka, Kaihō Shuppansha.

Central Executive Committee for the Establishment of Buraku Liberation
and Human Rights Policies. (2008). *Zenkoku no aitsugu sabetsu jiken*

nisenhachinendoban [2008 Edition of Continuing Discrimination Incidents across the Country]. Osaka, Buraku Kaihō Jinken Seisaku Kakuritsu Yōkyū Chūo Jikkōiinkai.

Davis, John. (2000). Blurring the Boundaries of the Buraku(min). In *Globalization and Social Change in Contemporary Japan,* ed. J. S. Eades, Tom Gill, and Harumi Befu. Melbourne, Trans Pacific Press.

Hinamoto, Masahiro, ed. (1984). *Enzai Sayama jiken* [A Case of False Accusation: The Sayama Case]. Tokyo, Gendai Shokan.

Johnson, David. (2002). *The Japanese Way of Justice: Prosecuting Crime in Japan.* New York, Oxford University Press.

Kamata, Satoshi. (2004). *Sayama jiken: Ishikawa Kazuo, yonjyūichinenme no shinjitsu* [The Sayama Case: Ishikwa Kazuo, the Forty-first Year of Truth]. Tokyo, Sōshiya.

Komori Megumi. (2010). The Sayama Case: Another Step Forward. *Connect* 13.4 (May): 19.

Kitano Futoshi. (2006). Sayama jiken no moto tyōekisyō Kazuo Ishikawa: Shakuhō sareta no ni mienai tejyō ga omoi [Ex-Convict of the Sayama Case Kazuo Ishikawa: Though Released from Prison, Invisible Handcuffs Weigh Heavily]. *AERA*, December 18.

Neary, Ian. (1989). *Political Protest and Social Control in Pre-War Japan: The Origins of Buraku Liberation.* Manchester, UK, Manchester University Press.

New York Times. (2009). Japan's Outcasts Still Wait for Acceptance. Online ed., January 16. <http://www.nytimes.com/2009/01/16/world/asia/16outcasts. html?_r=1&scp=1&sq= Japan's%20Outcasts&st=cse>

Noma Hiroshi. (1997). *Sayama saiban* [The Sayama Trial]. Tokyo, Fujiwara Shoten.

Repeta, Lawrence. (2009). U.N. Committee Faults Japan Human Rights Performance, Demands Progress Report on Key Issues. *The Asia-Pacific Journal,* May 20.

Rohlen, Thomas. (1976). Violence in Yoka High School: the Implications for Japanese Coalition Politics of the Confrontation between the Communist Party and the Buraku Liberation League. *Asian Survey* 16.7: 682–99.

Sōmuchō. *Tenkanki o mukaeta Dōwa Mondai: Heisei gonendo dōwa chiku jittai haakutō chōsa kekka no kaisetsu* [A Turning Point for the Dōwa Mondai: Analysis of the Results of the 1993 Survey to Assess Conditions in Dōwa Districts]. Tokyo, Chūōhōki Shuppan.

Tomonaga Kenzō. (2006). *Ima aratamete "Buraku Chimei Sōkan" sabetsu jiken o tou* [Revisiting the Discriminatory "Buraku Lists Incident" Again Now]. Osaka, Kaihō Shuppansha.

Upham, Frank. (1987). *Law and Social Change in Postwar Japan.* Cambridge, MA, Harvard University Press.

World Human Rights Research Center. (1999). *Jinken rekishi nenpyō* [Chronology of Human Rights History]. Tokyo, Yamagawa Shuppansha.

CHAPTER 4

Becoming Unforgettable: Leveraging Law for Labor in Struggles for Employment Security

Christena L. Turner

> When the owners of their parent company dissolved Universal[1] they had a strategy, an expectation. They would declare the company bankrupt, and, if the union opposed it and occupied the place, they would just wait. They compared it to making canned food (*kanzume*). They would just close the gates and let them stay sealed up inside for a while. They thought that most workers would give up and leave, especially the older workers and the part-timers. If the union tried to resist, they would just call the police and have them clear the premises.

This statement was later recounted by a union official from the parent company, Custom Shoes, who participated in the initial meetings with Custom management when the decision was made to let the Universal Shoe Company go bankrupt. The effort to dissolve Universal Shoe Company failed. It did not fail quickly, but in the end it did fail.

Immediately after the announcement at work that Universal was to be liquidated as a company, and, as a consequence, jobs would be eliminated, workers were led by their union leaders into the office of the Universal company president. They refused to leave or to let him leave until he signed a "factory use agreement" giving them the temporary right to use equipment and premises to continue production. Rather than disbanding, fifty Universal workers plus supporters from affiliated unions and labor movement networks occupied the Universal factory and resisted efforts by the parent company to force the evacuation of the buildings, the liquidation of assets, and the dissolution of this small subsidiary

---

1. To insure anonymity for participants in this research, the names of companies used in this chapter are pseudonyms. I chose these pseudonyms to sound like English language names because the real names are taken from English and transliterated into Japanese to sound English.

company. During these early days of the struggle even neighborhood residents and businesses came out in support of the Universal workers and their refusal to vacate the factory premises and give up their work and workplace. The supportive relationship with their neighborhood continued throughout the decade of labor struggle that followed. These disruptive and defiant actions were wrapped in legal cases that defined their struggle as a labor dispute and permitted them to continue to exercise self-production until all court cases could be concluded.

The account of management strategy that begins this chapter is one that leaked out through a sympathetic figure from the parent company. It summarizes a conversation held at a local coffee shop between the owners of the parent company and the owners of Universal, a meeting at which Universal's bankruptcy was planned. According to these owners and managers, that plan was an inevitable result of economic upheaval and could not be avoided. There was simply not enough work to maintain Universal. The workers through their union argued that this was untrue and that insufficient effort had been made to adapt to current economic conditions. Issues raised in this account illustrate the fundamental point that tied eight separate court cases to nearly ten years of collective action for the Universal Shoes labor union. The most radical form of social change that the Universal union pursued was greater employment security through the establishment of a worker-owned production company. The more modest form of social change they demanded was adequate efforts to guarantee employment security on the part of employers during times of economic upheaval. The court cases could not argue that workers had the right to run their own companies, but they could argue that under Japanese employment law they had the right to every possible effort on the part of management to protect their employment.

More specifically, the Universal Shoes union was fighting what, beginning in the 1970s, came to be known as *kubikiri gorika,* or the rationalization of employment dismissals. Their collective action rhetoric accused employers of discarding workers, treating them as invisible and as exchangeable commodities rather than as human beings in their business calculations. The legal arguments charged the parent company, Custom Shoes, with "fabricating" the bankruptcy of their subsidiary Universal Shoes, resulting in unfair dismissal of all Universal workers. Both labor lawyers handling the legal cases and the union leaders managing the near decade-long dispute spoke with passion about their drive to force employers to remember the rights of their employees when adjusting to economic changes. In the rhetoric of Universal's collective action, workers must become "unforgettable" (*wasurerarenai*). In the language of their lawyers, Japanese employers must be required to take workers' livelihood seriously, respect their legal rights, and use liquidation of a company or dismissal only as a last resort.

A dispute as legally complex and as organizationally challenging as this one required both agile leadership and deeply felt commitment to a cause on the part of the rank and file. Strategies for leveraging Japanese labor law and strategies for maintaining the solidarity necessary to an ongoing labor dispute shifted in tandem. Nearly four years into a bankruptcy-related labor dispute that would eventually last almost ten, one of the lawyers prosecuting the court cases for the Universal Shoe Company union said, "I believe that the true struggle does not take place in the court but in the actions of union workers and their families, and if we can continue more collective action, we might realize a positive settlement." At the same time, leaders of the labor movement saw the court cases as essential both to the ongoing self-managed production that sustained them in the short term and to the eventual settlement they hoped would offer compensation, continued employment, and an opportunity to reopen the small company under management of their own choice.

The president of the Universal union liked to say, "They tried to throw us away—like waste paper—just toss us out. We had to fight to become unforgettable." In demonstrations this simple idea took the form of demands for rights guaranteed both by Japanese constitutional provisions and by Japanese employment law. It also took the form of shouts aimed at financial institutions and their parent company to take responsibility for their employment and to treat them as human beings. Becoming "unforgettable" was, according to their legal team, critical to the court cases. They had been, according to these lawyers, "underestimated from the beginning," expected to just give up, disperse, and disappear.

Here I will suggest ways in which court cases set limits on collective action and influence the forms of that action, and also ways in which this union strategically used court cases to achieve labor dispute goals related to employment security and entitlements, as well as more radical goals aimed to challenge the very structure of Japanese employer-employee power relations. In the context of the global reach of marketization that has progressively exposed Japanese workers to greater and greater employment insecurity, these early bankruptcy disputes and those that followed over the subsequent decades called attention to the precarious position of workers in times of economic instability and demanded responsible actions to safeguard the livelihood of those affected. These demands were embodied in collective action and articulated in legal arguments.

In previous publications I have written extensively about the Universal labor dispute, along with a very similar dispute carried out by the labor union of Unikon Camera (Turner 1995). Subsequently, detailed information concerning their legal cases became available and has made it possible to examine these cases and the critical links between legal and political arguments and strategies that provided a measure of shared meaning between the rank and file, union leaders, lawyers, and others in their extensive support networks. Here I will analyze the relationship between legal rights and political power, and the complex strategies required to get ordinary people involved in disruptive actions aimed at exercising either one.

GLOBALIZATION, ECONOMIC INSTABILITY AND EMPLOYMENT SECURITY ISSUES

The globalization of the Japanese economy has brought widespread economic, political, and social changes, which have affected Japanese workplaces. What in Japan were called "Nixon Shocks" and "Oil Shocks" in the 1970s were just the beginning of a series of economic crises that included the so-called bursting of the bubble economy and recession. These crises ultimately ushered in an era of reform and restructuring aimed at economic recovery that began the new millennium. Beginning in the 1970s, the Japanese economy faced a series of challenges to its postwar high growth economic policies, its customary practices of labor-management relations, and its workplace values and frames of thought. Unemployment rose to 3 percent in the 1980s, 5 percent in the 1990s, and to nearly 7 percent by the turn of the century. These rates have been dropping since 2003 in response to aggressive economic restructuring, changes in employment practices such as increases in nonstandard workers, and gradual attrition as people drop out of the labor market altogether. Some of these changes were themselves responses to rapidly growing labor activism like that addressed in this chapter.

Unionization rates have been dropping since the beginning of the 1980s, and in 2003 they fell below 20 percent for the first time in postwar history, hovering at about 18 percent through 2009. This reflects the increase in nonunionized service sector jobs and nonstandard employment in all sectors at the expense of the more stable and lucrative industrial, financial, and transport sector jobs. Rengo, the Japanese Trade Union Confederation, which represents more than 60 percent of all union members, is challenged to design ways of safe-guarding employment and workplace practices in an economy where increasing proportions of the work force are in part-time, temporary, postretirement, or contract worker status instead of regular full-time employment.

Bankruptcies of small and medium-sized firms climbed in the 1970s, leveled off in the middle 1980s, and climbed steadily again in the post-bubble decade of the 1990s. Revisions in bankruptcy law just after the turn of the century have helped bring these rates down after 2003 as economic recovery began to take hold. This recent economic recovery has been crafted out of responses to crises experienced in workplaces throughout the society. Recent challenges regarding excessive overwork and over the rights of stockholders in corporate governance, which emerged in the 1980s and 1990s, have similarly challenged Japanese social practices and cultural concepts regarding economic activities and appropriate measures of value. These signal challenges to cultural notions about work and about the social importance of stability of livelihood for workers.

Reforms in corporate structures, employment practices, labor union organizations, and employment and business law have emerged throughout this period. In this context activist workers and their unions organized labor disputes and filed legal cases to protest against bankruptcy-related job loss. People have struggled to cope with changes visited upon them by taking some measure of control over their own work organizations and by appealing to the legal structures that help define legitimate labor-management relations in a period of economic and political change. Social change in these struggles is not always the result of efforts to bring about something new. It is sometimes about trying to hold on to something of value that is perceived to be in danger of undesirable reform or loss. Legal cases are used as a means to struggle against the market when the marketization of labor seems to challenge fundamental cultural values of stable employment.

The connections between daily life, a secure livelihood, and the changes in the world economy were reflected in daily conversations among workers at Universal as well as at other small and medium-sized companies in which I conducted fieldwork through the 1980s and 1990s. The rank and file worried that the success of conservatives like Margaret Thatcher in the United Kingdom and Ronald Reagan in the United States would have a negative impact on their own labor movement and ultimately on labor conditions and the labor market in Japan. The emergence of global market forces and Japan's vulnerability to them was of central importance in their evaluation of their prospects for the success of their own collective action. These connections were made regularly both in daily conversation and in organized union events where films about labor struggles in Europe or the United States were shown and discussed. Visitors from Eastern European labor unions came to the factory during the time I was there, and the Universal union itself made a documentary about its own struggle to distribute through national and international networks. The rank and file and their union leaders shared with workers elsewhere in Japan and around the world concerns about the economic disruptions related to transnational integration of markets that were troubling labor everywhere.

Similarly, Universal union leaders who were in charge of making production decisions as well as designing labor dispute strategies worried that "There isn't much we can do when we have to compete with European shoe design. Especially Italian! We have to make better, cheaper, more locally appealing shoes, and we have to study the designs from abroad." Sympathy for the challenges facing the entire shoe-making industry was great, but anger at the reckless way in which their parent company attempted to cope with their own business problems by dissolving Universal and dismissing its workers was even greater. The ties between their own lives and these larger changes were clear, and they were convinced that while the changes in national and international policy might be beyond their control, the strategies used by Japanese employers to cope with them should not be void of the "responsibility" to protect the livelihood of their employees.

This sentiment was widespread, and unions throughout Japan began to learn from one another how to cope with bankruptcy-related job loss. Universal was one of the earliest to engage in an antibankruptcy labor dispute, and their case inspired other unions to be watchful. For example, Unikon Camera's union began, even before their owners declared them bankrupt, to prepare the ground for such a dispute. As the market for cameras slowed and they began to worry about the outlook for their own company, they commissioned an independent analysis by university professors of the global market and the outlook for camera production and their place in it (Turner 1995). This study provided solid evidence about the nature of the industry and the possible ways in which the company could continue to succeed as a producer, an issue directly related to the argument made in the legal cases that bankruptcy and job loss were not unavoidable business strategies. Court cases filed by the unions fighting bankruptcy disputes often claimed that changes in the business environment should have been met with changes in management strategy, not with dissolution and unfair dismissals.

The Universal union is just one case in which a labor union successfully challenged the way in which a Japanese employer eliminated jobs by declaring bankruptcy. Theirs was one of the first of a series of antibankruptcy labor disputes beginning in the late 1970s that combined social movement tactics with legal battles. By 1982 there were ninety-four such struggles, and throughout the 1980s and 1990s small companies continued to organize such disputes as recession and economic restructuring threatened employment security (Gordon 1998, 190). Labor disputes involving working conditions and employment security issues have continued to rise, reaching over one million by 2005, and they and have inspired tripartite negotiations between government, business, and labor over ways to stem this trend through improved economic policy and labor law reform (McNamara 1996). The Universal case demonstrates the power of collective action coupled with court cases to place limits on employer rights to dissolve companies or make structural changes that lead to job loss.

FROM BANKRUPTCY TO COURT:
LEGAL LEVERAGE AND COLLECTIVE ACTION STRATEGIES

The Universal Shoes Workers' Cooperative Company operates as a small shoe-manufacturing company in Tokyo with about fifty employees. It was established under union ownership and management as a result of the 1986 year-end settlement of a nearly ten-year-long legal battle in tandem with an active labor dispute. Opened in 1946 immediately after World War II, Universal Shoes operated as a subcontractor for Custom Shoes, the third largest shoe manufacturer in Japan, until becoming its subsidiary in 1967. The liberalization of trade policies which opened the domestic Japanese market in shoes and leather goods to more imported products and the increasing sluggishness of the domestic economy associated with globalization led Custom to begin a process of "rationalization of production" (*gōrika*) in their factories. In 1977, as part of that effort, they made the decision to shut down their subsidiary, Universal, altogether. Some claim that this was also designed to intimidate their own unionized employees into accepting further unpopular rationalization measures, including forced retirements and layoffs.

The response of the Universal union was swift and decisive and is itself illustrative of the way in which social movement action and legal action worked in concert in this struggle from the very beginning to make a powerful and ultimately successful labor movement strategy. As described at the outset of this chapter, union members immediately forced the Universal Company president to sign a factory use agreement. The factory use agreement gave the union the temporary right to use land, buildings, and equipment, pending resolution of union demands for appropriate bankruptcy-related liquidation and dismissal, a "temporary right" that was the basis for use for nearly a decade. This innovation on the part of the Universal union was emulated by other unions in subsequent bankruptcy-related disputes because it facilitated the maintenance of production and thus of both economic solvency and social solidarity during legal and political battles, battles that in Japan are normally long and drawn out. Furthermore, it effectively marked all subsequent actions on the part of the union as *sōgi kōdō,* or "dispute actions." These *sōgi kōdō* are protected under trade union law as legitimate union actions so long as a dispute is ongoing and unsettled. Legal precedent in Japanese courts have allowed even otherwise illegal actions to go unpunished so long as they are construed as part of an ongoing dispute (Gould 1984).

The *jishuseisan,* or "worker-managed production" disputes, were strategically smart, largely successful, and culturally characteristic of Japanese labor-dispute tactics. They illustrate the significance of maintaining the relationship between employer and employee as a legitimate platform from which to enter and prosecute a dispute. Even the shell of the relationship, if preserved, is sufficient to continue to make claims, to engage in "dispute actions," and to assure a legitimate negotiating position on the part of workers until resolution can be reached. The simple unilateral declaration on the part of the owners of an enterprise is not sufficient to break this relationship. Indeed, the continued production at the factory itself, although managed by the union, served to preserve not just the livelihood of the workers enabling their continued activism, but also the existence of the enterprise and its employer-employee relations, guaranteeing the continued relevance of employment law to their legal cases as well (see Gould 1984; Totsuka 1984; Gordon 1998).

The propensity of labor-relation cases to be mediated until some conciliatory settlement can be reached commonly leads to very lengthy negotiations. This "legal informality" of the Japanese judicial process is credited by Frank Upham with shifting power to control and manage social change to the state through the court system, making the court a relatively conservative force in considering social change in Japan (Upham 1987, 22). It permits resolution without reference to universal principles or clear statement of right and wrong, thus situating social change firmly in particular circumstances. Hiroshi Itoh makes a related point in his evaluation of judicial activism in Japan when he claims, "actual and concrete disputes must exist before the court can adjudicate. No declaratory or advisory opinions are allowed in Japan" (Itoh 1990, 173). He goes on to suggest that courts are conservative in the sense that they do not wish to be active policymakers, opting whenever possible to act within established case law.

While case law may be influenced by a collection of resolutions, few grand gestures toward universal standards are made in Japanese court cases. The process is long, drawn-out, complex, and heavily reliant on the particular circumstances of each case. Such procedures generally tend to favor those with more power and more status within organizational and institutional hierarchies. Labor union leaders claim that the sheer length of court proceedings can in many cases be a significant factor in losing the requisite rank-and-file support for going to court in the first place, and even more so in keeping people engaged in the dispute long enough to reach a satisfactory settlement. Companies can often benefit by simply stalling because workers cannot maintain either the social solidarity or economic resources to persist to resolution.

As a platform from which to launch the dispute and to persevere for nearly ten years until resolution, self-managed production is the most important and powerful site where social movement and legal cases intersected. Here the court case and the social movement are mutually formative of one another. The legal limbo of the self-managed production dispute had two important consequences. First, it permitted the union to guarantee for an indefinite period of time a living wage and daily work routines to participating workers. As a result, the union managed to keep nearly all their workers for the duration of the dispute. This made daily contact around both production and movement solidarity building activities possible and was crucial for maintaining movement solidarity. Second, it situated the legal cases within the context of an ongoing employer-employee relationship because continued production acted as a de facto stall in the process of bankruptcy, preventing liquidation and all associated procedures.

RIGHTS AND POWER: CREATING FRAMEWORKS TO MOTIVATE ACTION

While Japanese labor law has developed extensive legal and even constitutional provisions to protect workers, their rights to collective bargaining, and even their right to stable employment, it is not the case that the rank and file necessarily understand these provisions, act on assumptions about rights, or even conceptualize their own agency in such terms. Indeed, in the Universal struggle, as in other struggles of its kind that I have studied, union leadership has had to undertake extensive educational activities as an integral part of mobilization strategies. Assumptions about lifetime employment norms in Japanese culture notwithstanding, Universal workers began their struggle with a stronger sense of resignation than entitlement. For some this was due to simple assumption that under bankruptcy law they had no legal basis for action. For others, it was rooted in a sense that even if a legal case could be made, their small fifty-member union would not have the resources and the power to make it.

Universal workers were accustomed to working under conditions of unequal power as relatively low-wage workers in a very small subsidiary company. Ideas about their own legal rights as workers were at the least counterbalanced by and sometimes outweighed by common sense understandings of their own positions of relative political, social, and economic weakness. Their education through participation in this movement involved learning about their rights as employees under Japanese law, regardless of income, size of company, gender, or age. The task for Universal's leaders hoping to motivate the rank and file was to uncouple notions of economic marginalization from notions of political marginalization. Workers in small companies like this one already differentiate themselves from workers in large companies with respect to the privileges of secure employment, fringe benefits, and high salaries. During Universal's struggle, workers frequently expressed their feeling that the judges in the courts, like the financial institutions that backed their parent company, would all just expect them to disappear from the scene.

While union leaders and lawyers urged the rank and file to stick together to make themselves known, to make it impossible for the financial institutions and the parent company to forget about them, the rank and file easily slipped back into a sense of vulnerability. They often explicitly talked about being "small" and being afraid that they had been "forgotten" when expressing their feelings of marginality.

As part of their efforts to change the culture and consciousness of the rank and file and make them powerful agents in the legal and political struggle, union leaders and the lawyers handling the Universal case convened large general meetings, held smaller seminar-style meetings, and engaged in study sessions before and after court dates. In addition to discussing specific legal strategies and the progress of ongoing cases, union leaders, lawyers, and/or national union federation organizers discussed Japanese employment law with the rank and file. This included Japanese constitutional provisions like those guaranteeing the right and obligation to work (Article 27) and the right to collective bargaining and collective action (Article 28). They also educated the members about the body of trade union and employment law within which their own cases fit, especially the legal limitations on employers concerning the dismissal of workers. Because so much of this is case law, union leaders and lawyers strove to educate workers about the postwar history of Japanese legal cases, the statutory protections available, and the ways employment law could be applied after a declaration of bankruptcy. This history itself involved activism on the part of unions to bring cases into the courts, a history that has established a body of law relevant to labor disputes that, once in the hands of the judiciary, union activists see as favorable to workers in matters related to termination of employment and the failure of management to negotiate or consult with workers.

Beginning as early as 1950 Japanese courts have, in Daniel Foote's words, "built a complex and sophisticated body of law providing workers strong rights against dismissal" (1996, 638) and establishing conditions that must be met before employers may exercise their rights to dismiss an employee or employees. While the Civil Code provides employers the right of dismissal without a requirement that cause be stated and the Labor Standards Act of 1947 adds that employees must have only thirty days notice, case law has ensured that specific conditions be demonstrated, even in the case of dismissal for economic reasons, and particularly in cases of collective dismissal. These include a necessity for reduction of the workforce, an employer good-faith effort to avoid discharge, the fair implementation and selection of workers to be discharged, and a consultation with the trade union or workers involved (Foote 1996; Yamakawa, 2001). If these conditions are not met, employers may be found to have engaged in "abusive dismissals." There is, in Foote's evocative description, "an iceberg of precedent underneath the small tip of Section 20 of the Labor Standards Act" that gives Japanese workers much greater rights under settled case law than might be apparent from a strict reading of the text of the law (1996, 707).

These rights and understanding of the history of judicial decisions in structuring Japanese employment relationships over the course of the postwar period gave union leaders within Universal and those in local, regional, and national federations a common ground for creating legal and social movement strategies and for being reasonably optimistic that if they could survive as a union long enough they would eventually win their case. Japanese law and legal precedent in matters of job security served, in other words, as a critical frame within which labor movement organizers made decisions about legal cases and created strategies to increase their political power relative to their parent company and adversary, Custom Shoes. The understanding of their potential for political power provided by this framework was crucial in mobilizing the rank and file for the lengthy and economically difficult personal struggles that constituted a labor dispute like this one.

The activist labor movement struggles of the 1970s and 1980s were compared to those of the fifties by union leaders and their legal teams. They saw the legacy of that period's labor activism in proving that workers could manage their own production. However, the new struggles were viewed quite differently in that they were taking place in times of settled employee-employer relationships rather than in times of enterprise disorder. They believed that this made their own struggles more complex because they required workers to struggle with established and powerful employers and management teams in order to take charge of production. They saw similarities, however, in the struggle of workers to have a stable workplace, to have a say in production decisions about adjustment to economic trouble, and to take over in order to save the company from failure. The history that leaders and lawyers emphasized in mobilizing workers favored the immediate and early postwar period.

Nimura Kazuo argues that the spread of struggles for the control of production in the immediate postwar period hinged on the appeal of the strategy to save the company from dissolution and on worry over the economic livelihoods of employees. Production control was a form of struggle "that had no adverse affects on company results. They thus easily gained the support of all employees, including that of managers who were concerned for the company's future, as well as the understanding of society at large" (Nimura 1994a, 65). In the case of the struggle by Universal workers, this was certainly an important factor especially in the early days when they had to refuse the order to evacuate the premises and had to make the case for their right to stay put and begin to manage their own production. The primary motivation for production control in a time of economic upheaval is to continue production and to secure employment, something that was as appealing at the end of the century as it was in the immediate postwar period. That legacy of the early Japanese labor movement was an inspiration for most of the Universal workers and a personal memory for many. Nimura argues that postwar workers "for their part . . . had entrusted their livelihoods to the company, [and] were afraid for the company's future, and their lack of faith due to their employers' feebleness only increased" (1994a, 64). He argues that the first struggle for production control, that at Yomiuri Shinbun, showed workers a way forward.

> The Yomiuri dispute showed such workers a way to address the problems that faced them. The dispute, which began with criticisms of employers' irresponsibility and developed into a takeover of production at the enterprise by the employees' union, taught many people that the way forward was to form a union and reconstruct companies themselves. Anger at a management that showed neither "sincerity" nor any understanding of employees' demands turned the dispute into a ferocious struggle that proved to be highly significant. (p. 64)

These early postwar struggles were infused with the chaos of a time where management had often left a vacuum into which union activists stepped. Kumazawa Makoto (1996) discusses these struggles in his history of postwar labor movements, pointing out that they were powerful and exemplified labor's ability and core concern with production. He writes that although such struggles faded away in the high-growth period of the sixties, between 1952 and 1957, "when management was in a general state of shock and bewilderment immediately after the war, unions exercised strong authority over production and personnel matters" (Kumazawa 1996, 66). The immediate postwar period was a time of economic crises, political change, and extensive realignment of Japan's relationships with the world, especially with the United States. The social movements of this time were powerful, and their gains contributed to the workplace practices of employment security and collective bargaining to which the Universal case referred (see Gordon 1998; Kumazawa 1996; Niimura 1994a, 1994b).

The majority of workers at Universal had personal memories of that time. Over one-third had vivid memories because they were old enough during the war to participate in social life as adults and to experience the transition from war through economic devastation and political turmoil. At Unikon, the camera company where I did research first, the Universal union was respected as the architect of the model that the Unikon union had used for their own labor dispute, and even more as a model for what their young leaders liked to call "real Japanese workers." It was at the urging of the Unikon people that I came to Universal in the first place. They said that I couldn't really understand activism and workers' consciousness without working with them. What I came to believe myself was that I had not fully encountered the lived history of the postwar worker until I met the Universal workers.

Personal adult memories of the immediate postwar period do not explain the organizing strategies, the successful legal battles, or even the ultimate success of their dispute, but they do allow us to understand some of the cultural models for thinking about employer-employee relationships, the importance of stability, the rights of workers not to be forgotten even in times of crises, and the sense of the possibility of social change itself. These cultural models helped people imagine activism and the power of collective action. It was commonplace to have conversations in which people laughed about the past where everything was "for the sake of the emperor, for the sake of the company" (*tennoheika no tame, kaisha no tame*), followed by comments that would begin with "thanks to losing the war" (*senso ni maketa okage de*) and would go on to remark about improvements in Japanese social and political life that they themselves had witnessed.

The frank lament that "democracy" had come to Japan but that Japanese people didn't know how to use it yet was a frequent refrain (Turner 1989, 299–323). References to that postwar economic chaos through which people had lived were used to contextualize their current struggles. One worker told me that it was impossible to know if you would live or die and that coming through experiences like that made you "used to struggling" (*narete kuru*). The older workers who were in positions of responsibility in the factory were even frustrated that there were no younger workers who knew how to do everything. One man in his sixties told me, "By our age we should be able to let the young ones run the place, but somehow it is always we, the older ones (*toshiyori*), who have to get involved.*"*

The legacy of the postwar activism of labor and the production control struggles of the immediate postwar period were on the minds of lawyers and union leaders. For the rank and file, the hardships, the experience of struggling to get by, and the importance of what they considered the "importation" of democracy from America dominated their memories. These memories of both hardships and positive political change and the ways in which personal lives could be changed by political action and legal institutions grounded the commitment of many of the Universal workers. One of the younger workers told me that she felt "lucky" to work with "these men who just do what they have to do and go on working for something." She said that maybe she wouldn't have "stuck it out" for all those years "if it weren't for them."

THE LEGAL CASES:

GOOD FAITH EFFORTS, EMPLOYMENT SECURITY, AND CONSULTATION

There were eight legal cases associated with the Universal dispute. Six were filed in Tokyo District Court, one with the Tokyo Labor Relations Board, and one in Yokohama District Court. None of these was settled prior to the final settlement nine years and nine months later. Each of them has a very specific claim based on some specific provision under Japanese labor law, and each of them had a specific set of arguments and evidence to support that claim, developed by labor lawyers handling the case, union leaders, and the Joint Struggle Committee (Kyōtōkaigi).

The first two cases were filed simultaneously, three months after the company announced bankruptcy proceedings. The union filed a formal case with the Tokyo Labor Relations Board against Custom for unfair labor conduct and a separate case in Tokyo District Court (Civil Suit Section 19) against Custom and Universal management for unpaid wages. The content of this appeal was based on two main arguments. First, because of massive wealth and multiple factories, Universal claimed that Custom had not demonstrated the economic necessity to close this small plant and eliminate the jobs of these few workers. The union claimed that Custom Shoes had at least two hundred million yen and factories in nine other locations throughout Japan. Thus, they claimed Custom was involved in "abusive dismissal" because they did not make "good faith efforts" to avoid bankruptcy or to relocate employees to other jobs (see Gould 1984; Foote 1996). Consequently, the union demanded, Custom must begin negotiation over reopening of the factory and over unpaid wages.

Second, the union argued that Custom was an employer. This was a critical claim, one that had to be accepted before labor law regulating employer-employee relationships could be invoked to settle all other disputes. Here they argued that because Custom owned two-thirds of Universal's stocks and five-sixths of all assets and property, they were, as a matter of practice, in an employer-employee relationship even though the formal business status of Universal Shoes was that of a subsidiary. This charge is, of course, an important challenge to one of the ways in which many Japanese companies try to guarantee long-term secure employment for a core of their own regular workers by creating a more flexible source of labor in small and medium-sized subcontractors and subsidiaries.

There were also, included in this case, charges of unfair labor conduct alleging that Custom forced the bankruptcy of Universal through intentional misman-agement as part of a policy of rationalization of production with a reckless disre-gard for the loss of jobs and an unwillingness to consult with the union represent-ing their workers about solutions to existing economic problems. There was, it is worth noting, no claim that rationalization or other organizational changes were themselves outside the rights of the employer, but rather that reckless disregard of the employment security of the workers combined with unwillingness to negotiate or consult violated workers' rights under Japanese employment law.

Japanese labor law does not guarantee workers freedom from market strain or other economic upheaval, but it does set limits beyond which employers may be charged with violating their responsibility as employers for their employees. The legal notion of "abusive dismissal" is about setting constraints on treatment of employees especially during times of economic crisis and collective dismissal. The responsibility of employers to act responsibly toward their employees has been established over the past six decades and has become the subject of record numbers of court cases, extensive legislative debate, and some legal reform over the past few years as postwar labor law and practice has been challenged by un-precedented economic crisis. The idea that employers must make "good faith ef-forts" to find alternative employment raised in the Universal dispute is an issue still debated today in the context of employment policies related to economic restructuring. Interestingly enough, in spite of reforms in labor law, commercial laws, and civil codes, the core features that allow workers to go to court to fight against unreasonable dismissals have remained largely unchanged (Yamakawa 2001). Foote quotes the legal scholar Nakayama Ichiro who claimed, in 1959, that "there is no other country in the world where dismissal is as strictly regulated as in Japan," and Foote goes on to argue himself that "the limitations on dismissal in Japan have become even more strict over the intervening years" (1996, 638).

The Universal union also filed charges against Custom for refusal to negoti-ate in a document that went before the Tokyo Labor Relations Board (TLRB). They outlined their own efforts at collective negotiation and claimed that they could do nothing without the cooperation of Custom and that their requests on six separate occasions to their "real employer," Custom, to enter into collective negotiation were met with refusal. On the one occasion when they did meet infor-mally, the discussion became contentious and Custom ended up calling the police and accusing the union members of violent behavior. The attempt on the part of the parent company to charge violent behavior on the part of the union members was to no avail. Many have noted that it is common in Japanese labor disputes to forgive otherwise disruptive actions—even marginal or illegal ones—so long as they can be shown to be part of a set of dispute actions (*sōgikōdō*) (Gould 1984, 40). Ultimately, the TLRB called on Custom to come and engage in negotiations aimed at settlement of the case. Custom refused to negotiate, however, claiming that they were not an employer and that they were in fact a separate legal entity from Universal. In response to this refusal, the Universal union formally requested assistance from the TLRB in settling the dispute.

The second case brought by the Universal union was a suit in Tokyo District Court (Civil Section 19) against Universal owners and Custom for unpaid wages. Once again, the central and critical claim was that Custom is the "real employer" and was thus a reasonable entity against which to bring suit. Universal owners responded by acknowledging their debt but claiming that they had no ability to pay. Custom rejected the obligation to pay based on their legal status as a separate entity. In this case, the evidence and arguments made over the following months and years were specifically aimed at proving the "parent/child company" (*oyako gaisha*) relationship and arguing the status of Custom as an employer. The court met approximately once every two months to hear this case. Over time, other claims were added to include unpaid wages for subsequent months.

The second and third legal cases were linked. and both were in Tokyo District Court. Universal's union petitioned the court (Civil Section 9) for permission to seize and auction unsold products to pay workers their unpaid back wages. The court granted this petition within a month, but Custom brought a third-party objection suit in Tokyo District Court (Civil Section 4) and halted the process. Once again the union argued that because Custom was an employer it had the obligation to pay back wages; Custom argued that as an independent entity and a major stockholder in the bankrupt Universal company, it was entitled to property as part of settlement for its own financial investment claims. This case was heard about once every two months over the course of several years.

The fifth, sixth, and seventh cases were all brought by Custom against the Universal union demanding settlement of debts through access to assets and properties of Universal, including cash savings in a bank account (Civil Section 12 and 23), buildings and land (Civil Section 15), and equipment (Civil Section 24). The final suit was brought by Custom against the Universal president in Yokohama District Court claiming that he had repaid debts incurred by Universal to a creditor bank using Universal assets and demanding that he reimburse them from his personal funds.

However favorable Japanese employment law may be for employees in any one of these cases, the process of litigation and negotiation presented a challenge requiring human, organizational, and financial resources possible only through the social movement practices of the Universal union and the extensive activist network within which they were situated. While fighting the legal battles in court, the Universal union and its network of supporters created and maintained resistance to asset liquidation, the economic context to maintain workers' livelihood, and the cultural context to understand the legal strategy and motivate people to become agents of social change over nearly a decade of struggle.

UNION-MANAGED PRODUCTION, COMMITMENT, AND ENDURANCE AS EVIDENCE

Labor movement leaders and the lawyers representing Universal frequently talked about the "three pillars" of union-managed production struggles: "living, working, and struggling." For union leaders these three pillars helped organize their efforts to maintain a strong collective sense of purpose and motivation, whereas lawyers saw them as good for their court battles. They claimed that maintaining the livelihood of the rank and file gave them time to gather evidence and construct stronger and stronger arguments as they engaged in the slow-moving process of court proceedings. They saw the length of time it took to settle as a mixed blessing. The continued production under worker management was in and of itself evidence for the feasibility of continued operation of the company as a business, and although they wanted to bring the cases to a successful close as soon as possible, the longer the production and sales continued the harder it was for the other side to argue the necessity of bankruptcy in the first place. Finally, the struggle both in its collective action forms and its production form gave them a client that was visible, tenacious, and "unforgettable."

One of the lawyers for Universal claimed that after four years of struggle their cases were actually stronger because the worker-managed production had enabled the legal team to gather more evidence and to make stronger arguments about the careless way in which the parent company had treated the Universal workers. "What we need for our court cases is evidence," and "nearly four years of self-management of production had made it possible to produce more and more evidence together." Of course no one wanted this case to last nearly a decade, least of all the union members who lived with uncertainty and personal economic struggles to sustain their families or the union leaders who had to maintain the solidarity necessary to outlast the legal negotiations and reach a favorable settlement. However, from the lawyers' point of view, time passing was not necessarily an indication of the likelihood of defeat. This, of course, is why they saw such significance in the activities of the union that stabilized the livelihoods, work, and social lives of the workers themselves and the Universal factory as a union managed plant.

The "living" and "working" aspects of this labor dispute created remarkable counterpoints to the disruptive actions and court hearings organized by the union. The combination of stable daily routines of production, sales, company management, and maintenance of the plant resembled the pre-bankruptcy routines to which all were accustomed. Given the goal of the eventual reopening of the company as a worker-owned production cooperative, these two "pillars" of normalcy were particularly important. One of the most striking things about the atmosphere of Universal during its struggle was its feeling of normalcy. In my own field notes, I remarked on this the first time I visited them. Aside from the small red flags adorning the fence that ran around the factory property, one would not know that anything unusual was going on inside. People and machines were active, and normal routines of work, breaks, friendly games, exercise, and even factory gardening were repeated daily. Following a very brief period of less than three months after the declaration of bankruptcy, workers had returned to routines with which they were already familiar. They shared these routines with people with whom they had already established ties of workplace collegiality and friendship. If I were to try to describe these daily routines it would make for tedious reading, but ironically it was largely that tedious stability of daily work life that grounded the Universal struggle and gave the union traction in pursuing a settlement of their dispute.

Periodically the festivals, parties, and factory bazaars opened the premises to neighbors, networks of social movement supporters, academics, representatives of political parties, and of course their legal team. One of the members of the union's Joint Struggle Committee joked at a general meeting that "rumors are running around the neighborhood about Universal workers—you are supposed to have gone bankrupt and to be engaged in a harsh struggle, but in fact you are working and partying as usual. What's going on?" He talked about numerous social events of the past year that had contributed to strengthening their reputation as a healthy small company. They had convened a New Year *mochi*-making party, a summer *obon* festival, a bazaar where they sold their shoes at a discount to those in their immediate neighborhood, and a factory festival. Not only had these activities demonstrated the continued existence of the company itself, they had also become a direct and powerful defiance of the order to go bankrupt and disband. As such they had become "an embarrassment to the parent company" against whom they were fighting.

The collective actions that support the "struggle" element in the dispute were dramatic, disruptive, and infrequent. Each effort to bring the rank and file into disruptive actions required renewed persuasion, framing, encouragement, and mobilization on the part of union leaders and their Joint Struggle Committee. These collective actions were largely unfamiliar and uncomfortable for people at first. Over the years they became adept at carrying them out although for most there was at best an uncomfortable fit between their lives as workers and their actions as demonstrators and activists (see Turner 1995).

In the beginning of their disputes workers were convinced to stay, to join in the court case, to continue production under their union's management, and to commit to a plan of action aimed at financial settlement, job security, and publicly correcting unfair treatment on the part of their parent company, Custom. In daily conversations and interviews over the course of many months, all the Universal workers reported that they experienced a gradual change in their motives for joining the struggle, staying with it for the first few years, and then persevering through to the end. One woman told me, "At first we had no work. We had no right to even be at work. But we were worried about our jobs and about the possibility of finding other jobs. Even the parent company had dismissed workers from its own factories. How could we expect to find work?"

The strength of union-managed production as a strategy for pursuing court cases about unfair dismissal lies in its creation of a short-term solution to the immediate problem worrying many of the workers involved. In order to keep the rank and file motivated over the long term, however, the leadership of the union had to offer more than a temporary solution to the problem of employment. Many workers expressed their anger at their parent company for treating them as "less than human" (*ningen to shite atsukarete inai*) and their worry about finding other jobs in a sector of the Japanese economy deeply affected by changes in international economic policy. However, as one worker put it to me, "What works in the beginning won't work after a few years or even months." Over time workers needed to find reasons to stay with this struggle, not knowing for sure that it would settle to their advantage. There were several things that sustained people. The most common was a deeply felt connection to other workers who had not quit. When I asked people why they stayed even after so many years, the most common response was, "I couldn't quit after all that time when others were sticking it out." These others were sometimes labeled as "even the young guys with families" or "even the older workers who should be retiring," but they were always a reference to a sense of shared purpose based on ties of common experience. Ironically, it seemed that time was on the side of staying even longer. There was a certain logic to staying put once a significant investment of time and effort had already been made.

In addition to the grounding of the struggle in bonds of shared experience, daily life routines of work, special occasions, and life, there were many for whom seeing this struggle through to the end held meaning beyond their own local dispute. The notion that they were doing something of value by standing up for Japanese workers and their rights to fair treatment even in times of economic hardship was tangible and provided for many a sense of purpose (*ikigai*) in their own lives. This was primarily developed in the process of finding, through the experience of participation in the dispute itself, that they were part of the very extensive network of the Japanese labor movement, a movement that had a history to which they might contribute. This was an explicitly argued message heard from lawyers, union leaders, and other labor movement activists. As a motivation for participation it was more salient for some rank and file than for others, but for everyone it was part of the cultural environment of their struggle. The legal cases themselves explicitly tied these workers and their collective purpose to the larger world of Japanese society and the historical evolution of important values and norms about workers' rights.

Clifford Geertz called law a way for society to "imagine the real" (Geertz 1983, 173). In the Universal case and in others like it that I have studied, I think that going to court has also been a way for ordinary citizens to realize the imagined or at the very least to exercise their agency to that end. In considering social change, in other words, it is not just the activist intention to transform that is in question, but also the process through which ordinary Japanese workers come, through specific political actions, to realize their legal and social positions within national institutions and Japanese society as a whole. It is in this union of legal action to achieve organizational goals and cultural action to create common sense categories for social agency that the role of the labor dispute as a social movement becomes critical for success legally, politically, and culturally.

Universal built an extensive local, national, and even international network of unions and labor federations that supported their collective action and their court cases, including the then powerful and progressive Sohyo, or General Council of Trade Unions.[2] The first thing the Universal union president did when he was notified of the bankruptcy declaration was to call the Custom Shoes union, the Federation of Shoe Manufacturers Union, to which they both belonged, and the national federation Sohyo. He claimed years later that while people always talk about the great efforts and accomplishments of the Universal workers in pursuing their labor dispute, there should be much more attention paid to the very extensive network of labor movement organizations that "propped us up" and made it possible to go to court, to pursue union-managed production, and to organize effective collective actions. In these early days, help was immediate and took many forms, all of them concrete in terms of resource sharing, advice, and mobilization of networks. Young workers from affiliated unions came to work at Universal,

2. Sohyo, the General Council of Japanese Trade Unions, took an active role in supporting labor disputes even in small and medium-sized industries. It was dissolved in 1989 when it joined the newly organized Rengo, or Japanese Trade Union Confederation. This newer organization now represents nearly 70 percent of Japanese unions.

federation personnel came to help organize the Joint Struggle Committee, network lawyers were brought in to handle legal cases, and organizational resources were made available.

As is common in disputes of this nature, the "Joint Struggle Committee," made up of representatives from the most important affiliated unions, political groups, and legal advisors, worked with the Universal leadership to plan their dispute actions and help lawyers plan their legal strategies. In addition, there were many other support committees (*shienkai*), organized by many different groups that joined in the network of protest for Universal. These included representatives from national level labor federations, the union organizations for shoe and leather manufacturers, Tokyo area labor union networks, Socialist Party organizations, neighborhood activists, and a wide range of progressive lawyers, academics, and social activists. They also joined the Tokyo Sōgidan, an organization made up of all companies undergoing labor disputes, which organized large-scale demonstrations and actions by joining forces and scheduling multiple site demonstrations over a single day. This extensive network of support integrated this small company's workers and their legal and political struggle into networks of labor that reached far beyond their own workplace.

Throughout the years of the Universal struggle, the organizations in this network continued to be involved in planning and execution of collective action as well as in production and sales. There were always people working on the shop floor who had been sent by one of the network organizations. Some of these people were there to help when additional human resources were needed, but more often they were workers engaged in either individual or very small disputes who needed employment while waiting for their own court cases to settle. Raw materials for Universal's production and all of their sales of the finished products were handled through union networks that stretched across Japan. I was interviewing a union president in a large electronics company, and when I mentioned I had worked previously with the Universal union, he cheerfully pointed at his Universal made shoes, telling me how much he liked them and how well made they were. He had purchased them from one of the lunchtime sales that his company authorized. Universal sold all their products by delivering or sending them to unions nationwide for sale to their members.

In addition, these networks conveyed in every interaction with Universal workers the increased potential for their struggle to be successful as well as the broader significance of their cause. The strategies Universal could pursue were of course constrained by their small size, but with the help of their supporters they kept up an ongoing series of actions ranging from large demonstrations in downtown Tokyo at the financial institutions backing Custom, weekly picketing of the Custom's Tokyo factory, and weekly pamphleteering in Custom's neighborhood.

Workers who felt "small" and largely invisible came away from demonstrations excited about what to them were "unbelievable" numbers of workers who came to demonstrate with them. Just before their first experience at one of the largest demonstrations (a day of coordinated demonstrations with thousands of workers) in which they participated, many rank and file worried about how insignificant their small company would be when they showed up in front of the banks and companies in downtown Tokyo. By the time they came back from that collective action, however, conversation was animated and excited about the extensive network of Japanese workers within which they had a place. One worker who had been dreading the event conveyed how surprised she was by the absolute numbers. "It was the first time for me, so putting on that thing [she motioned toward where the chest sign where their union demands were written] was something I was dreading. But you're not alone doing that, and even if something is unpleasant when you do it alone, when you do it with everyone else it is all right. There were so many people there yesterday. I didn't realize. It was amazing."

Even if the legal cases technically could have been carried out without these political actions and networks of extensive ties, it is unlikely that they would have been successful. Workers themselves claim that their dispute could not even have begun without this extensive network of protest supporters, much less could it have reached a satisfactory conclusion. These groups provided financial resources, expertise, experience, and credibility that pushed the parent company Custom and the financial institutions backing them to take seriously the cases against them and eventually to negotiate and work toward settlement. In addition to the tangible resources shared within these labor movement networks, there is an intangible experience of connection in the physical sharing of activities with one another. These networks conveyed a sense of being part of something larger than their own struggle, an experience of collective purpose that embodied the arguments made by union leaders and the legal team, arguments claiming that the Universal struggle was a more general struggle for Japanese workers' rights as well. The decade-long history of the Universal dispute is one not only of collective action and union victory but of a transformation in the rank and file's understanding of concepts of legal rights and political power made possible only through their shared experience of both the social movement and its related legal cases.

The Settlement and Its Significance

The irony of the Universal workers' struggle is that the legal case was about rights as employees and responsibilities of employers for the livelihood of their workers, while the political battle was ultimately to lead the Universal union to reopen as a workers' cooperative company, to become its own employer, and to take responsibility for its own future economic viability and thus the livelihood of its workers. Furthermore, it is unlikely that the legal cases could have been settled in as advantageous a way as they were had the labor movement actions not continued to demonstrate the power of this union and the network of social movement activism into which it had embedded itself. The assets won in the final settlement went to establish a cooperative company in which all the employees owned shares.

The final settlement of the Universal dispute was reached in negotiations at the Tokyo Labor Relations Board. Its wording carefully avoided any attribution of blame, any fault, or any conclusions about right and wrong. It included the agreement for both sides to withdraw all cases in Tokyo District Court and Yokohama District Court, and it specified that they would do so without further comment. It transferred substantial capital assets, land, and machinery to the Universal union—enough to pay all back wages and to reopen a factory able to employ all involved workers. The Universal Workers Cooperative Company operating today is the result. Its legal history lies in the liberal legal framework and precedents of Japanese case law favoring the right of workers to fair treatment and good faith efforts by their employers to do all they can—even in times of economic hardship—to preserve their employment and to engage in consultations and achieve some measure of agreement before restructuring the enterprise or moving to dissolve it. Their political and cultural history lies in what the union proudly and idealistically called "tiny socialism," a local practice of worker control with roots in the ideologically idealistic and strategically effective Japanese labor movement of the immediate postwar period. This history continues to frame progressive models aimed at moving Japan and Japanese labor relations toward a future founded on more "human-centered" values.

Assessing the significance of this small struggle and its contributions to significant social change is a complex task that generates equivocal conclusions. I think the actions of this small group of workers were important both as social movements and as court cases, and their achievements suggest the power that lies in this combination. As a labor movement action, Universal was one of the first struggles to oppose liquidation and loss of employment due to economic "rationalization," or *gōrika*. It became one of several model struggles in the 1980s and 1990s (see Totsuka 1978). Most of these had some measure of success in recovering assets, and several succeeded in reopening factories and reemploying workers. Many are still in business. For the workers involved in these struggles, the short-term impact was great, and it is easy to call them successful and to see ways in which they influenced grass-roots social change in Japanese labor relations practices. They clearly established models of protest with successful track records in the courts that became available for emulation by workers in the increasingly large number of small and medium-sized companies that fell into bankruptcy during the 1980s and 1990s as the Japanese economy fell into recession. Through the networks of labor and social movement actors that supported them, they also provided inspiration for agency for many other activists trying to grapple with the social changes that accompany economic change. In settings as diverse as medical activism, established labor unions at large stable corporations, and small citizens' movements, I have been surprised to hear people refer directly to these antibankruptcy struggles in general and to the Universal struggle in particular. It is possible that these cases may provide models for combining legal cases with social movements to create particular local solutions to particular social problems.

As a court case, Universal's success in enforcing labor laws through the courts demonstrates the power of law to frame and to legitimize labor movement action. The Universal court cases and those that followed contributed to the body of case law that defends employees against unfair dismissals by dealing directly with the problem of job loss through bankruptcy dissolution. There was an explicit intention on the part of Universal workers to force Japanese capitalists to act "responsibly" toward their workers when rationalizing or reorganizing their production in response to economic crises. These goals were clearly met in the final successful settlements and in the broader evaluation of their struggle within the labor movement, and beyond that in the world of social activism and civil society.

Yet there were unintended consequences of their struggle that stemmed from the accumulated pressures on employers as these and other labor disputes involving employment security proliferated during this period. Union leaders and workers alike comment now, with appreciation for the irony, that their struggles taught capitalists "how to go bankrupt" while avoiding worker initiated legal action and disruptive dispute actions. This too has contributed to efforts by employers to find more flexible ways of dealing with their work force and their networks of subcontractors and subsidiaries. In other words, the legal settlements of cases like Universal's helped to define the limits to employment elimination, dismissals, liquidation, plant closings, and bankruptcy for employers, subsidiaries, and subcontractors. Corporations learned the legal limits to their actions. Certainly, say the labor movement people, employers learned what they had to do to cut back their workforce without facing massive labor movement action and lengthy court battles. Foote generalizes about what he labels the "ongoing dialectic" process in the history of employer-employee legal struggles over dismissal practices: "businesses have devised new strategies designed to maintain flexibility, to which the courts have responded by developing the doctrine further" (Foote 1996, 638).

One obvious consequence of restrictions on the dismissal of workers has been the pressure for proliferation of new categories of employment beginning in the 1980s. Since the case law has tended to place more restrictions on regular full-time workers than on other categories of employment, businesses have responded by trying to create more flexibility in managing their work forces through reductions in the relative number of regular employees and increases in the number of workers in so-called "nonstandard" categories like temporary, contract, and part-time. Businesses can take precautions and show good faith efforts to protect jobs for the more protected regular work force and increase the nonstandard workers for whom employment security is less regulated. In recent interviews, in fact, Rengo officials readily admitted their frustrations about the increasing weakness of organized labor in the face of work-force restructuring. It is no longer, they say, a climate that favors radical action. In fact, their new efforts are focused largely on coping with the proliferation of new categories of employment created by employers trying to replace a large portion of the regular, full-time work force with more flexible categories of workers who are structurally kept in relationships without full protection of employer-employee relationships as customarily and legally defined.

Ironically, the success of cases like these in the 1980s and 1990s undoubtedly influenced the economic and political reform efforts aimed at reducing the record-breaking number of employment disputes, which ushered in the new millennium and set the stage for Japan's economic restructuring. The social activists involved in Universal's labor movement and their allies in related social movements lament that social recovery has not yet followed economic recovery. They see social ills and loss of meaning and value to be a continuing threat to Japanese workers and an important set of issues to be addressed by movement activities as marketization and its associated economic upheavals challenge the ability of people to find stable work, secure a reasonable livelihood, and understand their position in a rapidly changing social world.

ECONOMIC UNCERTAINTY, EMPLOYMENT STABILITY, AND SOCIAL CHANGE

In one sense these social movement activities were not so much about going to court to change things as they were about leveraging the law to keep things from changing. Of course, in the area of employment, because of its constitutive role in daily life itself, stability is a primary goal for workers. In times of economic crises the use of collective action and court cases to further the cause of employment stability resonates with the histories of both legal and social activism in Japan. Judicial activism around employment security began in the early postwar period to establish the case law that is still used to address "economically motivated dismissals" during the most recent "new wave" of economic upheaval (Foote 1996). Bankruptcy struggles used this body of law to their advantage. Safeguarding the livelihood of Japanese workers during economic restructuring is a complex problem. The Universal dispute and others that followed it in the 1980s and 1990s aimed to set limits on employer actions during times of economic crisis. The Universal workers, their union leadership, and federation allies did not set out to change Japanese labor law, but to benefit from and expand the application of those already in existence. They meant to force capitalists to be responsible for workers even in times of *gōrika*—or rationalization of production. They meant to enforce limits on dismissals, liquidations of production facilities, and elimination of jobs associated with the economic crises that were lining up off Japan's shores as globalization ushered in unprecedented demands for marketization in this "new wave" of economic upheaval.

Throughout the struggle, the language of the social movement emphasized both the particular issues reflected in the court cases and larger issues of what the union called "social responsibility." This echoes, in friendlier language, the legal concept of "social rights," but it shifts the balance to the more powerful side of a relationship with a nod toward paternalistic assumptions about moral action within institutional hierarchies. They accused Custom of being irresponsible and claimed that the company was responsible for the livelihood of the Universal workers and their families. The particular justice they demanded was summed up in the slogans like "Custom! Take responsibility for Universal's bankruptcy!" "Custom! Take responsibility for the livelihood of Universal workers!" Greater labor movement justice was imagined in "Big capital! Stop destroying small and medium-sized companies!" In a time when enterprises were trying to find ways to increase flexibility in their work forces, this was an important challenge, resonating with the resistance within larger companies of their regular, full-time workers asking for limits to be placed on offshore production and increases in nonstandard employment.

Much of Universal's legal battle was directed at establishing workers' rights as employees, at recovering lost wages and benefits, and at opening negotiations about a reestablishment of employment. Whereas the arguments regarding Japanese labor law were particular and exclusively context bound, avoiding, even in settlement, generalizing about right and wrong, or good and bad, the local disruptions of the social movement were infused with the discourse of broad national and international social change to improve the welfare of workers in Japan and around the world. The issues addressed in framing the local labor movement actions resonated with the tone of national legislative, business, government, and labor federation debates, as well as broader social discourse concerned with reforming Japanese social institutions in the context of marketization and economic restructuring. Both aimed to enforce existing protections and to advance additional protections for workers in Japanese society.

The most idealistic arguments that supported these actions were universal ones about rights as workers, employees, and citizens of Japan. The global economic change that compelled Custom to take measures to disband Universal was met with national legal actions and was supported by local social movement activity. Universal's disruptive actions were, of course, aimed in part at demonstrating their determination to fight until settlement could be reached in the court cases themselves, but they also aimed at a series of loftier goals. These included regaining employment for all Universal workers, reopening a Universal company under worker control of production, and demonstrating to Custom, to other Japanese capitalists and employers, and to workers around Japan that workers—even in small numbers and in economically vulnerable positions—can exercise power and can be at least a modest force for desirable social, economic, and political change ensuring safeguards for the livelihood of ordinary workers. None of these goals was addressed directly in any legal case and yet, without the legal cases asserting the very specific rights of these particular workers as employees, none of these goals could have been pursued. The pursuit of these general issues through the specific cases acted to legitimize the disruptive actions, especially in light of eventual victory in the court cases, and to signal a powerful message of support for employee rights to stable employment and a secure livelihood even in circumstances of economic crisis.

This discourse of social responsibility rests on an uneasy intersection of paternalistic notions of being taken care of by a powerful employer and liberal, even radical, notions of employee protection from rash disregard in the course of employer economic action. Daniel Foote (1996) says of the "abusive dismissal" case law that it lies on an assumption of a stronger employer and weaker employee and the corresponding necessity of assuring some measure of responsibility on the part of the employer and rights to protection for the employee. Fundamentally, he argues, in Japanese law employment is seen as a "stable relationship" that carries with it both rights and responsibilities. Frank Upham (1987) and William Gould (1984) have both written about the importance in Japanese court cases of social contracts within long-term relationships. Both argue persuasively that these are not traditional, conservative, reactive positions but in fact constitutive of the process of defining and protecting Japanese concepts and practices of social relationships and social rights.

Domestic and international economic pressures have led to recent reforms in Japanese employment law pushing toward more business flexibility and the opening of labor to more market forces. The reforms themselves, however, continue to use the language of employer responsibility, employee consultation, and preservation of the stability of the relationship between employers and employees even under conditions of economic stress, enterprise crisis, or organizational restructuring. Yamakawa (2001) argues that while revisions in commercial codes since 2000 have made it easier for corporations to restructure, revisions in labor law "have not touched upon the limitation on the employer's right to discharge established by case law, which is one of the most fundamental elements of the Japanese labor law." Foote concurs and suggests that although in the current economic climate erosion of employment security is likely, it will be market pressures rather than any change in judicial application of legal standards that will be responsible (1996, 706).

In this context of increasing transnational integration of labor and capital markets, there are many forms of social change in Japan not unlike those in the rest of the advanced industrialized world. What is particularly interesting about the Japanese response is the way in which economic, legal, and cultural institutions are being engaged in debate about the reconfiguration of both specific economic practices and cultural understandings of the role of work and stable employment relationships in constituting social life and identity for Japanese citizens. This debate goes on throughout society. A leader in the government organization charged with revitalizing Japanese companies recently wrote, "Japan, a nation of few natural resources, continues to rely on people as its primary source of wealth generation into the twenty-first century. Yet, the system for tapping that potential, a twentieth century *harmonie preetablie* [preestablished harmony] . . . is getting old. . . . If we accept this, what kind of system should we create for the twenty-first century?"

The response of activist unions to bankruptcy related loss of employment, supported by national federations and networks of social movement actors, constituted an important voice in the process of social adjustment by making demands for reasonable treatment of workers during restructuring or dissolution of companies. Because these demands were made both legally through court cases and politically in social movement actions, they became powerful enough to contribute to the critical social discourse regarding the consequences of subjecting employment to an unregulated labor market, and they have asserted the need for appropriate social, cultural, and legal limitations on economic action.

REFERENCES

Foote, Daniel. (1996). Judicial Creation of Norms in Japanese Labor Law: Activism in the Service of Stability? *University of California, Los Angeles, Law Review* 43.3 (February): 635–710.

Geertz, Clifford. (1983). *Local Knowledge: Further Essays in Interpretive Anthropology.* New York, Basic Books.

Gordon, Andrew. (1998). *Wages of Affluence: Labor and Management in Postwar Japan.* Cambridge, MA, Harvard University Press.

Gould, William B., IV. (1984). *Japan's Reshaping of American Labor Law.* Boston, MIT Press.

Itoh, Hiroshi. (1990). Judicial Review and Judicial Activism in Japan. *Law and Contemporary Problems* 53.1 (Winter): 169–79.

Kumazawa, Makoto. (1996). *Portraits of the Japanese Workplace: Labor Movements, Workers, and Managers.* Boulder, CO, Westview Press.

McNamara, Dennis. (1996). Corporatism and Cooperation among Japanese Labor. *Comparative Politics* 28.4 (July): 379–97.

Nimura Kazuo. (1994a). The Labor Movement at the Beginnings of Post-War Society in Japan. In *Nihon Kin-gendaishi* 4 (January). Tokyo, Iwanami Shoten.

Nimura Kazuo. (1994b). Post Second World War Labor Relations in Japan. In *Industrial Relations in Australia and Japan*, ed. Jim Hagan and Andrew Wells, 64–91. St. Leonards, NSW, Australia, Allen and Unwin.

Totsuka Hideo. (1984). Kokusaiteki ni mo susunda nihon no tosan toso [Japan's Advanced Antibankruptcy Disputes]. In *Ashira no ase kagayaitemasu: Jishu seisan tatakai no kenjitsu to kenkai* [Our Sweat Glistens: Evolution of Self-management and Struggle in a Labor Dispute], ed. Hataraku Nakama no Kojosai Jikko Iinkai. Tokyo, Rodo Kyoiku Sentaa.

Totsuka Hideo. (1978). Chūshō kigyō tosan hangai sōgi jirei chōsa [Antibankruptcy Disputes in Small and Medium-sized Companies]. *Shakai kagaku kenkyū* 30.1: 206–21.

Turner, Christena L. (1995). *Japanese Workers in Protest: An Ethnography of Consciousness and Experience.* Berkeley, University of California Press.

Turner, Christena. (1989). Democratic Consciousness in Japanese Unions. In *Democracy in Japan*, ed. Takeshi Ishida and Ellis S. Krauss, 299–323. Pittsburgh, PA, University of Pittsburgh Press.

Upham, Frank K.. (1987). *Law and Social Change in Postwar Japan.* Cambridge, MA, Harvard University Press.

Yamakawa, Ryuichi. (2001). Labor Law Reform in Japan: A Response to Recent Socio-Economic Change. *The American Journal of Comparative Law* 49.4 (Autumn): 627–51.

CHAPTER 5

Suing for Redress: Japanese Consumer Organizations and the Courts

Patricia L. Maclachlan

Since the mid-1960s, when "Citizen Nader" first exploded onto the scene, civil litigation has been a high-profile political tactic for the American consumer movement. In numerous instances, the courts have forced recalcitrant businesses into changing their behavior toward consumers and encouraging national and state governments to introduce or amend consumer protection laws and regulations. The value of the courts as an avenue for articulating the American consumer interest can be attributed to such factors as a broad standing to sue, liberal class-action rules, the ready availability of legal counsel, comparatively low court fees, and user-friendly court procedures for civil cases, to name just a few. Although Americans are quick to find fault with their judicial system, it stands alone in terms of its accessibility not only to lone citizens with private grievances, but also to organized spokespersons of the public interest.

In Japan, by contrast, litigation has historically functioned as a tactic of last resort for consumers. As others have shown, the reasons for this include a narrow standing to sue for most civil and administrative suits, a shortage of lawyers, economic and procedural barriers to litigation (see Haley 1978), and the psychological stigma attached to airing one's grievances in public (Taniguchi 1984, 34). These observations are borne out by statistics. Between 1896, when the Civil Code was enacted, and the introduction of the new Products Liability Law in 1994, the courts ruled on only 150 or so products liability lawsuits; in the United States, by contrast, there were approximately 13,000 products liability lawsuits before the federal courts in 1991 alone (Hamada 1996, 12). For "public interest" suits launched by consumer organizations, the contrast is equally pronounced; whereas movement suits against both business and governmental authorities are more or less routine in the U.S., Japan's leading consumer organizations resort to the courts only occasionally. Shufuren, the housewives' organization and a leading player in the consumer movement, has taken to the courts only a handful of times in its more than sixty-year history; the more radical Consumers Union (Shōhisha Renmei) routinely resorts to litigation to publicize its agenda, but its cases have attracted far less media attention than Shufuren's. For both organizations, litigation usually ends in defeat.

These observations notwithstanding, civil litigation has functioned as a significant tactic for Japanese consumer organizations—particularly those with legislative goals, and in ways that may strike some observers as surprising. To make this case, I explore consumer movement litigation in three issue areas (antitrust, products liability, and information disclosure), and with reference to the following questions. How receptive has the postwar Japanese judicial system been to consumer action on behalf of the public interest? To what extent does litigation serve the interests of consumer activists seeking political change? How do those activists relate to their constituents, political allies, and the general public during the course of a lawsuit, and what are the implications of these linkages for the movement's long-term development? Finally, how has the relationship between the consumer movement and the courts changed since the mid-1990s with the introduction of a national information disclosure law, amendments to the Code of Civil Procedure and other legal reforms, and what do these changes suggest about the future of litigation on behalf of public interest goals?

THE ANTICARTEL CRUSADES

Contrary to conventional wisdom, Japanese consumer organizations are deeply concerned about high consumer prices and have targeted lax antitrust enforcement as one of the root causes of that phenomenon. Accordingly, activists campaigned long and hard since the early 1950s for amendments to the 1947 Anti-Monopoly Law that would lessen the incidence of cartels and other forms of collusive business practices in the marketplace. As might be expected in a country where the interests of businesses and their bureaucratic spokespersons had a profound influence on virtually all facets of economic policy, consumer campaigns on behalf of Anti-Monopoly Law reform usually fell on deaf ears. By the early 1970s, however, a confluence of political and economic events opened a window of opportunity for expanded governmental discussions on reform that heightened the movement's determination to publicize the law's importance as a guarantee of the consumer's rights to both product choice at competitive prices and adequate administrative redress. Unfortunately, however, advocates lacked the necessary inroads into the mainstream policy process to convey that message to both the powers that be and the general public. It was against this political and institutional backdrop that a number of activists took to the courts in the so-called "juice trial" of 1971–78 and the "kerosene trials" of 1974–89, all of which showcased the perceived inadequacies of Japan's antitrust regime in terms of fulfilling basic consumer rights. As the following pages illustrate, both suits had a significant impact not only on public opinion surrounding the issue of Anti-Monopoly Law reform but also on movement solidarity and relations with movement allies (see also Maclachlan 2002a, chap. 6).

The Juice Lawsuit

In 1968, Shufuren's product testing center launched an investigation into canned and bottled juice products on the suspicion that artificial fruit juices were being falsely designated as "100 percent pure." Completed the following year, the tests revealed that of 100 samples marked "100 percent juice," only 3 percent had been accurately labeled; about a fifth of the samples consisted entirely of artificial juices, while the remainder fell within the 10 to 30 percent pure juice range (Nihon Hōsō Shuppan Kyōkai 1980, 168). To rectify what Shufuren viewed as a case of deceptive labeling and a violation of the consumer's rights to choose and to know, the organization appealed informally to the Japan Fair Trade Commission (FTC) for the introduction of more stringent labeling standards over the bottled juice industry.

In March 1971, the FTC announced that it had concluded a "fair competition agreement" (*kōsei kyōsō kiyaku*) with juice manufacturers under the 1961 Law to Prevent Unjustifiable Premiums and Misleading Representations (Futō Keihinrui Oyobi Futō Hyōji Bōshi Hō, or Keihyōhō) that was designed to clarify the industry's labeling standards. Fair competition agreements were usually drawn up by industry leaders and then approved (*nintei*) by the FTC. Although not subject to binding arbitration by the FTC, these agreements functioned as informal rules for promoting a "fair and competitive" economic order (Shōda and Sanekata 1976, 213). Shufuren, however, refused to endorse the commission's 1971 agreement with juice manufacturers on the grounds that it did virtually nothing to prevent the application of the term "pure juice" to products containing artificial ingredients.

Arguing that the new labeling standards still deceived consumers, Shufuren filed a formal "statement of dissatisfaction" (*fufuku mōshitate*) with the FTC under Article 10 of the Keihyōhō (Shufuren 1978, 4). It was the first time in Shufuren's history that it had ever taken such a step. The move conformed to Keihyōhō stipulations that parties—including consumers—whose interests (*rieki*) were adversely affected by violations to the law had the right to register such statements with the commission and to demand corrective measures (Kaneko 1974, 15)—in this case, the abolition of a fair competition agreement that Shufuren maintained was illegal under the Keihyōhō.

After thirty months of hearings that movement activists called the "juice trial" (*jūsu saiban*), the FTC ignored the substantive content of the complaint and ruled that Shufuren was not qualified to file a statement of dissatisfaction. The commission ruled that since the fair trade agreement governing the labeling of juice products had been drawn up with the interests of businesses in mind, the consumer interest was not directly pertinent to that agreement. The commission also concluded that it could not be established that the agreement had violated the consumer's right to product choice—a position that flummoxed the housewives' association. To add insult to injury, no sooner did the FTC rule on the case than it announced that juice manufacturers would have to comply with stricter and more accurate labeling standards after all—standards that reflected Shufuren's demands almost to the letter.

Although Shufuren was pleased that several years of activism had finally led to the imposition of proper labeling standards over the juice industry, the commission's alleged mishandling of the appeal enraged the organization. Since ignoring the ruling would be tantamount to tacitly approving it, the women sought review by the Tokyo High Court. Known as the "consumer rights trial" (*Shōhisha no kenri no saiban*), the suit was a test case of the consumer's right to be heard—of the right of ordinary consumers and consumer organizations to appeal administrative decisions pertaining to consumer protection.

After several months in court and with the financial and moral support of other consumer organizations and scores of lawyers and legal scholars who served as volunteer counsel, Shufuren lost the case. In its July 1974 ruling upholding the Fair Trade Commission's decision, the Tokyo High Court found that consumer protection was an important aim of the Law to Prevent Unjustifiable Premiums and Misleading Representations and that consumers did indeed have the right to contest administrative decisions that violated the interests of consumers. Consumers did not, however, have the legal standing to demand a repeal of the "fair competition agreement" that had set the juice industry's labeling standards, since the purpose of such nonbinding agreements was fair competition within the industry rather than the consumer interest (Kokumin Seikatsu Sentaa 1997, 97).

Not to be outdone, Shufuren appealed the case to the Supreme Court with the backing of forty prominent legal scholars. In 1978, the Supreme Court upheld the decision of the Tokyo High Court, holding that neither consumers nor consumer organizations were qualified to lodge formal complaints against administrative measures designed to protect the "public interest" (*kōeki*) (Yamane et al. 1998, 70). Clearly, the "public interest" in this case had been equated with the interests of producers.

Shufuren's defeat in all phases of the juice trial highlighted the judiciary's tendency to interpret the consumer's standing to sue very narrowly. As such, the defeat was a crushing disappointment for consumer organizations, not to mention a telling example of both governmental and court efforts to marginalize consumers as citizens in matters relating to the business community. That said, the suit had some positive side effects for consumer activists. First, the consumer movement's broad support for Shufuren's actions helped soften many of the ideological differences among its constituent organizations—differences that had hindered intramovement cooperation in the past. As the 1970s progressed, "joint action" (*renkei no purei*) on behalf of common goals became increasingly effective (Interview, Ono Shōji, Shōdanren, Tokyo, March 9, 1994).

Second, the voluntary participation of lawyers and legal scholars as advisors and legal counsel in the case helped forge a relationship between the movement and the legal community that is still in place today. This is not to suggest, however, that lawyers have flocked to the consumer movement. In marked contrast to the U.S., where lawyers routinely assume leadership positions in consumer organizations, few Japanese lawyers get involved in consumer movement affairs. Reasons for this include the dearth of opportunities for consumer-related litigation in Japan, resource deficiencies within movement organizations, and the traditionally low level of prestige attached to participation in postwar social movements. Also significant are the lack of a "public interest law" tradition in Japan and the country's perennial shortage of lawyers, although this is slowly changing. Although there are no statistics on this issue, based on personal observations and interviews with consumer activists, I would estimate that only twenty to twenty-five lawyers were regularly providing pro bono services to consumer campaigns by the early 2000s. Motivated in part by altruistic concerns for individual rights and the interests of Japanese consumers, these lawyers exhibited an entrepreneurial spirit insofar as they forged relationships with consumer organizations in their efforts to create broader legal and organizational opportunities for advancing the consumer interest.

Lawyers' contributions have been enormously important to the consumer movement. Unlike their American counterparts, Japan's cash-strapped consumer organizations consist almost entirely of volunteer housewives, few of whom have formal legal or other advanced academic training. They therefore have no choice but to rely on volunteer legal counsel for guidance on the finer points of the law. In the juice case, lawyers would assemble observers after every hearing to explain the legal significance of the day's proceedings; this practice continues today not only in the context of consumer litigation but also during complicated legislative campaigns. Without this logistical and educational support, it is highly unlikely that the movement would have accomplished as much as it has politically over the past three decades.

Last but not least, the juice trial helped galvanize the movement to reform the Anti-Monopoly Law and the Fair Trade Commission. By symbolizing the FTC's lack of accountability to consumers, the issue helped raise the public's consciousness of their rights as consumers and of the commission's frequent inability—if not unwillingness—to uphold them. The timing of the Tokyo High Court's ruling, moreover, proved highly propitious for Anti-Monopoly Law reform; handed down just as the FTC was fielding its own proposals for reform, the ruling attracted extensive media coverage and increased public support for the burgeoning legislative movement that eventually culminated in the amendments of 1977. In sum, the juice trial may have ended in legal defeat, but it was nevertheless an effective avenue of interest articulation for a politically marginalized social movement intent on reforming the legal system.

The Kerosene Trials

Another landmark consumer campaign that overlapped with and fed into the movement to strengthen the Anti-Monopoly Law involved three lawsuits against Japan's powerful oil cartel. Like the juice trial, these cases highlighted the difficulties confronted by consumer organizations within the court system and ultimately ended in defeat. More significantly, the cases had a major impact on public opinion vis-à-vis antitrust—at least during the early stages of litigation.

The primary trigger behind the kerosene trials was sharp increases in consumer prices following the 1973 oil shock and a concomitant drop in the supply of such basic consumer necessities as paper, soap, sugar, and toilet paper (Chifuren 1986, 127). To many activists, the inflationary effects of the oil shock had been exacerbated by an expanding oil cartel that was in turn symptomatic of lax antitrust enforcement. Taking their cue from the FTC, which by year's end had announced a decision to launch a formal investigation into allegations of collusion within the oil industry, a number of national consumer organizations took steps of their own. Their target was kerosene—a clean, relatively safe, and increasingly popular fuel for space heaters. In 1974, the Consumers Union (Shōhisha Renmei) took the first step by organizing 343 of its members into "The Consumer Association for Getting Back What Was Taken Away" (Torareta mono o Torikaesu Shōhisha no Kai), a plaintiffs' group that filed suit against the kerosene manufacturers with the Tokyo District Court in September 1974. Two months later, 96 members of Shufuren and the Kawasaki Consumer Cooperative filed a similar suit; in short order, 1,654 members of consumer cooperatives did the same in Tsuruoka in Yamagata Prefecture. The plaintiffs in the two Tokyo cases filed under Article 25 of the Anti-Monopoly Law, and the Tsuruoka plaintiffs filed under Article 709 of the Civil Code (Kokumin Seikatsu Sentaa 1997, 153).

These suits marked the first time in history that consumer organizations employed the legal tactic of "group litigation" (shūdan soshō), the details of which are specified by Article 47 of the Code of Civil Procedure. Group litigation is a Japanese version of the American class action suit, but with at least two important differences. Like the class action suit, the device enables plaintiffs to avoid the inconvenience of suing individually by allowing them to litigate as a group. Until recently, however, and in contrast to class action, all members of that group had to be specified before the case went to trial. One or more of the plaintiffs would be chosen by the rest of the group to represent that group in court (Davis

1996, 146 and 191); unlike class action, lawyers were forbidden from acting on those plaintiffs' behalf. The kerosene suits were particularly noteworthy because in each case, judges allowed either Shufuren or the consumer cooperatives to represent their members in court; normally, the courts do not permit third parties to assume such functions (Boling 1997, 471).

In all three cases, the consumers-as-plaintiffs requested no more than 2,400 yen per person (Yamane et al. 1998, 75). Since the plaintiffs were required to establish the relationship between their individual rights and the defendants' actions in order to effectively claim damages, they had to prove that they had purchased kerosene from cartel members in the wake of the oil shock. The requirement disqualified hundreds of potential plaintiffs who had long since discarded their receipts. Many of those who requested duplicates were turned down by kerosene retailers who feared retaliation from their suppliers (Nihon Hōsō Shuppan Kyōkai 1980, 182), a development that simply underscored the extent of the cartel's control over the distribution system.

As is wont to happen in Japan, the trials dragged on for years. In 1981, the Consumers Union's case was settled via conciliation (*wakai*); after a series of appeals that ultimately reached the Supreme Court, the other cases ended in defeat by 1989. In the Tsuruoka case, the Sendai High Court ruled in favor of the plaintiffs in a landmark decision in 1985; the Supreme Court subsequently overturned that decision.

Like the juice trial, the kerosene trials highlighted how difficult it can be in Japan to obtain compensation for alleged violations of consumer rights and interests through the court system, a problem that is at least partly attributable to the legal ambiguities and requirements of the statutes under which most consumer-related suits are filed. Article 25 of the Anti-Monopoly Law, for example, is unclear about the circumstances under which consumers can sue for damages; nor, for that matter, does it specify the meaning of "damages." Not surprisingly, few suits have been filed under these provisions. Between 1947 and 1984, for instance, only seven suits were filed under Article 25 of the Anti-Monopoly Law; in the United States during the early 1980s, by contrast, over one thousand private antitrust actions were filed each year (Iyori 1986, 75n21). To complicate matters, Article 709 of the Civil Code requires that the alleged victims of business behavior prove business negligence—an onerous task before the mid-1990s given the weak discovery provisions and the strength of measures to protect business secrets. Small wonder, then, that most consumer-related suits ended in legal defeat.

In politicized suits involving large numbers of plaintiffs who have suffered severe bodily damage at the hands of corporations, the courts have been known to suspend the plaintiff's burden of proof and to allow public opinion and moral considerations to influence their rulings. This was certainly the case in the Big Four environmental lawsuits of the late 1960s and 1970s (see McKean 1981) and suits involving large-scale damages caused by tainted foods and pharmaceutical products like thalidomide. In lawsuits involving questions of political principle and small amounts of damages, by contrast, the courts leaned toward conservatism. That said, litigation has been an effective tactic for educating citizens about their rights as consumers and attracting both media and public attention to consumer-related political issues. As one consumer activist once put it, consumer organizations will file suits that are destined to fail simply because there is no better forum for publicizing the status of consumer rights in Japan (Interview, Nishikawa Kazuko, Consumers Union, Tokyo, March 22, 1992).

During the mid-1970s, the use of the courts for political purposes was further legitimized by a number of progressive local governments that passed consumer ordinances permitting local government subsidies for consumer lawsuits. In the kerosene case filed by Shufuren and the Kawasaki cooperatives, for example, Shufuren received a total of 1.8 million yen—a significant amount in the 1970s—from the Tokyo Metropolitan Government to help cover some of their legal expenses (Shufuren 1998, 55). These measures can be interpreted as an official acknowledgement of the almost insurmountable barriers to litigation, an assertion of local governmental authority in the consumer realm, and the tacit rejection of national governmental efforts to control the extent of citizen litigation in Japan.

SUING FOR SAFER PRODUCTS

Unlike the movement to amend the Anti-Monopoly Law, consumer movement activism in support of new products liability legislation did not involve direct use of the courts. Instead, activists allied with members of the Japan Federation of Bar Associations (Nihon Bengoshi Rengōkai, or Nichibenren for short) to amass data on nearly one hundred years of products liability litigation and to publicize the fate of plaintiffs in contemporary suits in an overall effort to create a climate of public opinion that favored reform. Their efforts, in many ways, were very successful.

In the past, the victims of accidents caused by defective products had access to several avenues of recourse, including one-on-one negotiations with manufacturers (a procedure known as *aitai kōshō*), conciliation services administered by semigovernmental consumer centers at the local level, or ministerial compensatory schemes (see Maclachlan 1999). Consumers who were dissatisfied with these procedures, however, could sue the manufacturer in question for damages.

As proponents of reform were quick to point out, litigation under the pre-1994 products liability system was an almost impossible undertaking. For one thing, plaintiffs in most cases had to file suit under Article 709 of the Civil Code, which stipulates that plaintiffs must prove: (1) that manufacturers were *negligent* in the planning or manufacturing of the products in question; and (2) that the damages incurred were the direct result of product defects. To fulfill these legal obligations, plaintiffs required detailed information about the planning and manufacturing processes pertaining to those products. But neither the Civil Code nor consumer-related statutes provided for access to this kind of information; nor did the court system, which lacked adequate discovery mechanisms. As a result of these constraints, the vast majority of victims of defective products avoided the courts altogether by relying on alternative dispute resolution (ADR) programs, or, failing that, by simply "crying themselves to sleep" (*nakineiri*) in frustration.

Consumer activists saw in this dismal state of affairs an opportunity to educate the public on the deficiencies of Japan's system of consumer redress. Shufuren, for example, joined forces in 1991 with Nichibenren to carry out an annual three-day telephone service designed to solicit consumer feedback on consumer redress mechanisms. Established by the bar association the previous year, the service, which was known as the Defective Products Hotline (*Kekkan shōhin 110 ban*), collected data from over thirty locations around the country. The hotline was an ingenious idea that accomplished at least two goals. First, since the annual event was well covered by both the national and regional newspapers, it proved to be an effective mechanism for reaching the citizenry and educating them about both strict liability and their rights to safe products and adequate redress mechanisms. This function was particularly important given the complicated legal technicalities surrounding products liability reform and the resulting tendency for average citizens to ignore the issue altogether. Administering the hotline was also one of several tactics that enabled consumer leaders and their allies in Nichibenren to gather rough but compelling statistics about the perceived inadequacies of the judicial system in products liability cases—statistics that were disseminated to politicians and bureaucrats within the policy-making process.

The most prominent lawyer in the movement to enact a products liability law was Nakamura Masato. Nakamura first got involved in consumer litigation in 1975, when he helped represent the plaintiffs in suits involving damages incurred by a tainted antidiarrhea medicine (the SMON case). He participated in a number of products liability suits after that time and achieved national prominence as Nichibenren's leading spokesperson for consumer issues. An eloquent speaker and highly trustworthy activist, Nakamura was frequently asked by newspaper editors to review articles on products liability before they went to press (Interview, Nakamura Masato, Nichibenren, Tokyo, February 9, 1994).

Nakamura and a number of other lawyers joined forces with consumer leaders to publicize the results of their surveys on the state of Japan's products liability regime. One such survey revealed that of the 250 cases involving defective products handled by lawyers in 1989, 166, or 66 percent, never made it past the consultation stage. Of the remaining 84 cases, most were resolved through conciliation; only 4 lawsuits—many of them launched years beforehand—had resulted in victories for the plaintiffs (Nakamura et al. 1992, 26–30).

Finally, the alliance with Nichibenren contributed to an informal dialogue between the movement and the legal community that helped educate the general public as well as movement members. During private conversations and tactical planning meetings for those participating in the products liability reform campaign, lawyers frequently provided information on pending products liability suits—information that was in turn disseminated to other movement members through movement literature, lectures and symposia, and the National Consumer Rally (*Zen Nihon Shōhisha taikai*) held each November in Tokyo. The national and regional dailies, which occasionally reported on these developments, served as a link between intramovement discussions on products liability reform and the general public.

In June 1994, after several years of campaigning, consumer activists and their Nichibenren allies achieved their ultimate goal: the enactment of products liability legislation based on the concept of strict liability. Under the new system, plaintiffs in products liability suits are only required to prove the existence of a product defect and the cause and effect relationship between that defect and damages incurred. Theoretically, the new law facilitates access to the courts by loosening the consumer's legal burden of proof. In practice, however, consumers-as-plaintiffs are being encouraged to settle their disputes in an expanding network of nonstatutory ADR programs administered by both business associations and local governments (see Maclachlan 1999). These procedures can be a mixed blessing. For the aggrieved consumer, they are far less costly and time-consuming than formal lawsuits. For consumer advocates, however, they are nothing short of disappointing. The emphasis of ADR procedures on compromise solutions rather than the "winner-take-all" approach of the courts has enabled many corporate defendants to escape their legal responsibilities as stipulated under the new law. ADR procedures also tend to be quite opaque, thereby preventing valuable information about consumer protection and consumer rights from reaching the public at large (Maclachlan 2002a, 229). As such, products liability ADR procedures help privatize potentially controversial cases of consumer-related damages in much the same way that local governments helped privatize environmental disputes following the pollution crises of the 1960s and early 1970s (see Upham 1987). For those who view the courts as a nation's most effective arbiter of consumer rights, bureaucratic and corporate dominance of products liability redress has dampened the movement to strengthen consumer voices within the Japanese political economy.

THE DISCLOSURE CASES

Since the early 1990s, a new kind of consumer movement has been materializing in Japan. While the postwar movement was centered in institutionalized advocacy organizations led primarily by women and, to a lesser extent, the consumer coop-eratives, this new branch of the movement is situated primarily at the grass-roots level and is far more fluid in terms of its membership and political objectives. Consisting of relatively young, often college-educated women and men, these new, local groups and single-issue networks champion such issues as environmentalism, good governance, and citizenship, as well as traditional consumerism. As such, they resemble local wings of the contemporary American consumer movement.

Many of these groups were involved in a movement to enact a national information disclosure law that was fueled by a widespread determination to guarantee the consumer's professed right to know (see Maclachlan 2000). These groups are particularly significant for our purposes because many were involved in litigation in the context of loose, prodisclosure alliances with both lawyers and national consumer advocates. The activities of this alliance constitute a fascinat-ing case study of the changing relationship between social movements and the judicial system and the capacity of the latter to serve as a harbinger for political change.

Between 1982 and the mid-1990s, most Japanese prefectures and many city and town governments had enacted disclosure ordinances that authorized the limited release of local bureaucratic documents to local residents. While those ordinances served very positive functions for the advancement of citizen-government relations at the local level, they were far from perfect; users frequently complained of sloppy procedures, lengthy delays, and bureaucratic denials of formal requests on legally dubious grounds. To highlight these deficiencies, bands of citizens requested various kinds of information under local disclosure ordinances—information that they never expected to receive: safety data on controversial consumer products, information on the conduct and results of school entrance examinations, data on the entertainment and travel expenditures of local officials and heads of government, and the like. When local bureaucrats refused to comply with those requests, citizens had access to two avenues of recourse: first, they could appeal the decisions to local governmental inspection committees (*fufuku kansa iin*) established to deal expressly with disclosure cases; or, they could file suit at the district court level. By 1996, there were approximately sixty suits before the courts, and many were ultimately resolved in the plaintiffs' favor. Some cases even went as far as the Supreme Court, although few of these resulted in victory for the plaintiffs (Boling 1997, 128).

Many of these local litigants were linked to lawyers and national advocacy groups in nationwide networks such as The National Liaison Council for Citizen Ombudsmen (Zenkoku Shimin Ombuzuman Renrakukai) and The Citizens' Network to Demand the Establishment of an Information Disclosure Law (Jōhō Kōkaihō no Settei o Motomeru Shimin Nettowaaku). National advocates rein-forced the activities of these local litigants by conducting surveys of their own on the weaknesses of local disclosure ordinances. All told, their efforts had a profound impact on public opinion in the movement to enact national disclosure legislation, as well as on the willingness of local bureaucrats and politicians to reform their disclosure ordinances.

In May 1999, the Diet finally enacted the Information Disclosure Law after almost two decades of public debate, thereby opening national bureaucratic documents to systematic scrutiny for the first time in history. What is significant about the law is that it outlines procedures for appealing bureaucratic denials of disclosure requests to the country's eight High Courts. This provision—which was introduced as a concession to opposition parties in the Diet—is a significant guarantee of citizen supervision of Japan's national administration, not to mention a stunning expansion of judicial functions in ways that may deter governmental efforts at social control in the future. Consumer and citizen activists at both the national and local levels, meanwhile, remained partially mobilized and worked hard to encourage average citizens to test both the national and local disclosure systems not only to ensure bureaucratic accountability, but also to obtain information that could be used in citizen campaigns on behalf of anticorruption, safer products, and a host of other issues (Interview, Ohta Yoshiyasu, Nisseikyō, Tokyo, June 29, 1999). In contrast to past examples of environmental and consumer litigation, lawsuits relating to information disclosure requests have the potential to spark new types of litigation in the future, as opposed to a clamp-down on this method of interest articulation by governmental authorities interested in localizing and privatizing conflict.

Consumers as Plaintiffs: The Postwar Record

While financial, legal, and procedural constraints have rendered litigation a political tactic of last resort for both consumers in general and the organized consumer movement, the above case studies indicate that the tactic can provide movement activists with a significant opportunity to accomplish a number of political objectives. First, litigation can effectively highlight violations of the consumer's rights to information, product safety, product choice, and political representation in ways that legitimize the political objectives of the movement. Second, and related to the first point, litigation is often instrumental in galvanizing public opinion in support of long-term legislative objectives. What is ironic about the outcomes of these lawsuits is that plaintiffs did not have to win in order to accomplish their political aims. In fact, defeat actually worked to the advantage of consumer advocates by stoking a sense of outrage among movement members, their allies, the general public, and even erstwhile opponents of consumer causes; these sentiments in turn translated into pressure on the political system for comprehensive legislative reform.

Litigation also served as an effective instrument for forging a sense of solidarity within the organized consumer movement. From the movement's inception during the early Occupation period, cooperation between the ideologically diverse groups of the movement was at times next to impossible. Shufuren's juice trial, however, raised an issue that all consumer activists could agree on, namely, the importance of guaranteeing such basic consumer rights as the right to information ("the right to know") and the right to be heard in both governmental and business circles. Galvanized by Shufuren's mission, erstwhile rivals banded together in support of a common cause and helped build the interpersonal networks that proved so instrumental to political cooperation in later years.

Finally, these consumer trials helped build a mutually beneficial alliance between consumer activists and legal professionals. This alliance has been an invaluable one over the years for consumer activists, the vast majority of whom are poorly versed in the fine art of lobbying politicians and bureaucrats. In many of the single-issue political campaigns of the past two to three decades, prominent lawyers accompanied consumer advocates in their visits to Nagatachō and Kasumigaseki, serving as eloquent spokespersons of the consumer interest.

While the alliance with lawyers certainly has its advantages, it also reflects one of the movement's most glaring weaknesses: its lack of political and legal expertise. This in turn can have far-reaching implications for the movement's standing among the general public. As one consumer law expert once noted, excessive reliance on lawyers and other outside specialists as the movement's *chiebukuro* (fountain of wisdom) may actually diminish the movement's credibility in the eyes of ordinary consumers and hence its overall impact on public opinion (Interview, Shōda Akira, Sophia University, Tokyo, December 8, 1993). But for as long as the movement lacks these internal resources—and this will no doubt remain the case for as long as the movement struggles to attract younger talent—dependence on the legal community may constitute the only logical option for activists seeking to influence the direction of political events in Japan.

SIGNS OF CHANGE

In September 1996, on the heels of the implementation of the Products Liability Law and in anticipation of a national information disclosure law, the Japanese Diet passed the first series of comprehensive amendments to the 1890 Code of Civil Procedure since 1926. The amendments, which went into effect on January 1, 1998, were in part a response to mounting public criticisms of the judicial system in the wake of a series of controversial lawsuits. Among those lawsuits was a group action suit filed in 1989 by a number of hemophiliacs who had contracted HIV from the nation's blood supply as a result of negligence on the part of the Ministry of Health and Welfare. The plaintiffs in the case had successfully secured a court order for the ministry to release pertinent documentation during the early stages of the trial. Ironically, after the ministry refused to comply with that order, the plaintiffs obtained the necessary documentation through the American Freedom of Information Act. For many onlookers, there was no better proof of the court system's inaccessibility to ordinary Japanese citizens.

From the perspective of consumer rights and consumer movement access to the courts, the new code includes at least four significant features. First, it establishes a more streamlined pretrial procedure that enables both parties in a dispute to clarify points of contention and the applicability of those points to pertinent bodies of law. This represents a marked improvement over the more haphazard pretrial procedures stipulated by the old code—procedures that often contributed to confusion and unnecessary delays during subsequent stages of the trial (Mochizuki 1999, 295). Second, the new code provides for a small claims court for damages less than 300,000 yen. In the past, small claims suits with damages up to 900,000 yen were heard at the summary court level, where complicated procedures and lengthy delays were usually the norm. The new system is not only simpler but also less time-consuming, since most small claims cases must now be settled within one day. In theory, at least, this provision assists plaintiffs in products liability lawsuits involving small claims.

Third, the new code loosens the requirements for group action. While in the past all members of a group action had to be individually identified before a suit could be filed, the new code enables plaintiffs to sign on after proceedings have begun (Taniguchi 1997, 783). This is a small but important change that facilitates group actions in the consumer, environmental, and welfare realms.

Fourth, and perhaps most significantly, the new code takes a significant step toward correcting one of the court system's most glaring weaknesses: narrow provisions for the discovery of evidence. In contrast to the highly restrictive system that was in place under the old code, all documents are now subject to discovery unless they qualify for specific exemptions. Those who fail to comply with discovery orders are subject to more stringent penalties than they were in the past (Mochizuki 1999, 297–301). These provisions benefit plaintiffs in all kinds of civil suits.

Consumer advocacy organizations and plaintiffs in consumer cases more generally also stand to benefit from the 2004 amendments to the 1968 Consumer Protection Basic Law. The revised law marks a significant victory for consumers by explicitly recognizing the existence of basic consumer rights. The new law also provides for the establishment of two organizations that are designed to promote those rights: the Consumer Policy Conference, a cabinet-level organ led by the prime minister that meets yearly to discuss and coordinate national consumer policy; and the National Consumer Affairs Center, an independent administrative agency that works closely with local governments and consumer centers to carry out ADR functions, information dissemination, and a number of other tasks relating to consumer protection. Although in practice these developments have yet to produce major changes in either the filing or success rates of consumer-related suits, in theory, at least, they empower consumers vis-à-vis business interests in both the political and judicial spheres.

Finally, Japan introduced a series of changes to the legal profession over the past decade that further facilitates access to the courts. These include the establishment of professional law schools modeled loosely on the American system and a governmental commitment to increase the number of admissions to the legal profession (Feldman 2006, 12). The most dramatic result of these changes has been a steady increase in the number of attorneys in Japan, which rose from 16,731 in March 1999 to 28,789 in March 2010 (Japan Federation of Bar Associations 2010, 1). Also noteworthy was the 2004 passage of the Comprehensive Legal Support Law that in turn led to the establishment of the Japan Legal Support Center, an independent administrative institution that provides legal advice to Japanese citizens in civil as well as criminal legal matters. As Feldman observes, these developments could lead to a "change in public perceptions about the desirability and appropriateness of using the courts to settle disputes" (2006, 20).

Although the changes noted above promise to open the courts to more meaningful access by ordinary Japanese citizens, a run on the courts is unlikely to occur. For starters, while legal aid services for criminal cases have expanded in recent years, comparable services for civil cases remain underdeveloped. Moreover, the new Code of Civil Procedure does nothing to lower Japan's notoriously high court-related fees (Taniguchi 1997, 788)—fees that will continue to channel would-be plaintiffs into cheaper ADR procedures. Third, products liability plaintiffs with small claims will continue to shy away from the courts. In keeping with custom, most small claims cases will be settled via *aitai kōshō*—corporate dispute resolution procedures based on one-on-one negotiations between consumers and company representations. The vast majority of other products liability cases will be diverted toward more user-friendly ADR facilities. While these noncourt procedures certainly have their advantages, the fact that they are carried out behind the scenes is problematic for the fulfillment of consumer rights—a task, many analysts argue, that is best carried out by courts (see Maclachlan 2002b).

It is also likely that plaintiffs in civil suits will encounter problems with the code's new discovery provisions. Those who are asked to produce documentary evidence to the courts can claim exemptions if disclosure: (a) has the potential to incriminate either the holder of those documents or the relatives of the holder; (b) violates statutory or judicial secrets; or (c) involves documents that were generated exclusively for self-use. This last exemption is the most problematic. "Self-use documents" are those produced by professionals like lawyers, doctors, bank employees or company executives during the routine course of performing their professional duties. While it is unclear exactly what sorts of documents fall under this category, bureaucrats and corporations have strong incentives to activate this exemption to prevent the disclosure of potentially embarrassing information in court. As one analyst points out, documents that are "for sole use by the possessor" could include intracompany memos or proposals and internal reports covering consumer complaints (Mochizuki 1999, 301). Needless to say, this sort of loophole can have very damaging effects on plaintiffs in products liability suits who require documentary evidence in order to prove the presence of product defects and the cause and effect relationship between those defects and damages incurred.

THE COURTS, SOCIAL MOVEMENTS, AND THE QUESTION OF SOCIAL CONTROL

From the increasing incidence of tainted imported food products to the consumer-related implications of the devastating nuclear accident in Fukushima in March 2011, Japanese consumers and their advocacy organizations continue to grapple with challenges that affect basic consumer rights. As they do so, they face a court system that is significantly more accessible to consumer litigation than it was in the past. The Information Disclosure Law, for instance, is a surprising piece of legislation that guarantees access to district courts for consumers/citizens seeking to appeal bureaucratic rejections of disclosure requests. Although the law has enough loopholes to prevent bureaucrats from being completely exposed to public scrutiny, it nevertheless marks an unprecedented opening of the court system.

The new Products Liability Law and Code of Civil Procedure are also likely to expand consumer/citizen access to the courts, but their significance should not be exaggerated. For the most part, civil procedures under the new code remain costly and time consuming; these features, combined with the presence of low-cost ADR procedures manned by business and government, continue to deflect most aggrieved consumers away from the courts and into venues where pro-business interests will be able to privatize conflict. The implications of these observations for the broader relationship between the court system and social movements in Japan are significant. In his landmark 1987 study, Frank Upham explained how the state managed to divert social and political conflict away from the court system by creating alternative bureaucratic venues for dispute resolution—venues that enabled the state not only to privatize conflict but also to control the direction of future social and political change (Upham 1987). The history of consumer and consumer movement access to the courts suggests that while the state's grip on society has loosened since the mid-1990s following the downfall of the 1955 system and the passage of pertinent legislation, it still retains the upper hand in many instances. The beneficial effects of the Products Liability Law on the relationship between the victims of defective products and the court system, for example, have been offset by a sophisticated network of nonstatutory ADR programs, while the failure of the Code of Civil Procedure to remove many of the financial barriers to litigation will act as a deterrent to potential plaintiffs in a host of civil cases. For consumer activists, the partial opening of the courts to Japanese citizens may not be enough to motivate the movement into accessing the courts more regularly. Now, as before, the courts will constitute a tactic of last resort for activists with a political mission to fulfill.

REFERENCES

Boling, David Alan. (1997). Information Disclosure in Japan: Local Governments Take the Lead. Paper presented to the Fifth International Conference on Japanese Information in Science, Technology, and Commerce, U.S. Library of Congress (July 30–August 1), Washington, D.C.

Chifuren. (1986). *Zenchifuren: Sanjūnen no ayumi* [Chifuren: Thirty Years of History]. Tokyo, Zenkoku Chiiki Fujin Dantai Renraku Kyōgikai.

Davis, Joseph W.S. (1996). *Dispute Resolution in Japan*. The Hague, Kluwer Law International.

Feldman, Eric. (2006). Legal Reform in Contemporary Japan. *Scholarship at Penn Law*. Paper 155. http://1sr.nellco.org/upenn_wps/155

Haley, John O. (1978). The Myth of the Reluctant Litigant. *Journal of Japanese Studies* 4.2 (Summer): 345–70.

Hamada Koichi. (1996). Consumers, the Legal System and Product Liability Reform: A Comparative Perspective Between Japan and the United States. Paper presented to the Conference on Regulation in Japan, Columbia University (March), New York.

Iyori Hiroshi. (1986). Antitrust and Industrial Policy in Japan: Competition and Cooperation. In *Law and Trade Issues of the Japanese Economy: American and Japanese Perspectives*, ed. Gary R. Saxonhouse and Kozo Yamamura. Seattle, University of Washington Press.

Kaneko Akira. (1974). Shōhisha higai to fufuku moshitate [Consumer Damages and Statements of Dissatisfaction]. *Hōritsu no hiroba* 27.12.

Kokumin Seikatsu Sentaa. (1997). *Sengo Shōhisha undōshi* [A History of the Postwar Consumer Movement]. Tokyo, Kokumin Seikatsu Sentaa.

McKean, Margaret A. (1981). *Environmental Protest and Citizen Politics in Japan*. Berkeley, University of California Press.

Maclachlan, Patricia L. (2002a). *Consumer Politics in Postwar Japan: The Institutional Boundaries of Citizen Activism*. New York, Columbia University Press.

Maclachlan, Patricia L. (2002b). Japanese Civil Society in the Age of Deregulation: The Case of Consumers. *Japanese Journal of Political Science* 3.2: 217–42.

Maclachlan, Patricia L. (2000). Information Disclosure and the Center-Local Relationship in Japan. In *Local Voices, National Issues: The Impact of Local Initiative in Japanese Policy-Making,* ed. Sheila A. Smith. Michigan Monograph Series in Japanese Studies, no. 31. Ann Arbor, Center for Japanese Studies, University of Michigan.

Maclachlan, Patricia L. (1999). Protecting Producers From Consumer Protection: The Politics of Products Liability Reform in Japan. *Social Sciences Japan Journal* 2.2 (November): 249–66.

Mochizuki, Toshiro M. (1999). Recent Development: Baby Step or Giant Leap? Parties' Expanded Access to Documentary Evidence Under the New Japanese Code of Civil Procedure. *Harvard International Law Journal* 40 (Winter): 285–312.

Nakamura Masato, Tajima Junzō, and Yonekawa Chōhei. (1992). *Shōhisha no tame no seizōbutsu sekinin no hon* [A Products Liability Book for Consumers]. Tokyo, Nihon Hyōronsha.

Nihon Hōsō Shuppan Kyōkai. (1980). *Nihon no Shōhisha undō* [The Japanese Consumer Movement]. Tokyo, Nihon Hōsō Shuppan Kyōkai.

Shōda Akira and Sanekata Kenji. (1976). *Dokusen kinshi hō o manabu* [Learning About the Anti-Monopoly Law]. Tokyo, Yūhikaku Sensho.

Shufuren. (1998). *Shufuren: 50 shūnen kinen ayumi* [Shufuren: History at the Commemoration of the Fiftieth Anniversary]. Tokyo, Shufurengōkai.

Shufuren. (1978). *Shufuren: 30 shūnen kinen ayumi* [Shufuren: History at the Commemoration of the Thirtieth Anniversary]. Tokyo, Shufurengōkai.

Shufuren. (1974). Jūsu saiban [The Juice Trial]. *Shufuren dayori* (August 15).

Taniguchi, Yasuhei. (1997). The 1996 Code of Civil Procedure of Japan: A Procedure for the Coming Century? *American Journal of Comparative Law* 45 (Fall): 767–91.

Taniguchi, Yasuhei. (1984). The Postwar Court System as an Instrument for Social Change. In *Institutions for Change in Japanese Society,* ed. George DeVos. Berkeley, Institute of East Asian Studies, University of California.

Upham, Frank. 1987. *Law and Social Change in Postwar Japan.* Cambridge, MA, Harvard University Press.

Yamane Hiroko, Seryō Shingo, and Mori Takashi. 1998. Shōhisha dantai wa dokkinhō kanren jiken o dō mita ka [How Have Consumers Viewed Incidents Relating to the Anti-Monopoly Law?]. *Toki to hōrei* 1579 (October).

CHAPTER 6

No Voice in the Courtroom?
Deaf Legal Cases in Japan during the 1960s

Karen Nakamura

Many foreigners puzzle as to why Japanese activist and minority organizations do not seem to use the court system to engage in social and legal change as profligately as their American counterparts. This was not always the case. As other chapters in this volume attest, the 1960s was a particularly dynamic period for Japanese courts. This chapter focuses on the history of one organization, the Japanese Federation of the Deaf (JFD), as it shifted from prewar passivity to postwar litigation in the courts. It looks at the emergence of the first deaf lawyer for the organization, as well as early court cases in which the organization engaged. Ultimately, however, the organization changed strategies to engage in legislative and bureaucratic lobbying in the 1980s, working more cooperatively with the government.

BACKGROUND TO POSTWAR DEAF ACTIVISM

There was not much political activism by deaf people in Japan before the war. The Japanese Federation of the Deaf, the main social and political organization of and for the deaf in Japan, describes the period from 1900–1940 as an "Era of Pleading," during which deaf groups would have to beg for social services from government officers or other people in power. This radically changed in the decades after the war as a new generation of activists took over the organization. This new cohort was active both in the courts and outside of them—filing lawsuits, organizing trial support groups, pushing their cause to newspapers, and running petition drives.

Why was there such an explosion of deaf activism in the postwar period? I do not believe that that deaf activists were politically repressed in the prewar and wartime period and were simply bouncing back after the change in government. The historical record shows that deaf groups were not particularly politically active before the war, and, as with most other groups, there is evidence of willing government cooptation into the war movement.

Nor was it the case that the situation facing the deaf in Japan became worse after the war and during reconstruction, forcing more political mobilization. Interviews with informants born before in the first half of the twentieth century almost unilaterally show that the situation improved after the war: more social rights, more employment opportunities, better education, better social mobility, and so forth (Nakamura 2006a). If anything, deaf people should have been happy with their higher quality of life in the postwar period.

As was noted in other chapters in this volume, the general social and political milieu of postwar Japan is critical for understanding the ability of minority groups in Japan to articulate new forms of activist politics. Steinhoff (this volume) has shown that after the end of the American Occupation in 1952, there was both a resurgence of the left amid strong government repression and violent internal political struggles among groups. Indicative of the growing enmity between the Japanese Socialist Party (JSP) and Japanese Communist Party (JCP), the Buraku Liberation League split in 1955 from the JCP-affiliated National Council for Buraku Liberation (Davis, this volume). The conflict surrounding the U.S.-Japan Joint Security Treaty (more commonly known in Japan as Anpo) in 1959–60 heightened the general sense of political crisis within the left, especially among student groups such as Zengakuren, the national student organization, which split into JSP and non-JCP affiliated (New Left) factions just before the Anpo crisis. This student activism continued well into the 1960s and early 1970s, creating a broader frame (Snow and Benford 1988) for leftist political activism during this period that created a contextual frame for organizing protest in Japan.

The Social Demographics of Postwar Deaf Cohorts

The fervent social context of the postwar period itself does not fully answer how a new generation of deaf political activists was able to take advantage of new framings made possible by the New Left. We also need to explore the special demographic characteristics of the deaf cohorts that emerged in this period. The deaf youth that emerged as leaders in the 1950s and 1960s were qualitatively and physically different from their prewar counterparts. Part of this shift was caused by changes in the epidemiology of deafness and part by changes in the education system (for deaf social movements sparked by similar shifts in other cultural contexts, see Christiansen and Barnart 1995; Baynton 1996; Monaghan 2003).

Immediately after the war and into the early 1950s, there was a mass migration of the population towards urban areas at a time when the physical, medical, and social infrastructures were still rebuilding. The birthrate skyrocketed, but so did various epidemics, some of which (such as rubella or meningitis) caused pre- or postnatal deafness. Compounding this, the Occupation under the Supreme

Command for the Allied Powers (SCAP) brought in powerful new antibiotics, such as streptomycin, which could cure many infectious diseases but which were for children ototoxic; that is, one of the drugs' side effects in young children was deafness. The combination of the rising birthrate, epidemic disease, and the use of ototoxic antibiotics caused the number of deaf children to increase dramatically in the turbulent postwar period. This was a mixture of both prelingually deaf children (those who were deaf at birth and thus never learned a spoken language as their native tongue) and those who were postlingually deaf (those who became deaf in childhood, after they had already acquired spoken Japanese as a primary language).

In 1948, SCAP instituted compulsory education for all citizens including the disabled, who had been excluded from general education up to then. Schools for the deaf (and other disabilities) sprang up in every prefecture in Japan. Because of the very large numbers of deaf children, the schools were crowded and tumultuous. Forty or more students to a single classroom were not unusual, according to my informants. Because transportation systems were quite poor, most of these new schools were residential in nature, and the dorms were similarly packed with students of all age groups.

Somewhat surprisingly, public schools for the deaf in Japan at that time (as more or less now) shared the same curricula as their hearing counterparts. In both hearing and deaf schools, students used the same textbooks, teachers emerged out of the same training programs with the same (lack of) qualifications, wrote the same things on the blackboards, and gave the same lectures. The only difference was that in schools for the deaf, no one could hear the teacher speaking. And when teachers had their backs to their classes, writing on the blackboards, no one could read their lips.

Sociologist Julian Dierkes (2003) explains this as a direct result of pressure by postwar leftists teachers organizations to guarantee equality of education in Japan. Under this mantra, egalitarianism was only possible by ensuring that every Japanese child in the public school system received the same lecture using the same textbook, regardless of social class or geographic region—or ironically, disability. While on the surface it would seem a laudable goal, ensuring that children would not be treated differently based on class status or school district, it entirely failed to accommodate the special education needs of deaf children by preventing them from using curricula based upon visual methods or bilingual programs (such as a mixture of sign language and spoken Japanese).

This pedagogic inflexibility under the mantra of equality created inequality in the classrooms. Compared to their prelingually deafened classmates, students who were postlingually deafened because of streptomycin injections as young children had a huge advantage under this regime; they already had a base of spoken Japanese on which they could build their lip-reading and speech skills, as well as general academic skills such as reading and writing since they had attended regular schools until they had become deaf.

Those who became deaf later in childhood were able to speak Japanese and lip-read with greater ease than their other counterparts. These students, with a strong base in Japanese language, rose to the top of the school system. In the land of the deaf schools, those who became deaf later in childhood were kings (Nakamura 2006b; 2010). For instance, one of these students would later on become the first deaf lawyer in Japan and a leader within the JFD.

Matsumoto Masayuki: First Deaf Lawyer in Japan

In 1939, Matsumoto Masayuki was born in Osaka with normal hearing, but in his third year of elementary school in 1948, Matsumoto contracted epidemic cerebrospinal meningitis and was deafened as a result. He was not allowed to resume schooling in his regular neighborhood school due to his deafness, and he was transferred to the Osaka City School for the Deaf, where he (of course) did extremely well. He recalls in his memoirs that in those days there was still a lot of signing used within the Osaka School for the Deaf, and he picked up signing rather naturally (Matsumoto 1997, 1).

After elementary school, Matsumoto ended up taking most of his junior high and high school classes at a regular (hearing) school. However, most of his friends remained at the school for the deaf, and he remained close to them. After high school, he entered Kyoto University and graduated with a Bachelor's in Law in 1963, passing the bar exam the same year. He spent two years (1964–65) at the Judicial Research and Training Institute, finally registering with the Osaka Bar Association in 1966.

During his college years, Matsumoto became politically active within the Kyoto regional association of the deaf. He became friends with some of the youth group leaders who would later stage the silent coup (pun intended) of the late 1960s that would change the direction of the JFD. These leaders had backgrounds very similar to Matsumoto in that they had also been deafened in childhood and then later attended Kyoto University. They also had strong leanings toward Marxist-Leninist ideals, a political dimension that they largely kept hidden from public view. That these deaf leaders were centered in Kyoto is significant for another reason—the Kyoto-Osaka area was also a central battleground for Buraku organizing and mobilization as well as a center of JCP and student movement organizing. Kyoto was a hotbed for multiple types of protests.

DEAF PROTEST ACTIVITY IN THE 1960s

Kyoto School for the Deaf Protests (1965)

In November 1965, the year before Matsumoto registered with the Bar Association, high school students at the Kyoto Prefectural School for the Deaf started to organize around the issue of high school education. The so-called "3.3 Movement" held a strike at the school on March 3 of the following year. One of the protest leaders, Ooya Susumu, described the motivations for boycotting school:

> We students talked with each other [about what we wanted]: we didn't want classes where there was favoritism toward the students with proper enunciation skills; we wanted classes where everyone could understand; we wanted a school [environment] that everyone could enjoy. We looked closely at the reality of our situation: [that the idea of] entering college was considered a silly fantasy. We weren't even given the option of looking for employment at large corporations; we were expected to work like machines without hope until the end of our lives. We eagerly wanted to meet with all of the teachers to ask the question, "What are we studying for?" (Zenkoku Shuwa Tsūyaku Mondai Kenkyūkai 1994, 14 [translation mine]).

Deaf activist Itabashi Masakuni contextualized the 3.3 Movement in the milieu of post-1960, post-Anpo Japan. He notes that the framing of the high-school student movement was clearly about discrimination from the very beginning. He recalls turning on the TV or opening the newspaper and having the following questions perpetually raised by other social activists in Japan (1991, 360):

- What is democracy?
- What are basic human rights?
- What does it mean to protect our dignity as equal human beings?

It was clear that questions being pushed by leftists and Buraku activists were affecting how deaf students also thought about their role in the new Japan. Under the heading "Why Did These Problems Occur," the Chōkaku Shōgai Kyōiku Kyōto Fōramu (Kyoto Forum on Deaf Education) wrote:

> The social environment surrounding the school for the deaf at the time was one in which the problems caused by the nation's rapid economic growth and environmental pollution were increasingly challenged by local movements and other movements fighting for the protection of various rights.
> The Kyoto Prefectural School Board published its Dōwa [Burakumin] Education Guidelines in 1963. In the year that the [3.3 Movement] "Student Strikes" occurred, the [school board] was making its first steps in the civilized advancement *(bunmeika)* of [equal] education based on the Constitution and the Fundamentals of Education Act. The Kyoto School for the Deaf established its first committee for Dōwa education in 1965. . . . The attitude toward signing was [becoming] stricter, and one week before the Strike, the principal announced at the morning assembly that "I would like you to stop that gesturing

with your hands and speak [with your lips]." (Chōkaku Shōgai Kyōiku
Kyōto Fōramu 1996, ii–iii)

In an environment where the rights of the former Burakumin were being
espoused while at the same time as the linguistic rights of the deaf were being
denied, deaf students felt they had no choice other than to strike. Although the 3.3
Movement resulted in some minor changes at the Kyoto School, the situation in
schools for the deaf did not improve appreciably. The most significant impact of
the 3.3 Movement was perhaps in its broader appeal to Japanese society. The story
was picked up by the major newspapers as well as local and national newsletters
for the deaf. Deaf activists described this and other incidents that occurred in the
same year as clarion call for a "Deaf Human Rights Proclamation" (Itabashi 1991,
360). Deaf organizations around Japan galvanized at the idea of these students
protesting to improve their situation. This led to a new sentiment within the generation emerging out of the postwar context: challenging law enforcement and court
systems was an essential next step in the development of their political acumen.

Deaf Ears at the Police Station
In order for people who are deaf to defend themselves adequately in the criminal
justice system, there need to be provisions made for sign language interpretation. The first mention of interpreters for the deaf appears in the Meiji Civil Proceedings Act of 1891, which was based on European legal codes: "When those
pleading before the court do not understand the Japanese language or are deaf or
otherwise mute, an interpreter shall be present. However, questions may be posed
through writing, and written statements may be obtained from those who are deaf
or mute" (Article 134 of the Civil Proceedings Act of 1890, cited in Zenkoku
Shuwa Tsūyaku Mondai Kenkyūkai 1994, 12 [translation mine]).

Itō Shunsuke, one of the founders of the Japanese Sign Language Interpreters
Association, recalls the first time he was called to interpret:

> In 1949, I became a teacher at the Kyoto Prefectural School for
> the Deaf. I started to learn how to sign and how to be an interpreter.
> The first time I used my sign interpreting skills in public was when I
> was called to the Kyoto City "N" Police Station one day. A young man
> had been arrested for theft. He was uneducated and couldn't read or
> write. Even his signing was difficult to understand. I'm not sure if I
> was really acting in the role of sign language interpreter at the time. I
> put my signature [on the statement] and listed my role as the "sign in-
> terpreter." (Zenkoku Shuwa Tsūyaku Mondai Kenkyūkai 1994, 12–13
> [translation mine]).

Japanese Deaf News (*JDN*), the monthly newspaper of the JFD, reported
with increasing frequency criminal cases involving the deaf in the postwar pe-

riod. This was likely a result of the increased numbers of people who were deaf mentioned earlier, the economic and social devastation of the country at the time, returning veterans with war injuries, growing urbanization, and weakening family support systems that had previously helped to shelter the disabled. I use the *JDN* archives as a primary source to understand how the nascent organization came to use the judicial system in Japan, first defensively and then offensively, in order to mobilize social change.

Early on, the JFD was relatively passive in reacting to court cases. For example, in the February 1952 issue, the *Deaf News* noted the final outcome of the trial of four deaf men arrested in 1948 for armed burglary. In this incident, the victim reported to the police that burglars told him to "Be quiet!" "Where's the money?" "Open the [bureau] drawers from the bottom!" "Shut up!" etc. As the arrested suspects were all reported to be "deaf and mute," there was some question about whether this was a case of mistaken identity. In the trial, which took four years to come to conclusion, two of the indicted men were found guilty while the other two were found innocent (*JDN* 1952 [February 1], 3). There was no mention of any trial support groups or of special legal aid rendered in this case, and the local deaf association did not mobilize to help them.

In the same month, the *Deaf News* also reported the murder of a mother and daughter by a deaf family of four in Gunma Prefecture (*JDN* 1952 [February 1], 2). Three schoolteachers from the Gunma Prefectural School for the Deaf apparently served as interpreters (*JDN* 1952 [March 1], 3). Again, in this case there is no mention of any special support groups or legal aid from the local or national deaf association. These two cases are typical of criminal suits in the 1950s and early 1960s. While the *Deaf News* questioned if the police and prosecutors understood the special circumstances of the deaf, larger issues of human rights had not yet been foregrounded. This was to change by the mid-1960s.

Janome Murder Incident (1965)

The year 1965 was a tumultuous one for the deaf community, and the issue of human rights was very much in the forefront. As mentioned earlier, the students at the Kyoto School were striking while the national deaf association was butting heads with bureaucrats over control of a welfare center for the deaf. There was also a pivotal court case: two deaf men stood accused of murder in what came to be known as the Janome Sushi Restaurant Incident.

Witnesses said the two defendants, Satō Yoshikazu (age 29) and Kido Takashi (age 32), had been provoked into a brawl at the Janome Sushi Restaurant in Tokyo by three hearing men who had been making fun of their deafness and use of signs. Trying to stop the potential fistfight, the owner of the sushi restaurant tried to reason with one of the deaf men. Unfortunately, the deaf man could not read the owner's lips, and further miscommunication ensued. Frustrated, the owner raised his thick wood *geta* sandals and struck one of the young men in the face. The young man fought back and knocked the owner to the ground. The owner apparently struck the back of his head on his way down and subsequently died. The two deaf men were arrested on charges of assault and bodily injury resulting in death (Kawai 1991, 380).

No sign interpreters were provided during their police interrogations, and Kido later signed a confession detailing his role in the incident. The defendants were not provided with any effective way of communicating with their (hearing) lawyers. Although under the constitution defendants in Japan are guaranteed the right to meet with their lawyers without police surveillance, the police held that the sign language interpreters were not legal counsel (*bengonin,* i.e., officers of the court) and insisted on monitoring any meeting with lawyers where interpreters were present. In addition, it was questionable whether the defendants understood their rights (of silence, for example) and were fully aware of the legal proceedings.

The issue of awareness of legal rights, especially the right to silence and non-self-incrimination, has proven to be a problem in the United States as well. Deaf defendants with minimal schooling may not understand the basic concept of "rights" as used within the court system. For example, in a murder case in Maryland in 1975 the defendant signed a Miranda waiver as well as a confession, but there were suggestions that he understood the sign interpretation of "you have the right to an attorney present" as meaning. "it is all right to have an attorney present" (Lane et al. 1996, 354–55). The charges were later dropped. Unskilled court interpreters have interpreted "the right to silence" as "the right to peace and quiet" (i.e., silent as in silent night) and not as "the right to not say anything using sign or any other form of communication in response to questioning."

In the case of the two Japanese deaf men, a trial support group named The Group to Protect Satō and Kido was immediately formed in their defense (see Steinhoff in this volume for the importance of trial support groups in Japan). The *Deaf News* reported that a fundraising campaign by deaf persons, teachers at schools for the deaf, relatives, other civic organizations, ordinary citizens, school students, and others collected ¥120,000 toward their defense costs (*JDN* 1966 [August 15], 6). Unfortunately, they quickly came across an unforeseen roadblock.

According to one of the members, the support group went to all of the law firms in the area in order to hire a private defense team, but one by one all of the lawyers they asked declined the case after they heard that it involved deaf defendants. Finally, the group found one firm that would accept deaf defendants as clients. The support group had similar problems finding qualified interpreters, and then they realized that their problems involved not only injustices within the court system but larger social prejudices and institutional barriers against the deaf as well (Kawai 1991, 381).

Kawai noted that when the parents of one of the defendants visited him in jail, she had to ask a classmate of the defendant to translate what was being said in sign. In those days, parents were told not allow their deaf children to use sign nor to learn it themselves. As a result, many deaf children had very little lingual skills—in both sign and written/spoken Japanese. Of the two defendants, one had graduated from a deaf middle school, while the other had only finished third grade in Taiwan and was functionally illiterate (1991, 381–82).

The Tokyo District Court ruled that Satō was guilty and sentenced him to ten months imprisonment with hard labor, suspended for three years. Kido was sentenced to five years imprisonment with hard labor without a stay of execution (*JDN* 1966 [August 15], 6). The *Deaf News* reported that, as a result, the trial support group changed its name to "The Group to Support Kido's Appeal." The JFD decided at its annual national meeting to lend its full support to this group. In Osaka, a general support group, "The Group to Protect Deaf Persons' Human Rights" was planned. One of the deaf activists involved in the 3.3. Movement recalls that the group eventually formed under the name "The Group to Protect the Legal Rights of Deaf Persons" (Itabashi 1991, 360).

Matsumoto Masayuki, who had just recently joined the bar association, rallied to the cause of the defendants and filed an appeal in late 1966. This was Matsumoto's first appearance as a lawyer for the deaf. His appeal questioned the qualifications of the interpreters provided by the court, especially in regards to whether they properly informed the defendants of the right not to have to provide self-incriminating testimony (e.g., Kido's signed confession). The trial support group protested under the banner of "Give Deaf Persons Justice in the Courtroom!" (*JDN* 1966 [December 15], 4).

According to Kawai Yohsuke, who was involved in the case, the case went to the Appeals Court. Kido submitted numerous personal appeals on his own behalf, but the justices were not able to understand the rather incoherent contents of these letters. The appeal justices affirmed the decision of the lower court but found Kido to have diminished mental capacity. They ruled the sentence be reduced (slightly) from five to four years hard labor (Kawai 1991, 382).

The lawyers were reportedly greatly disappointed at the shallow level of disability awareness shown by the justices. As Kawai points out, the justices did not realize that if Kido was functionally illiterate (as evidenced by his incoherent letters to the justices), there is no way that he could have understood and signed the written police statement/confession that condemned him. Kawai notes that when Kido communicated in sign with Matsumoto, his deaf lawyer, he showed intelligence and full comprehension (1991, 384).

The lawyers thought that, if the judges were able to understand sign language, they would have seen that Kido's mental and linguistic capabilities were normal and would have ruled on the basis of the actual appeal claims, thus setting precedence for the handling of deaf defendants. Instead, they had a pyrrhic victory based on a prejudicial view of Kido as mentally retarded because signing was his native language. Resigning themselves to the situation, the team did not file further appeal (Kawai 2002).

In 1966, at the First National Debate Meeting of the Deaf Youth, there was a panel debate on discrimination, and from the discussions that followed the Youth Section of the JFD was formed. Matsumoto's compatriots, the young Marxist-influenced leaders from Kyoto, took control and steered the JFD onto a new course. The *Deaf News* headline read, "Protecting the Human Rights of the Deaf" (*JDN* 1966 [August 15], 6). The following year, a new age was declared, "The Era of Fighting for Our Rights" (*JDN* 1967 [February 1], 1). One of the principal rights to receive attention on this new front was the right of deaf people to hold driver's licenses. This battle was first fought in the courtroom and, when that did not succeed, through administrative channels.

Taking the State Head On: The Case for Driver's Licenses for the Deaf
The original postwar Japanese Traffic Code prohibited driver's licenses to those who were "deaf, mute, or blind, and so forth." The first mention of driver's licenses in the postwar *Deaf News* was a very small article in 1957 enviously noting that a Swedish deaf man had won an automobile in a lottery. He had already obtained his driver's license, so he was excited by his prize (*JDN* 1957 [November 15], 3).

In the October issue the following year, the *Deaf News* had a front-page article on a Japanese deaf man who had successfully obtained a "Light Vehicle Driver's License" and had driven around the entire Japanese mainland. The article noted that in an "age of rocket ships" and "artificial satellites," it was ridiculous for deaf persons in Japan to have to use bicycles to relay information to each other. Even "the modern convenience of telephones" was not available to the deaf, despite having been invented by Alexander Graham Bell whose wife was deaf (*JDN* 1958 [October 15], 1). The article noted that deaf people in America were treated just like everyone else and were allowed to have driver's licenses. It was time, the author wrote, for Japanese deaf persons to claim their right to drive.

In the October 1960 issue, the *Deaf News* optimistically reported that the traffic law had changed in June of that year so that those who were not totally deaf were now able to obtain driver's licenses. However, in the November issue, the *Deaf News* noted that local prefectural offices had not yet received the proper information from the prime minister's office regarding the new regulations.

For example, Nagano Prefecture was apparently unwilling to issue automobile licenses but would grant moped licenses to deaf individuals who passed the test. The metropolitan police agencies (Tokyo, Osaka, etc.) were all reportedly unwilling to grant driver's licenses, citing the traffic problems found there. When the newspaper asked about those deaf people who had already obtained licenses (such as the aforementioned man who had driven around the mainland), the traffic agency reportedly replied that there might be some individual variation based on each person's hearing level, or that that man had simply been lucky. The newspaper was very unhappy that the situation was unequal based on location and individual circumstances (*JDN* 1960 [November 1], 3).

The January 1961 issue of the *Deaf News* brought more clarity. New driving regulations had been issued as of December of the previous year. Drivers would be required to undergo visual examinations as well as to be tested for their response to the sound of a car horn with a loudness of approximately 90 decibels at a distance of 10 meters (*JDN* 1961 [January 1], 1–2). Unfortunately, even by June of the next year (1962), there were complaints that local area offices were still not allowing deaf individuals to take the driving test (*JDN* 1962 [August 1, 5). Other test centers were apparently not permitting applicants to wear their hearing aids during the hearing tests, which would of course cause them to fail. Op-ed pieces compared Japan unfavorably to the United States and West Germany, where the deaf were allowed to drive (1962 [September 1], 2). A 1965 article even noted that in the United States, eight deaf persons were able to obtain aircraft pilot's licenses (*JDN* 1965 [January 1], 7).

In 1965, the Council on Problems Facing the Deaf announced four major issues that they wanted to see resolved (*JDN* 1965 [May 1], 5):

1. Obtaining driver's licenses
2. Certified social workers for the deaf
3. Captioning of television programs for the deaf
4. Expansion of employment opportunities for the deaf

In its report, the council conducted a survey and noted that while 787 deaf persons had reported that they wanted a driver's license, up to now, only 13 deaf persons in all of Japan had managed to obtain a regular driver's license, while 36 had managed to obtain a Light Vehicle License (*JDN* 1965 [May 1], 5). Clearly, the situation was not optimal for the deaf in Japan.

Frustration was clearly mounting. In late 1967, a young deaf man in Morioka Prefecture named Toishita Mitsuo was arrested for riding a motorcycle without a license (*JDN* 1968 [February 1], 1). The interesting thing was Toishita was more properly hard of hearing than deaf. That is, with a hearing aid he could hear and communicate fairly well. He held a job managing real estate and interacted with hearing people regularly (Matsumoto 1997, 110). Unfortunately, he could not use a telephone with his type of hearing aid, and thus he had to meet people face to face. He had previously applied twice for a driver's license, but he was not permitted to use his hearing aids and so failed the hearing exam both times. Because his job required him to travel all around the city to meet clients, he ended up having to ride his motorcycle without a license.

Toishita had already been fined numerous times for riding his motorcycle without a license (enough that his legal counsel recalls his company even ended up creating an accounting code for traffic code violations for him [Matsumoto 1997, 111]). But the latest citation was the straw that broke the camel's back.

Toishita reportedly came to the conclusion that "this is not only my problem. This is a problem that concerns deaf people all over Japan who are not able to obtain driver's licenses" (*JDN* 1968 [February 1], 1). Rather than accepting the usual summary judgment and paying a fine, he filed a claim in the Morioka District Court on March 15, 1968 arguing his innocence, for the right to drive, and for the invalidation of the law in question. He stated that he was ready to take this to the Supreme Court if necessary.

Matsumoto Masayuki decided to take this case on as Toishita's legal counsel. Matsumoto notes in his memoirs: "This court case was history making in that it represented the first time that institutional bias against those who could not hear was directly challenged. On a personal level, I will never forget the youthful energy that burned inside of me at the time" (Matsumoto 1997, 113).

Matsumoto was then only twenty-nine years of age. Court expenses were paid by a nationwide fundraising campaign on Toishita's behalf. Matsumoto acknowledged in an op-ed piece at the time that winning the case (a finding of innocence for Toishita, indicating the unconstitutionality of the law) "would be very difficult. However, what is important is to show [the nation] where the problems are. In order to unite the Driver's License Movement, we need to fight in the courts" (*JDN* 1968 [February 1], 1).

The arguments made by the defense were that: (1) the driving prohibition was illegal under the Constitution's right to free employment as well as equal treatment under the law; (2) the definition of "deaf person" in the law was left undefined in regards to the level of hearing/audiological ability, which is unconstitutional; and (3) while forbidding automobile licenses was one matter, the law also forbade obtaining motorcycle licenses, which was going too far and was unconstitutional as well (*JDN* 1968 [April 1], 1). The defense made the argument that given that people who are near-sighted were allowed to wear glasses, deaf people should be allowed to wear their hearing aids when taking the hearing test (*JDN* 1969 [January 1], 9).

The JFD created a "Central Headquarters for the Promotion of the Movement for Driver's Licenses" and organized a fundraising campaign with the minimum goal of raising ¥300,000. The estimated cost of the case was expected to be ¥500,000 (*JDN* 1968 [April 1], 1). By June, there was an organized trial support group based in Tokyo named "The Group to Support Toishita's Driver's License" (1968 [June 1], 2). At the third hearing later that month, around twenty deaf persons were in the audience. The *Deaf News* reported that their presence gave a "strong impression" of support for Toishita's case (1968 [July 1], 7).

By late July, the fundraising goal was raised to ¥1 million although only ¥108,667 had been donated by then (*JDN* 1968 [September 1], 1). The central headquarters also created petition forms and distributed them to the prefectural deaf associations. In an unsigned op-ed piece, the editors noted that there were three requirements for a successful social movement: "(1) That the matter being asked for is legitimate; (2) that there is support from the hearing community; and (3) that the movement comes from below [i.e., grassroots]" (*JDN* 1968 [September 1], 1). However, even the *Deaf News* was pessimistic about the chances of winning the case. The editors acknowledged that even if the courts found Toishita innocent on an individual basis, it was unlikely that the Court would rule the traffic law unconstitutional.

The prosecution demanded the maximum sentence of six months imprisonment with hard labor for the traffic infraction of driving without a license. On June 9, 1969, the Morioka District handed down a brief but strict verdict: "The traffic law is appropriate. Defendant Toishita is sentenced to six months hard labor with a two-year suspension" (*JDN* 1969 [July 1], 1). The legal team filed an immediate appeal to the Sendai High Court.

On the first day of the appeal, November 11, 1969, sixty-five deaf people from the neighboring deaf associations showed up at the Sendai High Court. In his opening remarks to the court, lawyer Matsumoto referred to the attention the trial was receiving all across Japan. He noted that many in the audience were deaf, and he asked for sign language interpreters to be present so that the audience could understand the proceedings of the court. The justices agreed to his request, and a Mr. Takahashi of Sendai City stood up and for the first time in Japanese history interpreted the court proceedings in sign for the audience (*JDN* 1969 [December 1], 1). Unfortunately, although this was a great advancement for trial support and deaf rights in the courtroom, the High Court ruled on July 11, 1972, that "in order to protect the safety of the general populace who use public roads, the legal restriction forbidding people who cannot hear from possessing driver's license is a reasonable solution" (*JDN* 1972 [August 1], 1). The legal team filed an immediate appeal to the Supreme Court.

While the appeal was pending in the Supreme Court, the situation outside the courtroom was changing due to political pressure from the media attention. The Police Agency issued new guidelines that stated if the response to the following two questions was positive then the applicant should be considered "not deaf" and allowed to take the examination (*JDN* 1972 [October 1], 7): (1) "Can the applicant understand a simple conversation?" (2) "Can they hear a car horn from ten meters away?"

Applicants were also allowed to wear hearing aids during the examination for the first time (Matsumoto 1991, 375). Rather than changing the law, the administrative definition of deafness was modified to include most (but not all) deaf people. This was yet another example of what Frank Upham (1987) has called Japan's propensity toward "bureaucratic informality."

In January and February of 1974, Toishita Mitsuo obtained not only a motorcycle license but also an automobile license under the new administrative guidelines. He mailed photocopies of both licenses to the Supreme Court as evidence for his case. A few months later, however, the Supreme Court agreed with the lower court rulings: "driving with a hearing aid [was] considered dangerous" (Matsumoto 1997, 123). This final ruling, however, was essentially mooted by the change in administrative practice by the police.

While the courtroom battle was lost, as the deaf political strategists had predicted, the case served to focus broader social and political attention on the right of deaf people to drive, as well as to unify the community around institutional injustices. And on a pragmatic level, it was clear that social change through legislative or bureaucratic action was more efficacious than seeking remedy through the courts.

NEW STRATEGIES IN THE 1970s

The courtroom experiences of the 1960s were important stepping-stones for deaf activists in Japan. They learned that they needed to react quickly to potential incidents, making sure that sign language interpreters were provided early during police interrogations and that defendants knew their rights under the law. They also became aware of broader institutional barriers to their full participation as citizens. In addition, the numerous high profile cases helped build up their competence in handling these cases as well as consolidating their central role in the community.

Even with limited voice in the courtroom, the 1960s were an extremely important growing and learning period for the newly reconfigured JFD. A new generation of leaders had emerged with a different set of values and a vocabulary of "human rights" and "discrimination." While they fought their first battles in the courts, they quickly realized that the public relations value of the courtroom drama was just as important as the actual cases themselves. Political alliances and mass mobilization were key strategies. Not only would they have to awaken the deaf community to what they believed was a class-based struggle, but they would also have to alert greater (hearing) Japan to the problems that deaf members of society were facing.

However, just as changing contextual frames and demographics caused the rise in legal activism in the postwar period in the first place, changing social circumstances led to a shift from the courts to political and administrative realms. The number of incidences of abuse within the police/judicial system dropped at the same time people realized that true power (and resolution of discrimination) would be found in changing the actual legal and administrative framework itself. The JFD realized that this sea change was occurring as early 1969 in the Toishita case. One leader wrote in the *Deaf News*: "The courtroom trial is a weapon in our fight to get a driver's license. But however important that weapon is, *you cannot change the law through the courts.* The [only] way to change the law is through the Diet" (*JDN* 1969 [January 1], 9; emphasis added).

The leaders of the Japanese Federation of the Deaf found the battleground shifting from the judicial system to politics. In 1975, the president of the JFD addressed the National Diet. In 1979, the JFD challenged the Incompetence Law, which held that all deaf and mute people were financially incompetent (i.e., were legally minors).

The 1980s and 1990s yielded a new era of "cooperative welfare" with administrative bureaucrats in the Ministry of Welfare (Nakamura 2002; 2006a). In this struggle, deaf leaders were forced to balance the fruits of closer cooperation with the government against the co-optation of the movement. They resolved it in part by bifurcating their organizational structure into two: local deaf associations functioned as nonprofit service providers in close cooperation with prefectural welfare offices while the national association kept a more activist stance toward the government, lobbying for legal and political change when possible. It is clear, however, that they would not have been able to gain this moral authority vis-à-vis the state without the significant structural frameworks they had established in the previous decades.

References

Baynton, Doug. (1996). *Forbidden Signs: American Culture and the Campaign against Sign Language.* Chicago, University of Chicago Press.

Chōkaku Shōgai Kyōiku Kyōto Fōramu [Kyoto Forum on Deaf Education]. (1996). *Kyotorō "Jugyō Kyohi" sonogo: kōtōbu no kyōiku wo chūshinni* [After the "School Strike" at Kyoto School for the Deaf: Focusing on Education at the High School Level]. Kyoto, Kyoto Forum on Deaf Education.

Christiansen, John B., and Sharon M. Barnart. (1995). *Deaf President Now! The 1988 Revolution at Gallaudet University.* Washington, DC, Gallaudet University Press.

Dierkes, Julian. (2003). *Teaching Portrayals of the Nation: Postwar History Education in Japan and the Germanys.* Ph.D. dissertation. Princeton University.

Garon, Sheldon. (1997). *Molding Japanese Minds: The State in Everyday Life.* Princeton, NJ, Princeton University Press.

Itabashi Masakuni. (1991). Rōa undō no rekishi [The History of Deaf Movements]. In *Atarashii chōkaku shōgaishazō wo motomete* [In the Search for a New Image of Deaf People]. Tokyo, Japanese Federation of the Deaf.

JDN = *Japanese Deaf News.* Monthly newspaper of the Japanese Federation of the Deaf, Tokyo. Although the Japanese title of the newspaper has changed through the years, I use the *JDN* abbreviation in citations to reduce confusion.

Its precedessors were: *Rōa Geppō* [Deaf Monthly Report] (1931; pre-JFD); *Nippon Rōa Shinbun* [Japanese Deaf Newspaper] (1948–49); *Nippon Rōa Nyūsu* [Japanese Deaf News] (1949–52); and *Nihon Chōryoku-shōgai Shinbun* [Japanese Hearing Impairment Newspaper] (1952–).

Kawai Yohsuke. (2002). Personal communication via facsimile and e-mail. May 17.

Kawai Yohsuke. (1991). Chōkakushōgaisha undō [Deaf Movements]. In *Atarashii chōkaku shōgaishazō wo motomete* [In the Search for a New Image of Deaf People]. Tokyo, Japanese Federation of the Deaf.

Kwon, Huck-ju. (1998). Democracy and the Politics of Social Welfare: A Comparative Analysis of Welfare Systems in East Asia. In *The East Asian Welfare Model: Welfare Orientalism and the State*, ed. Roger Goodman, Gordon White, and Huck-ju Kwon, 27–74. London and New York, Routledge.

Kyoto Prefectural Association for the Hearing Impaired. (1996 [1968]). *Jyugyō kyohi: 3.3 Seimei ni kansuru shiryōshū* [Student Strikes: Background Material on the "3.3 Proclamation"]. Kyoto, Kyoto Prefectural Association for the Hearing Impaired.

Lane, Harlan, Robert Hoffmeister, and Ben Bahan. (1996). *A Journey into the Deaf-World*. San Diego, Dawn Sign Press.

Matsumoto Masayuki. (1997). *Rōasha, shuwa, shuwatsūyaku* [Deaf Persons, Signing, Sign Interpreters]. Kyoto, Bunrikaku.

Matsumoto Masayuki. (1991). Hōritsu-mondai wo chūshin ni [Focusing on Legal Issues]. In *Atarashii chōkaku shōgaishazō wo motomete* [In the Search for a New Image of Deaf People]. Tokyo, Japanese Federation of the Deaf.

Monaghan, Leila. (2003). The Development of the New Zealand Deaf Community. *Deaf Worlds: International Journal of Deaf Studies* 19: 36–63.

Nakamura, Karen. (2010). The Language Politics of Japanese Sign Language (Nihon Shuwa). In *Deaf around the World: The Impact of Language*, ed. Gaurav Mathur and Donna Jo Napoli, 316–32. New York, Oxford University Press.

Nakamura, Karen. (2006a). *Deaf in Japan: Signing and the Politics of Identity.* Ithaca, NY, Cornell University Press.

Nakamura, Karen. (2006b). Creating and Contesting Signs in Contemporary Japan: Language Ideologies, Identity, and Community in Flux. *Sign Language Studies* 7.1 (Fall): 11–29.

Nakamura, Karen. (2002). Resistance and Co-optation: The Japanese Federation of the Deaf and Its Relations with State Power. *Social Science Japan Journal* 5.1: 17–35.

Snow, D. A., and R. D. Benford. (1988). Ideology, Frame Resonance and Participant Mobilization. *International Social Movement Research* 1: 197–217.

Tsukuba University School for the Deaf Alumni Association. (1991). *Tsukuba Daigaku Fuzoku Rōgakkō Dōsōkai Hyakunenshi* [The 100 Year History of the Tsukuba University School for the Deaf Alumni Association]. Chiba,

Tsukuba University School for the Deaf Alumni Association.

Upham, Frank K. (1987). *Law and Social Change in Postwar Japan.* Cambridge, MA, Harvard University Press.

Zenkoku Shuwa Tsūyaku Mondai Kenkyūkai [All Japan Sign Interpreter Research Center (AJSIRC)]. (1994). *Kakebita Zentsūken: 20nen no ayumi* [Keep Flying Zentsuken]. Kyoto, Zenkoku Shuwatsūyaku Mondai Kenkyūkai.

CHAPTER 7

Cause Lawyering in Japan: Reflections on the Case Studies and Justice Reform

Daniel H. Foote

Each of the case studies presented in this volume is an important and fascinating story in its own right. Taken together, the case studies enrich our understanding of cause lawyering and the relationship between law and social change in Japan. Despite their rather disparate subjects, the studies dovetail exceptionally well. They show numerous commonalities in the use of law to further social causes, as well as some important differences. They reveal a truly impressive level of creativity in the use of law, and they disclose several common barriers to successful litigation to promote social causes in Japan. As discussed below, a number of recently introduced reforms seek to ameliorate some of those barriers. As these case studies so eloquently show, however, the goal of socially oriented litigation at times is not victory in the court battle itself, but rather victory in the court of public opinion. In short, although this book is entitled *Going to Court to Change Japan*, the courts are only one locus in a much broader battle.

LAW AND SOCIAL CHANGE

For many years, the prevailing stereotypes in the West were that the Japanese people lacked rights consciousness, their courts were invariably passive, and their law played little role in social change. As Patricia Steinhoff observes in her introduction to this volume, the image of nonlitigious Japanese, culturally predisposed not to pursue claims in court, was set forth most notably by Kawashima Takeyoshi in a 1963 essay in English (Kawashima 1963) and later works in Japanese, and that image took firm root in the United States. In his path-breaking 1978 work "The Myth of the Reluctant Litigant," John Haley took direct aim at Kawashima's assertion of a cultural predisposition, pointing instead to numerous systemic factors as the primary explanation for low litigation rates in Japan (Haley 1978). Numerous subsequent studies have explored and elaborated on the impact of systemic factors. If the appearance of Haley's article was not enough, one might think the above stereotypes would have been laid to rest in 1987 with the publication of Frank Upham's outstanding book, *Law and Social Change in Postwar Japan* (Upham 1987). Through four case studies, that book provided seemingly irrefutable evidence of a deep relationship between law and social change. Other works (before and since) have explored that relationship in fields as diverse as health law, tobacco, labor, and even financial regulation. As with so many other stereotypes, however, the stereotypes of nonlitigious Japanese and of a legal system unresponsive to and with little influence on social change have proven deep-rooted, despite strong evidence to the contrary.

Needless to say, the authors included in this volume are all deeply familiar with Haley's and Upham's work. Many of the case studies refer prominently to Haley and Upham, and the authors of the studies contained here evidently have been influenced and inspired by their works. In these studies, the authors have extended the examination to several new fields and have offered many new insights into how social activism utilizes and influences the legal system in Japan. If there was ever any doubt, these studies should finally put to rest the notion that Japanese lack rights consciousness.

CREATIVE USE OF LAW

As Steinhoff and others have observed, the movements discussed in these case studies share a number of organizational characteristics, including use of hotlines, provision of legal assistance, creation of volunteer support groups, and wide-ranging media campaigns. The legal strategies employed in the cases, though, vary widely, and those strategies display a level of creativity that would likely impress even renowned U.S. litigators.

In the consumer cases discussed by Patricia Maclachlan, the various methods employed included civil lawsuits against manufacturers, formal and informal administrative challenges, and efforts to bring about legislative change at both the local and national levels. The union's efforts to combat the employer's bankruptcy, examined by Christena Turner, included no fewer than eight separate cases filed in two district courts and the Tokyo Labor Relations Board, all pursuing separate claims based on numerous different theories (including a lawsuit against the company president in his personal capacity). As discussed by Karen Nakamura, the Japanese Federation of the Deaf and other deaf activists pursued a number of different strategies, including boycotts, protests, and courtroom arguments aimed at educating the judges, as well as efforts at the administrative and legislative levels. In the Sayama case, as discussed by John Davis, Jr., the efforts of the Buraku Liberation League have extended to the international level, through appeals to the United Nations Human Rights Committee, in addition to petitions for retrial (including demands for full disclosure of all evidence held by the prosecution) at the domestic level. The *karōshi* efforts, examined by Scott North, included administrative challenges, civil lawsuits, and legislative efforts. Notably, the litigation strategy included what were, at the time, regarded as novel theories regarding causation of death (including the claim—ultimately recognized by the courts—that even suicide might be caused by excessive work). Finally, my personal favorite example of a creative legal strategy is the use of adult adoption in the Hannichi bombers case, discussed by Steinhoff, as a means for achieving access, *by family members*, for visits to prisoners. That the prison authorities rejected the attempts and then rewrote the regulations to explicitly exclude adopted family members from visitation rights does not make the strategy itself any less impressive as an example of creative lawyering.

The example of adult adoption, in particular, brings to mind two other examples of creative legal strategies in social movements in Japan: the so-called "one share" and "one tree" strategies. The "one share" strategy was used most prominently in the infamous case of Chisso, the corporation primarily responsible for the mercury pollution in Minamata. Victims and their supporters each purchased one share of stock in Chisso, so as to entitle them to attend the annual shareholders meeting, file a motion modifying a management-supported resolution, and voice their protest in person. The chairman of the shareholders meeting responded by declaring the meeting open, submitting the management resolution, declaring it passed by a majority vote, and then declaring the meeting adjourned—all in the course of four minutes, while ignoring those seeking to speak.

The "one tree" strategy also related to environmental issues, in the context of blocking development. In this strategy, each opponent of a development project purchased one tree on land proposed for development or on neighboring land, thereby forcing the developer to negotiate separately with each opponent and also ensuring each opponent a direct personal economic stake sufficient to confer standing to sue in an effort to enjoin the project. Of course, by agreeing to sell trees separately from the underlying land, the landowner greatly reduced his or her ability to manage or dispose of the property. Hence, adopting this strategy required the existence of landowners so deeply opposed to the development in question they would be willing to encumber their land in that way.

A similar strategy is the so-called "one *tsubo* landlord" campaign adopted by those opposed to U.S. military bases in Okinawa. In that strategy, owners of land being used, over their opposition, for bases agreed to transfer very small parcels of their land (in many cases even smaller than the "one *tsubo*," a Japanese measure equal to approximately 40 square feet, referred to in the name of the movement) to others opposed to the bases (Arasaki 1998).

SOLIDARITY

The adult adoption, one share, and one tree strategies each pursued specific legal aims, but all three also aimed at a broader common objective: achieving solidarity among supporters. That in turn ties to a broader commonality among all the case studies in this volume: all involve movements.

As the case studies reveal, solidarity plays a wide range of roles in these movements. One role, noted by nearly all the authors, is in overcoming the social stigma attached to filing lawsuits. With reference to the pollution and thalidomide cases of the late 1960s and 1970s, in "Myth of the Reluctant Litigant" Haley pointed to social stigma as one barrier to filing lawsuits, mentioning as causes for such stigma "a sense of 'shame' for physical and mental deformity, constraints on individual initiative and 'selfish' behavior imposed by the demands of community unity and group consciousness, and hostility against an association with . . . a leftist, antigovernment cause reflected in the politics of the lawyers who dominated the conduct of these trials" (Haley 1978, 367).

To a greater or lesser degree, the concern over potential stigma must have arisen in virtually all the cases discussed in this volume, as well. Toishita Mitsuo, for example, must have felt considerable trepidation when he elected not to take the easy route of simply paying a fine for driving without a license, but rather suing to invalidate the law prohibiting deaf persons from obtaining driver's licenses—in the process publicly highlighting his own disability. One can easily imagine that support from the Japanese Federation of the Deaf, providing the imprimatur that Toishita was acting not just so he himself could keep his job, but was representing the interests of the entire deaf community, greatly helped in overcoming that stigma. Similarly, if individual consumers had brought claims seeking damages for mislabeled "fruit juices" or overpriced kerosene, they might have been branded by the media and the general public as overly sensitive, selfish kooks. But when the claims were brought under the auspices of Shufuren, representing the interests of consumers from throughout Japan, the image shifted dramatically, from selfishness to upholding the public interest. To offer a parallel from the United States, when a single consumer sued McDonald's for burns suffered because her coffee was too hot and was awarded nearly three million dollars in damages, she was promptly labeled by the media as a greedy example of the excesses of the U.S. civil justice system. Had the claim been brought under the auspices of a major consumer organization, with public relations efforts highlighting the hundreds of other customers who reportedly also had suffered severe burns from scalding coffee, many to their genital areas, as was the case with the plaintiff in that case, the public reaction—and the resulting stigma—might have been far different.

In some of the other cases, it is more questionable whether the perceived stigma would have deterred lawsuits even if there had been no support groups. In both the *karōshi* and bankruptcy cases, for example, one of the reasons employees worked without protest in the first place was fear over the stigma of protesting publicly coupled with the concrete fear of loss of job. Once the employee had died (in the former case) or the company had expired (in the latter), the stigma presumably would have been greatly attenuated; there inevitably would be a great sense of outrage and there would also be far less to lose from bringing a lawsuit. To again offer a parallel from the United States, a number of years ago it was reported that, after a major meat-packing plant announced it was going out of business, over a quarter of the employees filed workers compensation claims, primarily relating to carpal tunnel syndrome. The employer sought to portray these claims as an abuse of the workers compensation system. At least equally plausible, though, is that the workers had been suffering in silence, fearing that filing claims might endanger their continued employment. Once the factory announced it was closing, they had little to lose from filing claims.

Needless to say, solidarity plays countless other roles in addition to lessening stigma. Among the notable other roles reflected in nearly all of these case studies are: providing financial support for litigation and other activities, assembling information (and thereby to some extent trying to fill the hole left by the dearth of effective discovery mechanisms), and offering mutual support through what in almost all cases were very long trials.

LITIGATION ONLY PART OF BROADER STRATEGY

This collection of case studies is entitled *Going to Court to Change Japan*. Yet the court proceedings were part and parcel of much broader strategies. In all the cases, efforts were aimed at administrative agencies or the legislature in addition to the courts. In every case, though, the ultimate target was the general public—or, in many of the cases, various "publics."

The activities on behalf of the Hannichi bombers and Red Army defendants, for example, were aimed in part at the community of other radicals and potential radicals, in an effort to give them heart and perhaps stir them into action. That objective presumably is the reason the Japanese authorities were so adamant about keeping the testimony closed in those cases; the Japanese government did not want to provide the defendants with a public forum. As examples of other "publics" to which the cases were aimed: The bankruptcy case was in part a call to other unions, in an effort to build union solidarity. The *karōshi* cases were an appeal to other victims, potential victims, and workers suffering long overtime hours in silence, as well as their families. And for decades, the Sayama case has served as a rallying cry for Buraku residents.

In all the cases, however, the ultimate objective was to reach beyond these narrow "publics" and influence the views of the public as a whole, and thereby to change Japan. The movements recognized that winning individual court battles, or even winning new administrative policies or new legislation, would be of limited value in achieving true reform unless accompanied by a shift in people's thinking and in society as a whole. At the same time, they recognized that one of the best ways to assure success at the judicial, administrative, and legislative levels was to bring about a shift in public views and demonstrate that shift to the relevant authorities. In short, public attitudes and meaningful legal reform go hand in hand. With this in mind, each of the cases involved coordinated efforts to raise consciousness and understanding, of which the court battles were one part.

As the case studies reveal, the movements utilized a broad range of tools in their efforts to influence public opinion. Hotlines not only served as a vehicle for gathering information, but the publicity surrounding them also helped to raise awareness of the relevant concerns among the general public, and coverage of the results of the hotlines helped to establish the gravity of the issues. Other direct means of spreading information included newsletters, letter-writing campaigns, public education sessions, and the like. By far the most important tool for influencing public opinion was the mass media, and the movements undertook a broad range of efforts to persuade the mass media to take up their causes. With respect to the trials themselves, each court session throughout the long proceedings provided a new photo opportunity—a chance for large crowds of supporters to appear with banners and placards in front of Tokyo District Court, the Supreme Court, or some other courthouse—and each session afforded a new opportunity for the lawyers and other representatives of the movement to appeal to the mass media for coverage and thereby keep the dispute in the public eye.

To these movements, the courts were just one part of the overall struggle. Indeed, there are striking indications that the courts were regarded as just another element in the policy-making structure, to be treated in much the same way as the other branches of government. In her chapter on the consumer movement, Maclachlan states that most consumer activists "are poorly versed in the fine art of lobbying politicians and bureaucrats." From reading these case studies, however, one receives the impression that courts, as well as politicians and bureaucrats, were viewed as a proper object for lobbying. In nearly all these cases, supporters undertook demonstrations, sit-ins, and letter-writing campaigns aimed at the courts and even at the individual judges themselves. The trial support groups described so vividly by Steinhoff are not limited to New Left criminal defendants, but are, as she notes, characteristic of all types of Japanese social movements that utilize the courts to press their claims. Davis provides one indelible image of these groups: the sculpture of Buraku Liberation League protesters hoisting the league's flag while demonstrating before riot police in front of the Supreme Court. And North offers a concrete example of efforts to influence judges' thinking through courtroom actions by supporters in a *karōshi* case: "The unionists attended the trial sessions and could be counted on to mutter and grunt derisively in response to the statements of defense witnesses. . . . Mrs. Hiraoka's lawyers thought that this peanut gallery behavior had a beneficial effect on the judges as long as it was kept within reason."

Judges are human; they are not insusceptible to the powers of suggestion, conscious or subconscious. Nonetheless, in Japan, as in the United States, judges regard themselves as neutral and impartial; they regard lobbying as highly inappropriate; and they view the courtroom as sacrosanct. Many Japanese judges also personally experienced disrupted trials in the late 1960s and early 1970s, when trial support group activity was at a peak. From this standpoint, it is little surprise that, as Steinhoff reports, half the prohibitions listed at the entrance to Tokyo District Court relate to protest activities and protest paraphernalia.

At the same time, the scope of trial support group activity in connection with litigation by all types of social movements in Japan serves as testament to the fact that the ultimate battle is for the hearts and minds of the public, which is not necessarily tied to success in any given case. Indeed, when one examines the various court cases discussed in these case studies, the losses by the social movements substantially outnumber the victories. Yet, when one expands the consideration to the role of the court battles in raising people's consciousness, and to the ultimate impact on society, the success rate is more impressive.

Many of the authors express pessimism about the relative lack of progress. Steinhoff, for example, states that, in the face of the protests, the "Japanese criminal justice system . . . has devised more severe policies to circumvent the resistance of suspects and defendants who use the support system." North observes that, with the current seemingly never-ending stagnation in the Japanese economy, pressure on workers is, if anything, intensifying. He points to business efforts to water down or eliminate many of the legal provisions that limit working hours, and he reminds us that, "in the absence of strong unions, it is widely believed that . . . revisions [to the Labor Standards Act], carried out in the name of gender equality, will put women in the same unprotected position [with regard to long working hours and *karōshi*] as men." "Union leaders," reports Turner, ". . . comment ... that their struggles taught capitalists 'how to go bankrupt' while avoiding worker-initiated legal action." And efforts to obtain a retrial for Ishikawa Kazuo, the defendant in the Sayama case, have been rejected yet again.

Even in these respects, though, one should not underestimate the impact the movements have had. In the criminal context, suspects today enjoy greater rights to meet with counsel than in the past, and, as discussed further below, important recent reforms have expanded access to publicly provided counsel and access to discovery. As North observes, the current economic climate has left many workers happy just to have jobs and unwilling to risk their employment by protesting over working hours. Yet, as he also observes, the *karōshi* movement has achieved major successes at the administrative level, with steady relaxation of the standards for recognizing *karōshi*, along with a great change in public attitudes. As Turner notes, employers may have learned how to go bankrupt without facing legal claims by workers, but in order to do so the employers have to meet certain legal standards, including showing good faith efforts to protect jobs. In this respect, union struggles of the type she discusses have helped to place limits on employer behavior. And, while Ishikawa has not won acquittal or a retrial, one can easily imagine that the mass protests may have played some role in the commutation of his death sentence and his release on parole. Given the lack of transparency regarding criminal investigations, one can only hope that targeting of Buraku residents as suspects for major crimes, as reportedly occurred in the Sayama case, is a thing of the past; there can be no doubt that the protests surrounding the case focused widespread attention on that issue.

Thus, even when the court cases themselves have ended in defeat, the movements frequently have achieved successes in administrative or legislative settings or in other ways. And the publicity surrounding the court cases often has played an important role in those other successes. Paradoxically, on occasion failure in court may be more effective in the long run than victory. As Maclachlan observes in connection with consumer litigation, "litigation is often instrumental in galvanizing public opinion in support of long-term legislative objectives. Plaintiffs do not have to win in order to accomplish their political aims. In fact, defeat may actually work to the advantage of . . . advocates by stoking a sense of outrage among movement members, their allies, the general public, and even erstwhile opponents of . . . causes; these sentiments can in turn translate into pressure on the political system for comprehensive legislative reform [tense changed]." A striking example from the consumer context is the juice trial, in which the courts' rejection of the suit out of hand helped to galvanize the movement for legislative reform. Similarly, in the context of the deaf discussed by Nakamura, Toishita's conviction for driving without a license, upheld by the courts in brief and seemingly unfeeling opinions, generated media attention and political pressure that led the National Police Agency to change standards for granting licenses. In sum, the court battles in these case studies had great significance, regardless of victory or defeat in the litigation itself.

Barriers to Litigation and Reforms

As mentioned earlier, in "Myth of the Reluctant Litigant" Haley noted the impact of social stigma as one factor discouraging litigation in some contexts, but the primary focus of that article is on systemic and structural factors that function as barriers to litigation in Japan. Each of the case studies in this volume confirms the impact of such systemic and structural barriers. Accordingly, in closing it may be worth reflecting on some of the common barriers to litigation faced by movements in the past, together with the likely impact of recent reforms.

Barriers

Each of the movements faced similar hurdles to pursuing litigation. These included, most notably, barriers to access to the litigation process, lack of legal and other technical expertise, and lack of information.

Barriers to access included difficulties in establishing standing and the lack of a class action mechanism. In the cases discussed in this volume, those concerns were especially problematic in the consumer context, but class action, standing, and other limitations on qualification to bring suit affect many other potential challenges to administrative and corporate actions. The single greatest barrier to access, however—and one that affected all the cases—was the cost of litigation. Even though legal counsel offered their services on a *pro bono* basis in nearly every case, pursuing litigation involved a host of other expenses. In each of the cases, the network of supporters provided contributions to help defray the costs of the legal battles, and some movements were able to tap into support from other sources, such as the Tokyo Metropolitan Government in connection with the kerosene litigation. Yet cost was a major concern in each of the cases.

A second common hurdle was lack of legal and technical expertise. Victims, defendants, and movement members, for the most part, had little knowledge of or experience with the legal system. The movements depended heavily on the involvement of committed lawyers. The lawyers not only helped plot legal strategy; they also educated supporters about the law, their rights, and other matters. In many of the cases, including *karōshi* cases and various consumer and deaf legal cases, medical or other expert knowledge also was essential, so the involvement of other experts was crucial. Locating lawyers and other experts willing to take on the causes—usually on a *pro bono* basis—sometimes was a matter of fortuity, as when Mrs. Hiraoka found attorney Matsumaru Tadashi when she placed a call to a *karōshi* hotline. But in many of the cases it must have been much more difficult to find committed lawyers. Moreover, one can easily surmise that many other movements were far less fortunate in finding competent and committed legal representation.

A major reason for this situation has been the scarcity of lawyers in Japan. Until 1991, only approximately 500 candidates per year passed the bar exam; of that number, between 100 and 150 became judges and prosecutors, leaving under 400 new practicing lawyers each year. The number of successful candidates gradually increased thereafter, but even as of 2003 fewer than 1,200 candidates passed the bar exam. As of that same year, Japan, with a population of over 130 million, still had fewer than 20,000 practicing lawyers, most of them located in the Tokyo and Osaka areas. Under those circumstances, finding lawyers willing to take on new causes was not easy. With broader access to legal representation, it seems likely that many more movements might have pursued litigation in their efforts to change Japan.

A third common hurdle for litigation was lack of information. In all of the cases, one of the great struggles was to obtain information necessary to prove claims or to refute claims of the other side. The Hiraoka *karōshi* case was unusual, in that Mr. Hiraoka had kept, in his own home, records of his working hours and duties, his medical records, a personal diary, and other documents. These alone would not have been sufficient to prove death from overwork, but they were instrumental in structuring the case, in pointing the way to other relevant information, and in refuting many of the company's allegations. In most of the other cases reported here, the litigants did not have access to such a treasure trove of information, but instead had to assemble information from a wide range of sources. Hotlines served as one means of collecting information, albeit largely anecdotal information. Supporters aided in providing information to which they had access and in searching for information from other sources. And lawyers and other professionals undertook extensive research, as well. Notably, the tool for collecting information that would be at the very top of the list in the United States—demanding disclosure of relevant information from the other side, through the discovery system—did not play a significant role in any of these case studies. Even after recent reforms, the civil discovery system in Japan remains limited in scope, and the criminal discovery system is even narrower. Indeed, expansion of access to information is itself one of the causes espoused in two of the case studies reported here: consumer groups were among the groups behind the push for information disclosure laws and an expansion in civil discovery, and one of the major objectives of the Sayama case movement has been an expansion of criminal discovery.

Reforms

Recent reforms affect all three of the above hurdles. As Maclachlan reports, amendments to the Code of Civil Procedure in 1996 expanded civil discovery, and the Information Disclosure Act, enacted in 1999, greatly expanded access to government information. Over the past dozen years, broad reforms to many other aspects of the justice system also have been undertaken. The prime reform agent was the Justice System Reform Council, a special advisory panel convened in 1999 by then-Prime Minister Obuchi Keizō, which undertook a comprehensive reexamination of the entire justice system. With the case studies in this volume in mind, it bears special note that the thirteen members of the Reform Council included Yoshioka Hatsuko, Secretary-General of Shufuren, and Takagi Tsuyoshi, at the time the Vice President (and later President) of Rengo, the Japan Trade Union Confederation. In the council's deliberations, they served as effective advocates for the interests of consumers, labor, and other social causes and sought to ensure proper attention was given to these types of concerns.

In its final recommendations, issued in June 2001, the Reform Council called for major reforms to civil justice, criminal justice, the legal profession, and other aspects of the justice system (Shihō Seido Kaikaku Shingikai 2001). The proposed reforms related to all three of the hurdles mentioned above, along with many other aspects of the justice system.

With regard to access, the Reform Council called for reductions in filing fees, the expansion of court services in the evenings and on holidays, and other measures to increase convenience of the courts. In addition, to provide greater access to legal services for those with limited means, the Reform Council recommended a major new system for provision of legal assistance. To facilitate the pursuit of claims in cases involving many victims, each with low individual damages (prime examples of which are the juice and kerosene consumer cases), the Reform Council called for consideration of introducing the right of group action, whereby an organization would be permitted to represent the interests of victims. In another broad set of reforms designed to make the justice system more accessible and effective, the Reform Council called for various measures to speed up trials.

Expanding the availability of competent legal services was another major aspect of the Reform Council's recommendations. With the goal of increasing both the size and quality of the legal profession, the Reform Council called for a major expansion in the number of lawyers, together with a fundamental change in the legal training system. On the former point, the Reform Council recommended increasing the number of passers on the bar exam to 3,000 per year by about 2010. At the same time, the Reform Council called for establishing a new tier of law schools, three-year professional schools at the graduate level bearing strong similarities to the U.S. law school system, intended to ensure better training for the legal profession and to enhance diversity of the profession (at least in terms of diversity in academic disciplines pursued at the undergraduate level and diversity in societal experience).

With regard to access to information, the Reform Council recommended further expansion in methods for collection of evidence for civil cases and improvements in access to experts for medical and other cases entailing technical knowledge. In the criminal context, the Reform Council called for expanded disclosure of evidence, with the adoption of rules clearly setting forth the timing and scope of discovery. Another important reform recommended for the criminal justice system was expansion of the right to publicly provided counsel for suspects upon issuance of a detention order (as opposed to upon indictment, as in the prior system).

In addition, the Reform Council recommended various measures to enhance the openness of the justice system and popular participation in it. The recommendation that received the most attention was the call for introduction of a system for lay participation in judging criminal cases. The Reform Council also called for greater participation by the people in a wide range of matters relating to the justice system as a whole, including the appointment of judges and the management of the courts, public prosecutors' offices, and bar associations, and for expanded disclosure of information by the courts, prosecutors offices, and bar associations.

One could easily imagine that proposals for reform of this scope would wither and gradually recede to a distant memory. That, after all, is essentially what occurred with the last prior major effort at justice system reform in Japan, the Provisional Justice System Investigation Committee. That twenty-member committee met for two years, from 1962–64, and issued a final set of recommendations that bore many similarities to the Reform Council's recommendations of nearly forty years later, including a recommendation for a major increase in the size of the legal profession. Most of that committee's recommendations soon faded into oblivion. Such was not the fate of the Reform Council's recommendations. To the contrary, Koizumi Shin'ichirō, who was Prime Minister at the time the Reform Council issued its recommendations, endorsed the recommendations; and the Cabinet promptly established a Headquarters for Promotion of Justice System Reform, along with twelve expert advisory committees for each of the major areas of reform, together with a detailed timetable for passage of essential legislation and implementation of the reforms.

Reform of legal training and the legal profession was deemed fundamental to the success of many of the other reforms, so that project was placed at the top of the agenda. The new system of legal education commenced in April 2004, and a new bar exam was instituted beginning in 2006. In the face of growing resistance, especially from members of the Japanese bar (many of whom are concerned over increased competition), the goal of increasing the number of passers on the bar exam to 3,000 per year by about 2010 has not been attained. After reaching somewhat over 2,000 passers in 2008, the number of passers has remained at that level ever since (and, as of this writing in 2014, there is considerable pressure to reduce the number of passers). Even so, by 2014 the total number of lawyers had risen to over 35,000—twice what it had been at the turn of the century.

Since the Reform Council went only so far as to recommend further study of the group action and class action systems, it is perhaps unsurprising those reforms have not yet been undertaken. Yet a very broad range of other reforms recommended by the Reform Council have been implemented. These include expansion in civil and criminal discovery, expansion of the right to publicly provided counsel for criminal suspects, establishment of a new nationwide legal assistance network, enactment of an act aimed at speeding up trials, establishment of a new system for handling individual labor disputes, and various reforms to the administrative litigation system, including some expansion in standing, increased access to evidence, and expanded rights to preliminary relief. In what is without question the single reform that has attracted the most attention, the new lay participation system for judging criminal cases—the so-called *saiban'in* system—went into effect in mid-2009. Under that system, mixed panels consisting of three professional judges and six lay members are responsible for judging serious criminal cases, with their shared responsibility extending to sentencing as well as determination of guilt. In another significant difference from the U.S. jury system, use of the *saiban'in* system is mandatory for cases subject to it; neither the prosecution nor the defense has the right to opt out. Taken as a whole, many of the reforms, especially those to the criminal justice system, reflect the desire to foster a more robust adversary system in Japan (Foote 2010, 35–40). It should be noted that even the above list of reforms is only partial. For an overview of the Reform Council and summary of the major reforms, see Foote (2007).

As the above list reflects, the past decade or so has witnessed a very wide array of reforms to the Japanese justice system, which touch in various ways on each of the case studies in this volume. These reforms seem certain to have a major impact on Japanese society and on the future of cause lawyering in Japan. In closing I might briefly address two of the developments that I regard as most significant: the push for greater transparency and the expansion in the legal profession.

The initial promise of the expanded civil discovery mechanism has been muted by highly restrictive judicial interpretations, such as decisions giving corporations broad leeway to refuse to disclose documents if they were drawn up only for internal use and "disclosure might impair the decision-making process." In addition, the new criminal discovery system is subject to numerous conditions. Nonetheless, the very enactment of these discovery systems reflects an important shift in thinking, and it is noteworthy that in an early decision interpreting the criminal discovery provisions, the Supreme Court construed the discovery duty rather broadly (Foote 2010, 35–36, 39). Furthermore, the Information Disclosure Act has proven to be a valuable tool for gaining access to government information. It—together with the change in public views it reflects—has resulted in greater transparency and has helped reduce the sense of unreviewable administrative discretion. Increased disclosure of information by the courts, prosecutors' offices, and bar associations and greater popular participation in the management of those institutions reflect and reinforce the same trends toward transparency and accountability.

The trend toward greater transparency is by no means absolute. As its title implies, the Personal Information Protection Act, passed in 2003, provides important protections for personal information. At the same time, its provisions are sufficiently broad to provide justification for refusals to disclose a wide range of information. In a more recent development, the so-called State Secrets Act (Act for the Protection of Special Secrets), passed in late 2013, has come under widespread criticism by the media, academics, transparency advocates and many others, as a vehicle that may allow the government of Japan to hide important or embarrassing information from the public.

Although fewer than 2,500 cases per year are subject to the *saiban'in* system, the introduction of that system has focused tremendous public attention on the criminal justice system. And, despite steadfast resistance by the police and prosecutors, in late April 2014 a major government council recommended mandatory taping (video or audio) of interrogations of detained suspects in two categories of cases. The debate that led to this recommendation arose in part from revelations of improprieties by police and prosecutors, including fabrication of evidence by a high-ranking prosecutor, in evident efforts to induce confessions supporting scenarios they had already concocted. The reform recommendation has been criticized for not going far enough. Still, in view of the past adamant resistance by police and prosecutors to anything smacking of transparency, achieving the taping of the interrogation process would be a major development indeed.

The increase in the size of the legal profession is itself closely connected to these same trends. The Reform Council positioned that increase as an essential step in a fundamental shift in Japanese society, from an "advance control/adjustment type society," premised on extensive administrative discretion, to "an after-the-fact review/remedy type society," with clear, publicly announced rules and a transparent decision-making process. The increase in the size of the bar has important implications for many other aspects of Japanese society, as well. While raising the number of lawyers will not ensure even distribution of legal services nor access to legal services for all who need them, the increase will help to alleviate the dearth of legal professionals. Moreover, the reforms in legal education had been expected to help bring broader perspectives into legal practice by facilitating entry into law school and thereafter into the legal profession for those who have specialized in fields other than law. As of mid-2014, the promise of facilitating entry into the legal profession by those who majored in fields other than law at the undergraduate level is in danger of being lost. To date, the pass rate on the new bar exam by those who majored in fields other than law has been only approximately half as high as the pass rate for those who majored in law, and on the 2013 bar exam, the pass rate for the nonlaw cohort was a mere 16.6 percent. Not surprisingly, given those statistics, applications to the graduate level law schools by nonlaw majors have plummeted. In part due to pressure to focus on bar exam subjects, the new law school system has not yet lived up to initial hopes in other respects as well, including clinical education and internationally oriented offerings. For detailed discussions of the legal education reforms and the challenges those reforms have faced, see Foote (2011; 2013).

Although the reforms have not fully achieved their initial promise, one might assume these developments, coupled with improvements for access to experts in technical fields, should help litigants involved in social causes in obtaining necessary expertise. Some members of the legal profession have suggested that just the opposite result might occur. The rationale for this view runs essentially as follows: "The relatively limited competition in the Japanese legal profession in the past has afforded lawyers with an assured livelihood. This, in turn, has helped foster cause lawyering. Lawyers concerned with social causes have enjoyed the wherewithal to undertake representation relating to those causes on a *pro bono* basis, without worrying about remuneration; the abundance of other well-paying work has afforded them that freedom. With the increase in competition resulting from expansion in the bar, however, that freedom will be lost. Even lawyers who are deeply concerned about social causes will feel that they have little choice but to devote themselves to paying clients and will be reluctant to undertake activities on a *pro bono* basis."

I have always felt these fears were vastly overblown, if not completely unwarranted. To the contrary, I have assumed, expanding the legal profession should lead to an increase in the number of lawyers committed to social causes. And, as one who has been heavily involved in the legal education reform process, I like to think the new system of legal education has much to offer, as well.

It remains too soon to offer a definitive assessment on this issue, but I believe the early returns vindicate my views. As one would expect given the magnitude of the recent increase in the size of the bar, legal services have become more widely available. As one example, the past few years have witnessed a substantial rise in the number of lawyers practicing in areas of so-called "lawyer scarcity." Developments with perhaps more direct relevance to cause lawyering include the following: In recent years a number of bar associations, including the Osaka bar association and all three of the Tokyo bar associations, have introduced mandatory *pro bono* requirements for lawyers registered in those associations. The number of lawyers taking on responsibility as publicly provided counsel in criminal cases has risen substantially. In addition to the government-established Japan Legal Support Center (the new legal aid network commonly referred to as Hō Terasu in Japanese, which has offices in every prefecture and branch offices in many additional locations), the bar associations have fostered the establishment of so-called *kōsetsu jimusho* (literally "publicly established law offices"). These offices actually are established under the auspices of and with financial support from the Japan Federation of Bar Associations or local bar associations in many locations throughout Japan. Most of these *kōsetsu jimusho* are located in areas of lawyer scarcity, but a recent development has been the establishment of urban *kōsetsu jimusho* specializing in criminal defense. In another recent development with potential significance for cause lawyering, some recent graduates of the new law schools have begun work at nongovernment organizations.

As a final note, legal education appears to be making a contribution to cause lawyering. Many of the new law schools have established special programs, clinics, or classes in such fields as human rights, environmental law, labor law, health and welfare, consumer rights, and *pro bono* lawyering. Here too, some of the initial impetus has been dissipated by the pressure to focus on bar exam subjects. Still, a number of lawyers who have been heavily involved in cause lawyering themselves—including lawyers who have worked on *karōshi, enzai* (miscarriage of justice), information disclosure, and consumer rights issues—are teaching at the new law schools. It seems safe to assume they are imparting to their students not only a broad range of skills needed for successful advocacy, but a sense of passion and commitment.

In sum, overall the reforms hold considerable promise for cause lawyering. The reforms do not go as far as many advocates would have wished, and they certainly do not guarantee success in litigation, but they should facilitate future efforts to go to court to change Japan.

REFERENCES

Arasaki, Moriteru. (1998). On One-*tsubo* Antiwar Landlords. *JPRI Critique* 5.3 ("Okinawan Activists in Their Own Words") (March). Accessed at: <http://www.jpri.org/publications/ critiques/critique_V_3.html>.

Foote, Daniel H. (2013). The Trials and Tribulations of Japan's Legal Education Reforms. *Hastings Int'l & Comp. L. Rev.* 36: 369–442.

Foote, Daniel H. (2011). Internationalization and Integration of Doctrine, Skills and Ethics in Legal Education: The Contrasting Situations of the United States and Japan. *Hōshakaigaku* 75: 8–70.

Foote, Daniel H. (2010). Policymaking by the Japanese Judiciary in the Criminal Justice Field. *Hōshakaigaku* 72: 6–45.

Foote, Daniel H. (2007). Introduction and Overview: Japanese Law at a Turning Point. In *Law in Japan: A Turning Point*, ed. Daniel H. Foote, xix–xxxix. Seattle and London, University of Washington Press.

Haley, John O. (1978). The Myth of the Reluctant Litigant. *Journal of Japanese Studies* 4: 359–90.

Kawashima, Takeyoshi. (1963). Dispute Resolution in Contemporary Japan. In *Law in Japan: The Legal Order in a Changing Society*, ed. Arthur T. von Mehren, 41–72. Cambridge, MA, Harvard University Press.

Shihō Seido Kaikaku Shingikai [Justice System Reform Council]. (2001). *Shihō seido kaikaku shingikai ikensho—21 seiki no Nihon o sasaeru shihō seido* [Recommendations of the Justice System Reform Council–For a Justice System to Support Japan in the Twenty-First Century]. June 12. Translation into English available at: <http://www.kantei.go.jp/foreign/policy/sihou/singikai/990612_e.html>.

Upham, Frank K. (1987). *Law and Social Change in Postwar Japan*. Cambridge, MA, Harvard University Press.

Contributors

John H. Davis, Jr. is Assistant Professor of Sociology/Anthropology at Denison University, where he is also affiliated with Black Studies, East Asian Studies, and International Studies. He is a sociocultural anthropologist who specializes in Buraku studies, ethnographic approaches to human rights, and the anthropology of race.

Daniel H. Foote has been Professor of Law at the University of Tokyo since 2000, specializing in sociology of law. As of fall 2014, he has assumed a joint appointment and is now also Professor of Law at the University of Washington School of Law. He has written on numerous aspects of Japanese and comparative law, with major research interests including the judiciary, the legal profession, criminal justice, labor and employment law, dispute resolution, and legal education. His works include *Law in Japan: A Turning Point* (editor and contributor) (University of Washington Press, 2007) and several books in Japanese.

Patricia L. Maclachlan is Associate Professor of Government and Asian Studies at the University of Texas at Austin. She is the author of *Consumer Politics in Postwar Japan: The Institutional Boundaries of Citizen Activism* (Columbia University Press, 2002) and *The People's Post Office: The History and Politics of the Japanese Postal System, 1871-2010* (Harvard University East Asia Center, 2011), as well as co-editor of *The Ambivalent Consumer: Questioning Consumption in East Asia and the West* (Cornell University Press, 2006).

Karen Nakamura is Associate Professor of Anthropology at Yale University and the author of *Deaf in Japan: Signing and the Politics of Identity* (Cornell University Press, 2006) and *A Disability of the Soul: An Ethnography of Schizophrenia and Mental Illness in Japan* (Cornell University Press, 2013). Her research focuses on disability, gender, sexuality, and minority social movements in contemporary Japan.

SCOTT NORTH is Professor of Sociology in the Graduate School of Human Sciences at Osaka University. His recent publications in Japanese and English include book chapters and journal articles on work hours, death from overwork (*karōshi*), the gendered division of labor in dual-income households, corporate labor welfare regimes, and fatherhood in Japan. Current projects include a study of work-family balance in Japan and participant observation in small social movements that use litigation to promote Japanese worker health and wellbeing.

PATRICIA STEINHOFF is Professor of Sociology at the University of Hawaii. Her primary research interest is social movements, civil society, and radical left groups in Japan. Most of the twenty books and monographs plus one hundred articles and book chapters that she has written, co-authored, edited, or co-edited concern Japan, including three books in Japanese. She recently edited *Destiny: The Secret Operations of the Yodogō Exiles*, an English translation of Takazawa Kōji, *Shukumei: Yodogō Bōmeishatachi no Himitsu Kosaku* (University of Hawaii Press, forthcoming 2015). She is currently writing a book on Japan's invisible civil society and co-editing a collection of studies of contemporary Japanese movements with David Slater and Nomiya Daishiro.

CHRISTENA TURNER is Associate Professor of Sociology and Director of the Program in Japanese Studies at the University of California, San Diego. She is the author of *Japanese Workers in Protest: An Ethnography of Culture and Experience* (University of California Press, 1995). She is an anthropologist whose research focuses on inequality, daily life, and transnational approaches to culture.

Index